HOLIDAY WALKS
in
PROVENCE

Judy Smith

Published by Sigma Leisure – an imprint of Sigma Press, 5 Alton Road, Wilmslow, Cheshire SK9 5DY, England.

British Library Cataloguing in Publication Data
A CIP record for this book is available from the British Library.

ISBN: 1-85058-789-2

Typesetting and Design by: Sigma Press, Wilmslow, Cheshire.

Printed by: Interprint Ltd, Malta

Cover Photographs: main cover picture – Montagne Ste. Victoire; smaller pictures from left – church and bay at St. Tropez; the 'perched village' of Méthamis; coastal path on Cap Lardier.

Photographs: the author

Maps: Bute Cartographics

Thanks: to the very helpful staff of Offices de Tourisme all over Provence.

DISCLAIMER

Preface

As a child in North Wales, I once sat through an Eisteddfod competition for baritone soloists in which the set piece was the catchy aria 'Di Provenza' from La Traviata – the song of a father pleading with his son to return to his homeland. 'Air and sunshine of Provence' were the words I heard carolled over and over again that morning – at least by those who chose to sing the English version – but they didn't mean anything special to me at the time. It was only many years later, when I first travelled south for myself, that I understood. The air of Provence is quite magical – clean and fresh with the scents of lavender, rosemary, thyme, eucalyptus, mastic and a hundred more aromatic shrubs. The light is clear and has a strange luminous quality, perfect for the many artists who settle here. And as for the sunshine – well, there is more than seven hours of it a day on average, which should be a good enough guarantee for any holiday.

The 31 walks in this book are scattered throughout Provence, encompassing the five *départements* of Bouches-du-Rhône, Vaucluse, Var, Alpes-de-Haute-Provence and Alpes-Maritimes. In no other region could there be a greater variety of terrain or more scope for every style of walking. The routes here have been chosen to cater for all tastes and abilities, and range from gentle family strolls along the coast and quiet rambles in the shady forests to more-demanding hikes in high mountains and paths through the gorges of wild rivers. In addition, most walks have possible short cuts or extensions, making them even more adaptable. And along with each route, there are suggestions for several more nearby – hopefully enough to keep you busy all holiday.

Once more my heartiest thanks go to my husband Eric for his company and for his never-failing enthusiasm for finding new routes. We both enjoyed the opportunity to explore this splendid region so thoroughly – and realised that we had done no more than scratch the surface on our previous visits. Our 'Year in Provence' had many highlights. One was certainly climbing to the cross on the top of Montagne Ste. Victoire on a windy day – breathtaking would describe more than the view. On another occasion we enjoyed a picnic under the umbrella pines, all alone in an idyllic rocky cove – yet just around the corner was St. Tropez. But the prize must go to the scene in the lonely valley of Fontanalbe with its ancient carvings, where we watched a pair of ibex coming out to graze in the late autumn sunshine. I hope you will gain as much pleasure as we have had from exploring Provence on foot. Good luck on your journey!

Judy Smith

Contents

Location Map

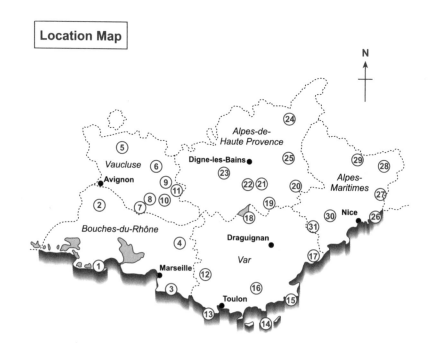

The Walks

Provence and its footpaths

Provence is a region teeming with life and colour. It brings to mind images of blue skies, red ochre earth, white limestone, purple lavender, yellow sunflowers and bright cotton prints. It is a land of vineyards, olive groves and cypress trees, warm sunshine and scented air; of cobalt sea, white-hulled yachts, fronded palms and spreading umbrella pines. Crumbling red-roofed villages perch on the hilltops while colourful and aromatic markets spill through their streets and old men play pétanque and drink *pastis* under the shade of huge plane trees. It is a place rich with legend, folklore and tradition, with more feast-days and festivals than any other part of France.

If you have visited Provence before it may well have been on a sun-seeking holiday in one of the resorts of the south, or perhaps on a cultural break in pursuit of the many Roman remains in the Rhône valley. Taking a walk off the beaten track here will show you a very different side of Provence – in walking you are getting closer to the land and its people. On foot you can take your time to admire the views or look closely at the farms you are passing, to watch the harvest in the vineyards or fishing boats going out to sea, to enjoy the rich colours of the Mediterranean vegetation and the scents of the herbs you crush underfoot. The multitude of visitors to this popular region will be left behind – you are likely to meet only a few locals and other walkers like yourselves. But Provence covers a large area and has a great variety of scenery – you can hardly visit it all at one go. So to help you choose your destination, here are just a few words about what you can expect to find on foot in Provence.

Walking books often stress contrasts in landscapes, but Provence has to be in a league of its own here, a place of infinite variety. Going first to the coastline, the western part is the Camargue in the delta of the Rhône – as flat a landscape as you can imagine, lakes and salt marshes stretching to the distant horizon and reflecting the brilliant blue of the wide sky. The paths here are raised tracks, from which you can watch the hundreds of flamingos that live and breed in this watery place. In the east the scene is very different – near the Italian border the tail of the alpine chain plunges into the sea from a dizzy height. Beneath these cliffs, the busy conurbations of Menton and Monaco are separated by the green peninsula of Cap Martin – and around that promontory a splendid balcony path curves above the azure sea. Between these two extremes of shoreline, the *département* of Var boasts a coastal path along almost its entire length and there are many more splendid sea-side walks on the idyllic Îles d'Hyères. One path that deserves special mention is the Grande Randonnée skirting the 'Calanques', the coves and creeks east of Marseille. This spectacular 28km long trail is quite demanding, but the short walk around the three most beautiful easterly calanques is one that should be on everyone's agenda.

Moving inland, the landscape is largely mountainous, but every range is different. The oldest mountains are the forested Maures and the red-rocked Esterel, both dating from the Primary Era, more than two hundred million years ago. The other Provençal ranges were formed along with the Alps and Pyrenees in the Tertiary Era and are less than sixty million years old. These ranges run from east to west – the rocky Ste Victoire so beloved by Cézanne, the Ste Baume with its legends and cave, the jagged peaks of the Alpilles, that inspired Van Gogh, and the gentle green Luberon where villages cling to the hillsides and the earth glows with the rich colours of ochre. Farther north is the huge bulk of stone-capped Mont Ventoux, the 'Sentinel of Provence', while to the east are the foothills of the Alps, cut through by the gorges of many rivers. The walk through the gorges of the Verdon is a classic, and one of the most popular hikes in France – but the slit-like gorges of St Pierre are more awe-inspiring, and the little-known Gorges de Trévans are perhaps prettier. In the neighbourhood of Digne, the 'pre-Alps' have been given the status of a geological reserve – you can investigate a wealth of curious rock formations here or walk out into the wilderness to find the fossilised skeletons of prehistoric creatures. Farther east, the mountains of the Mercantour National Park rise to 3000m along the border with Italy. Mountain torrents and waterfalls pour down the slopes, clear blue alpine lakes nestle high in the rocks, and the larch woods shelter chamois, ibex and mouflon. Walks in this remote place are well on the wild side, and perhaps most exciting of all are excursions into the valleys of Merveilles and Fontanalbe, where Bronze Age man left hundreds of engravings on the rocks.

Provence offers so many splendid walks that it has been nearly impossible to choose between them. But choice there had to be, and I hope you will enjoy the 'Lucky 31' that made it to the top. Almost all these walks are circular, and they range between 2 and 17km in length. Many good walks that didn't find a place here are included in the sections of 'More Walks' that have been provided with each route described. If you are planning to stay in an area, taking advantage of these extras should extend the scope of your holiday. The maps and leaflets referred to can all be found in the local Office de Tourisme – and if you need any help with the French, the 'Dictionary of Walking Words' on Page 10 might just possibly shed some light. Even so, in almost every case, the combination of an excellent map and good waymarking on the ground will get you round, so don't be afraid to have a go at these extra suggestions. And, perhaps surprisingly, a local Office de Tourisme will often be able to offer advice about the various routes – as well as providing bus timetables or help in finding a taxi if necessary. In these Offices de Tourisme you will also find a wealth of regional literature. The 'Places of Interest' section with each walk includes just a small personal selection, but there is so much to see and do in Provence that you will need to investigate the brochures and guide books for yourself. So now read on and find out about the holiday walks that await you in what is surely the most fascinating region of France.

Walking in France

France is almost certainly the best country for walking in Europe. The scenery is widely varied, the tracks are well-maintained and well-waymarked and every Office du Tourisme can offer you an assortment of routes and inexpensive maps of the area.

The excellence of the footpaths of France is due almost entirely to an organisation called the Féderation Française de la Randonnée Pédestre – The FFRP – who over the last half century have waymarked and described routes of all kinds throughout France. Many of the walks in this book are based on their routes, and you will undoubtedly be grateful for some of their waymarking as you follow them. Their long distance paths, the Grandes Randonnées (GR), are the best waymarked paths imaginable, and will invariably lead you past all the most interesting features and best viewpoints in an area. If there is something worth seeing, the Grande Randonnée will take you there. Next there are the Grandes Randonnées du Pays (GRP), round tours of an area or region which may take, in walking time, anything from a couple of days to a week or more. They aim to show you the best a region has to offer. And finally there are the Petites Randonnées (PR), the equivalent of our short circular walks, and these are sprinkled generously over the whole country. Each of these route types has its own waymarks, painted on trees, rocks, telegraph poles, or any other convenient surface– the Grandes Randonnées are marked white on red, the Grandes Randonnées du Pays yellow on red and the Petites Randonnées, yellow. You will meet all of them on the walks in this book, so here is all you need to know:

Path continues

Wrong way

Left turn

Right turn

Thus, you are warned of every turn before you reach it, and halted by a cross if you have missed it. Nothing could be simpler! In fairness, it must be said that although Grandes Randonnées are invariably superbly waymarked, the state of a Petite Randonnée may reflect the level of enthusiasm of the local tourist board or walking group. Even so, most are excellent. To accompany these fine routes, the FFRP produces a series of Topoguides, which offer all the relevant information from flora and fauna to history, geology and details of available refreshment. The pity is that only very few have been translated into English, and, oddly, these are generally of the long distance routes. For the rest, at least a working knowledge of French is needed. If you decide to tackle these – or any other described routes – a vocabulary of 'walking words in French' has been included in this book to help out.

Another excellent feature of walking in France is that most paths are open to you – only those marked 'Privé' deny you access. It is accepted that you will not wander on crops or gardens and that you will not leave litter or pick flowers. It should be mentioned that in winter some forest paths are temporarily closed for the period of 'la chasse' – the hunting season – generally from November to February, but these paths will again be marked. In France, farmers and landowners seem much more in tune with walkers than in England and will generally greet you cheerfully. If you can manage just a 'Bonjour' in return', it is certain to go down well.

And now the footpaths of France await you – and they are guaranteed to be addictive. Take one short stretch of a Grande Randonnée and you may well be hooked for life! It remains only to wish you 'Bonne route'!

A little history to set the scene

Early Days

In Provence, history goes a long way back – rock carvings in the Grottes de l'Observatoire in Monaco are thought to have been made around 1,000,000 years ago and are some of the oldest in the world. From here it's a giant leap in time to the first appearance of Homo sapiens around 30,000 BC Some of his earliest carvings, including seals and bison, are to be found on the walls of the Grotte Cosquier, a cave now hidden below the waters of the Calanque of Sormiou near Marseille. Almost recent by comparison are the engravings from the early Bronze Age (1,800 to 1,500 BC) to be found in the remarkable valleys of Merveilles and Fontanalbe in the Mercantour National Park. These valleys around Mont Bégo were sacred places of pagan worship for the Ligurian tribes who by this time had colonised the coastal regions and were early farmers. It was they who first built the circular dry-stone huts (*bories*) – and although we do not know the true purpose of these early buildings, their clever designs were reproduced as shelters for both men and animals until the 19th century.

By the end of the Bronze Age, the first Celtic tribes were arriving on the scene from the north, and mingling peacefully with the resident Ligurians. Around 600 BC Greeks landed on the southern shores and founded a settlement by the name of Massalia. Its site was that of modern-day Marseilles. These Greeks from Asia Minor brought the first olives, figs and vines to the region. They established trading posts along the coast (Antibes, Nice, Monaco) and inland (Avignon, Cavaillon). But the Celto-Ligurian tribes were rising against these incomers and threatened to attack Massalia from their own capital of Entremont (near Aix). The Greeks called on the might of Rome to defend them – and so the Romans first came to Provence in 125 BC.

The Roman Era and Christianity

The Romans were not fond of the Celts and Ligurians, who after all had helped Hannibal to cross the Alps for his campaigns in Italy almost a hundred years earlier. In 122 BC Entremont fell to the Roman armies, and soon all southern France from the Alps to the Pyrenees was under Roman control as the Provincia Gallia Transalpina. Only Massalia remained independent – but after the Greeks unwisely supported Pompey against Caesar, that city too fell to Rome in 49 BC. The Celto-Ligurian tribes continued to rebel in the east and were only finally suppressed by the Emperor Augustus in 14 BC. To commemorate his victory the huge statue called the 'Trophy of the Alps' or the *Trophée d'Auguste* was erected on the hilltop above Monaco. It can still be seen today in the town of la Turbie. In time the huge province of Transalpina was split into two for the purposes of government – Narbonne was the principal city of the west, and Arles that of the east. Undoubtedly Arles became the place to live – the magnificence of its arena, Roman theatre and much more can still be seen to this day. The Romans built roads, bridges and aqueducts in their conquest of Transalpina, and celebrated their victories with the occasional triumphal arch. Their rich legacy is well-preserved throughout Provence.

Provençal legend has it that Christianity was brought to the region with the landing of a boat in the Camargue, at the place now known as Saintes-Maries-de-la-Mer, in the year AD 40. In that boat were Mary Magdalene, Mary Jacobea, Mary Salome and a handful of others depending on the version you prefer (the gypsies believe their very own black Saint Sarah arrived that way). Be all that as it may, Christianity was originally seen as a threat to Rome and was actively suppressed over many years. It was the Emperor Constantine, himself a Christian convert, who in AD 313 first officially granted freedom of worship.

Medieval Provence and the Popes

The wealth of Arles attracted the attention of the Visigoths – they finally sacked the city in AD 471, by which time the Roman Empire was well in decline.

The next few centuries brought chaos as one barbaric tribe after another fought for territory. Visigoths, Ostrogoths, Burgundians and Franks in turn laid waste the land. At the end of the 8th century the Saracens arrived from across the Mediterranean and founded settlements on the southern shores. Their reign was short and bloody – in 974 their fortress at la Garde Freinet fell to the Count of Arles and in 1032 Provence was incorporated into the Holy Roman Empire. Even so, the land was still governed by local lords, the threat of attack was ever present and the population gathered together in fortified hilltop villages – the original *villages perchés* – for protection. The territory was divided between the Counts of Toulouse and Barcelona, the land east of the Rhône becoming the possession of Barcelona. In 1246 the propitious marriage of Charles of Anjou to Beatrice, the daughter of the Count of Barcelona, brought Provence under the control of Anjou. Charles and his successors governed well, and the following years saw prosperity with the building of churches and abbeys and a flourishing of the arts. Troubadours wandered between the great courts, singing (in Occitan) of the happenings of the time. In 1274, the land known as Comtat Venaissin was ceded to Pope Gregory X. A few years later Clement V moved his headquarters from Rome to Avignon and one of his successors later bought the town from the then Countess of Provence for 80,000 florins and an official pardon – she was said to have murdered her husband. The Papal Palace was built and Avignon enjoyed a hundred years of importance as a centre of political and intellectual life. The late 14th century saw Provence once again despoiled by warring lordships, but the accession of a ruler who loved Provence and became known as 'Good King René' restored peace, culture and economic prosperity to the region.

French Provence and the Wars of Religion

When Good King René died, Provence passed to his nephew who survived him but briefly and had no heirs. In 1481 Louis XI of France took possession of his territories – the Provence we know today with the exception of the County of Nice (approximately the present day department of Alpes-Maritimes) and the Comtat Venaissin. In 1539 French became the official language of Provence for the first time.

In the middle of the 16th century a wave of Protestantism was sweeping Europe. In Provence this new religious climate gave strength to the Vaudois or Waldensians, a dissenting sect whose roots went back some 400 years. Persecuted throughout that time, their strongholds were now the hill villages of the Luberon. From here they attacked and destroyed the Abbey of Sénanque, for which act more than 3000 of them lost their lives and others were sent as galley slaves, while their villages were razed to the ground. A measure of peace was achieved when Henry IV, a Protestant, came to the throne of France and granted freedom of worship with the Edict of Nantes (1598). When Louis XIV revoked this almost a century later, religious hatred and persecution were greater than ever in Provence. And to add to the troubles of these times, a trading ship from the east brought the plague to Marseille in 1720. More than half the population of that city lost their lives.

The French Revolution and Napoleon

The sympathies of Provence were divided – broadly as elsewhere the towns supported the Revolutionaries while the rural communities were Royalist. Provence is proud to have been the originator of the anthem, the Marseillaise, at this time. The Marseillaise was actually composed by a soldier in Strasbourg (Rouget de Lisle), and was entitled the Battle Song of the Army of the Rhine – but it was taken up by a volunteer corps of Revolutionaries from Marseille and sung as they marched to Paris in 1792. The new regime divided Provence into three departments and later annexed the Comtat Venaissin as a fourth. Nice and Monaco were conquered later. It was the subsequent Reign of Terror with its religious oppression that caused the people of Provence to produce the clay models that were the first *santons* (little saints). These tiny figures of the scene around Christ's crib gave a focus for worshipping at home, rather than in the forbidden churches.

After Napoleon seized power in 1799, France – and Provence – enjoyed a measure of ordered government. But defeat in foreign campaigns forced Napoleon's abdication and exile to Elba in 1814. He didn't stay away long. On March 1st 1815, he landed near Cannes with 1200 men and marched north through the mountains with amazing speed, reaching Sisteron in four days and Paris itself on 20th March. His brief reign ended at the Battle of Waterloo in June, after which he was sent to a more secure detention on St Helena.

The Nineteenth Century and the Belle Époque

The nineteenth century changed the face of Provence for ever. The advent of the railways favoured an industrial revolution, with the mining of ochre and bauxite among others, and the expansion of the perfume-making industry. The opening of the Suez Canal in 1869 brought increased trade to Marseille. The more rural scene fared less well, with silkworm farming ruined by disease and the vineyards decimated by the phylloxera beetle – although olives and wheat were still produced in large quantities. Village populations left for the towns. The new railways also brought the earliest tourists to Provence. Queen Victoria was one of the first to discover the delights of wintering in Nice rather than at home, and other nobility followed her example. Money came with them – and was soon spent. The opening of the Casino at Monte Carlo in 1865 changed Monaco from the poorest to one of the richest states in Europe. Others came for their health – the 'air and sunshine' were thought to be particularly good for the dreaded tuberculosis. And it was the exceptional clarity of the light that attracted the painters – Cézanne to Aix, Van Gogh to Arles and St Rémy and Signac and Matisse to St Tropez. The southern coast became the playground of the upper classes of Europe and was first dubbed the Côte d'Azur in an early nineteenth century guidebook.

The Twentieth Century and War

Although the territory of Provence was untouched by the First World War, the loss of its youth was felt both in the fields and in industry. After the war tourism again leapt forward and the coastal towns acquired their sophisticated image, attracting the rich, famous, intellectual and artistic of the day. The Second World War brought the party to an end. Provence was at first part of Vichy France, but after the German invasion of November 1942 became occupied territory. The Resistance movement was strong, with hundreds of cells hiding out in the remoteness of the hills. From the scrubland that gave them cover they were named the Maquis. On the 15th August 1944, more than two months after D-Day, the Allied forces landed on the southern beaches. It took them just fifteen days to take Provence before going on to meet their colleagues in the north. After the war, the Roya valley, originally part of Savoy and then Italy, was finally returned to Provence.

Since the war Provence's agriculture has seen modernisation and industry has thrived. The most important industry is undoubtedly tourism, and it is no longer just the coast that attracts the visitors. The Luberon was brought everyone's attention with Peter Mayle's *A Year in Provence* in 1989 – and since then crumbling old farmhouses in the region have been at a premium. Provence seems to have it all – the scenery, the weather and the wine – and at times it can seem that all Europe wants a share of it. The footpaths of Provence now offer the very best way get away from the crowds and reach the historic heart of this fascinating country.

How to get there

Provence has major airports at Nice and Marseille and many lesser ones throughout the region. With the advent of economy flights from regional airports in the UK, anyone living outside the Home Counties may well find that certain flights to Provence are less costly than a rail ticket to London. Inexpensive car hire can be included with the package. All this means that a long weekend on the Mediterranean coast is a very real possibility, and several walks in this book can be easily accessed from Nice or Marseille. Anyone wanting to travel further afield will find excellent train services along the coast. Main lines extend inland too, but there is one very special train that will give immediate access to the mountains without the need for car hire. The Train des Pignes ('Pine-cone Train' on account of its original fuel) runs four times a day between Nice and Digne, stopping at Puget-Théniers, Entrevaux, Annot, St André-les-Alpes and Barrême. All of these offer fine walking possibilities, some of which are included in this book. The train is operated by Chemins de Fer de Provence, starts from its own station, the Gare de Provence near the centre of Nice, and takes around 3 hours for the whole amazingly scenic journey to Digne.

By road, the journey from Calais to Avignon is of the order of 600 miles, with Marseille being another 50 miles farther on, and Nice another 100 on top of that. It is possible for cars – and their occupants – to be transported on the weekly overnight motorail service from Calais to Avignon or Nice (summer months only), but this tends to be an expensive option, despite being associated with reduced cross-channel fares.

Rail travel to Provence is relatively easy. Eurostar to Paris or to Lille can be followed by a TGV connection to Avignon. In either case the total journey time is around 6½ hours. The direct service from Ashford to Avignon – cuts very little off the journey time. Onward travel could be by TGV to Nice (3 hours approx) or by standard service to Marseille (1½ hours approx).

Weather

Provence boasts over 2500 sun-hours a year on average – that is, you can expect more than 7 hours of sunshine every day. If that makes you want to catch the next plane south immediately, take just a few minutes to consider exactly where and when you are going – it does make a difference.

On the south coast the winter is mild, and perfectly suited to walking.

Farther north, around the Luberon, you can expect at least a couple of cold months, whereas in the mountains, snow shoes may be in use for several months. But spring comes early to Provence, and, with it, the splendid 'Easter bouquet' of wild flowers. March, April and May are excellent months for walking in all regions – with the exception of the mountains of the Mercantour, where the highest peaks may be snow-covered until June. The one drawback is the dreaded Mistral, that icy blast that funnels down the Rhône valley and is strong enough to 'blow the tail off a donkey'. The wind is most common in late winter and spring, and may last a few hours or several days at a time. If the Mistral is blowing, walking may be difficult – and you should not even think of attempting some of the peaks in its path, Mont Ventoux, the Dentelles of Montmirail or Mont Ste Victoire. But even the Mistral has a plus side – it is accompanied by clear sunny skies.

Summer brings problems for the regions of the south. The average temperature in July and August on the south coast is around 24°C – but on many an afternoon will climb to the upper 30s. This is simply too hot for a pleasant walk – and in any case, most paths in the mountains near the coast (the Maures and the Esterel) will be closed to reduce the risk of fire. These areas have seen some horrendous blazes in the last 30 years, and whereas some paths may only be closed when the ground is tinder dry and the wind brisk, others are closed annually between fixed dates – most commonly, 1st July to 15th September. If not closed through fire risk, paths like that through the cedar forest of the Luberon will offer welcome shade, and deep gorges like those of the Siagne or St Pierre should remain cool. But summer is without doubt the time to head for the mountains – in the peaks of the Mercantour temperatures will be around 10°C below those at the coast.

Autumn is an excellent time to walk throughout Provence. Days are warm and mellow but not too hot, the sea retains its heat making a quick dip still a pleasure, and the warm earth brings a wonderful harvest of grapes and olives to admire. Deciduous woodlands take on their autumn colours and in the mountains the larches are at their scenic best in tones ranging from bright yellow to burning orange. On the downside, rainfall levels are highest in October and November – but the rain generally comes in heavy downpours of a few hours at a time, after which the sun comes out and business is as usual. And as spring arrives here early, so winter comes late – November temperatures are comparable to those of March, and, being much farther south, daylight hours are noticeably longer than in Britain.

Flora and fauna

Walking in Provence is immediately different on account of the Mediterranean vegetation and it would be a pity not come to terms with just a little of it. It is worthwhile investing in a book of trees and flowers. But to get you off the starting blocks, here are my top five of each – with apologies to all the rest. Let's start with the trees.

The olive tree. Almost a symbol of Provence, it had to come first. Its gnarled black branches and grey green leaves with silvery undersides are quite distinctive. White flowers appear in summer – and later in the year you can't miss the olives. Olives are cultivated and often seen in large plantations, but specimens are found growing wild as far north as the Luberon.

The Cypress. Tall, dark, straight and pointed, they are often planted around farmhouses, and are again classic components of the Mediterranean scene.

The Plane tree. It seems every village square is shaded by huge plane trees. They also frequently line the roads, becoming a traffic hazard as girth increases. Plane trees have distinctively mottled trunks, the thin grey bark peeling to leave yellowish patches.

The holm oak. Not an exciting tree, but there's a lot of it. Holm oaks have thin leathery leaves a bit like holly but less prickly, and furry twigs. They can grow to a great height but are often little more than shrubs. An obvious tree on any forest walk.

The umbrella pine. This is included simply because it is such a beautiful tree. Found along the coast, these spreading pines have thick velvety green domes of foliage – a whole hillside of them is a magnificent sight.

And if you've mastered those, go on to the characteristically aromatic mastic or lentisc, the strawberry tree with its simultaneous 'strawberries' and bell-shaped white flowers, the cork-oak, its bark stripped to an under-layer of orange, the prickly juniper with cones like berries, and the imported fluffy yellow mimosa and droopy-leaved eucalyptus. And that's only the beginning.

Now to the flowers:

Lavender. It had to be in poll position. But those bright purple flowers lined up in the fields may be either fine lavender or lavandin, a hybrid of lavender and aspic. Each has its uses and any lavender farm or museum will distinguish between them for you. In the wild, fine lavender is only found at altitudes greater than about 800m Lavender's short flowering season is the months of July and August – not the time you are likely to be walking in Provence.

Rosemary. A bushy shrub with narrow leaves and blue flowers, common throughout Provence on dry rocky soils and easily recognised by its smell.

Thyme. Much smaller than rosemary with pink flowers. Like rosemary it found on open rocky ground (garrigue) and can easily be identified by its smell

Tree heath. A very large heather growing up to 1 metre in height, bushy and with scented white flowers.

Cistus or rock rose. There are many members of this family. Most common is the Grey-leaved Cistus, descriptively called *Cistus Cotonneux* (Fluffy Cistus) in French. The leaves are grey and covered with downy hairs. In late spring the tall-ish stems bear bright pink flowers with yellow centres.

For all the rest you will need a book (Dorling Kindersley's 'Wild Flowers of the Mediterranean' is a good one). Spring is the best time for the floral display – summer is simply too hot and dry. But many flowers bloom for a second time in autumn.

Going on to the fauna, the rocky garrigue is home to lizards and grass snakes, wild-boar are found in the forests, while pink flamingos stalk the Camargue. The most exciting place is the Mercantour where the 'big 5' are possibly chamois, mouflon, ibex, red deer and marmot, and bird life includes black grouse, ptarmigan and golden eagles. Rare sightings are those of the Hermann's tortoise in the Maures and the Tyrrhenian painted frog on Port Cros. And as night falls, all Provence throbs with the insistent drumming of the cicadas, which is actually the mating call of the male of the species. Having spent more than ten years of his life under the ground, he has just one month in the open air to mate before he dies.

Dictionary of Walking Words

anse	a cove, a small bay
atteindre	to reach
balisage	waymarking
bifurquer	to fork
blanc (blanche)	white
bleu(e)	blue
bois	a wood
bosquet	a spinney, a copse
chemin	a way, a path
colline	a hill
contourner	to go around, to skirt
creux	sunken or hollowed out
dessous	under
dessus	above
droit (tout droit)	straight ahead
droite	right
église	church
empierré	stony or metalled (as in road)
emprunter	to take (as in direction)
étang	a pond, a pool
en face	opposite
fourche	a fork
franchir	to clear, to cross
gauche	left
goudronnée	tarmacked
grimper	to climb
hameau	hamlet
jaune	yellow
jusqu'à	as far as
longer	to skirt
mener	to lead
monter	to climb
niveau	a level
patte d'oie	multiple path or road junction
pente	slope
prairie	a meadow
rouge	red
route	a road
ruisseau	a stream
sentier	a footpath, a track
sous-bois	undergrowth
suivre	to follow
talus	a slope or bank
tourner	to turn
traverser	to cross
variante	alternative route
vert(e)	green
virer	to bend or turn

Offices de Tourisme and other useful addresses

Provence is a holiday region and every place of any size has an Office de Tourisme. In the larger towns they are open all year – elsewhere it may be the summer months, or, in some villages, just July and August. Out of season, the stock of the Office de Tourisme is usually transferred to the Mairie – and they won't mind you asking for it. The list below comprises the Offices de Tourisme referred to in each walk in this book. Every tourist office is happy to send you information on its region, and, where leaflets of walks are free, to include these if you request them. And whether writing or telephoning, in this holiday region there is almost always someone who can understand if you would prefer to use English.

Walk	Location	Address
1	Camargue	5, Ave. Van Gogh BP 73, 13732 SAINTES-MARIES-DE-LA-MER. Tel. 04.90.97.82.55
2	St Rémy-de-Provence	Place Jean Jaurès, 13210 ST. RÉMY-DE-PROVENCE. Tel. 04.90.92.05.22
3	Cassis	Place Baragnon, 13260 CASSIS. Tel. 04.42.01.71.17.
4	Aix-en-Provence	Place du Général de Gaulle BP 160, 13100 AIX-EN-PROVENCE. Tel. 04.42.16.11.61
5	Malaucène	Place de la Mairie, 84340 MALAUCÈNE. Tel. 04.90.65.22.59
6	Sault	Avenue de la Promenade, 84390 SAULT. Tel. 04.90.64.01.21
7	Mérindol	Rue du Four, 84360 MÉRINDOL. Tel. 04.90.72.88.50
8	Bonnieux	7, Place Carnot, 84480 BONNIEUX. Tel. 04.90.75.91.90
9, 10 & 11	Apt	20, Ave. Philippe de Girard, 84400 APT. Tel. 04.90.74.03.18
9, 10 & 11	La Maison du Parc du Luberon	60, Place Jean Jaurès, 84400 APT. Tel. 04.90.04.42.00
12	Nans-les-Pins	2, Cours Général de Gaulle, 83860 NANS-LES-PINS. Tel. 04.94.78.95.91
13	Six-Fours-les-Plages	Promenade Charles de Gaulle, Plage de Bonnegrâce, 83140 SIX-FOURS-LES-PLAGES . Tel. 04.94.07.02.21
14	Le Lavandou	Quai Gabriel Péri, 83980 LE LAVANDOU. Tel. 04.94.00.40.50

15	La Croix-Valmer	Les Jardins de la Gare, 84320 LA CROIX-VALMER. Tel. 04.94.55.12.12
16	Collobrières	Bd. Charles Caminat, 83610 COLLOBRIÈRES. Tel. 04.94.48.08.00
17	Fréjus	325, Rue Jean Jaurès, 83600 FRÉJUS. Tel. 04.94.51.83.83
18	Aups	Place F. Mistral, 83630 AUPS. Tel. 04.94.70.00.80
19	La Palud-sur- Verdon	Le Château, 04120 LA PALUD-SUR-VERDON. Tel. 04.92.77.32.02
20	Annot	Bd. St Pierre, 04240 ANNOT. Tel. 04.92.83.23.03
21 & 22	Digne-les-Bains	Place du Tampinet, 04000 DIGNE-LES-BAINS. Tel. 04.92.36.62.62
23	Les Mées	21, Bd. de la République, 04190 LES MÉES. Tel. 04.92.34.36.38
24	Barcelonnette	Place Frédéric Mistral, 04400 BARCELONNETTE. Tel. 04.92.81.04.71
25	Colmars	Place Joseph Girieud, 04370 COLMARS-LES-ALPES. Tel. 04.92.83.41.92
26	Menton	Palais de l'Europe BP 239, 06506 MENTON Cedex. Tel. 04.92.41.76.76
27	Sospel	Pont Vieux, 06380 SOSPEL. Tel. 04.93.04.15.80
28	Tende	Avenue du 16 septembre 1947, 06430 TENDE. Tel. 04.93.04.73.71
29	St Martin -Vésubie	Place Félix Faure, 06450 ST. MARTIN-VÉSUBIE BP 12. Tel. 04.93.03.21.28
30	Gourdon	Place de l'Église, 06620 GOURDON. Tel. 04.93.09.68.25
31	St Cézaire -sur-Siagne	3, Rue de la République, 06730 SAINT-CÉZAIRE-SUR-SIAGNE. Tel. 04.93.60.84.30

Map Supplies

Fédération Francaise de la Randonnée Pédestre (FFRP), 14, Rue Riquet, 75019 PARIS *(supplies Topoguides)*

Stanfords, 12 – 14 Long Acre, London WC2E 9LP *(Topoguides and maps)*

The Map Shop,15 High Street, Upton-upon-Severn, Worcestershire WR8 0HJ *(Topoguides and maps)*

Recommended Publications

Michelin Green Guides (3): French Riviera. ISBN: 2060000920; *Provence.* ISBN: 2060000297; *French Alps.* ISBN: 2060000882

Hachette Vacances: Provence and the Côte d'Azur. ISBN: 1842020064

Lonely Planet: Provence and the Côte d'Azur. ISBN: 1864501960

The Rough Guide: Provence and the Côte d'Azur. ISBN: 1858284201

DK Eyewitness Travel Guide: Provence and the Côte d'Azur. ISBN: 0751347078

Landmark Visitor Guides: Provence and the Côte d'Azur. ISBN: 1901522458

Lonely Planet: Walking in France. ISBN: 0864426011

Provence on the Internet

Here are just a few websites you might find useful

www.ffrp.asso.fr

This is the website of the French rambling association, the Fédération Francaise de la Randonnée Pédestre. Along with other information (in French), the site lists and describes the major topoguides and gives information on ordering direct – a cheaper option than buying in the UK.

www.easyjet.com

The website of Easyjet. Offers low-cost flights from Bristol, Liverpool, Gatwick, Stansted and Luton to Nice. Booking on-line

www.ryanair.com

Ryanair's website, offering low-cost flights from Stansted to Nîmes and on-line booking.

www.eurostar.com

The website of Eurostar, giving timetables, fares and on-line booking

www.voyages-sncf.com

The site of the French railway system, offering train timetables and reservations.

www.trainprovence.com

This is the website of the Train des Pignes, travelling between from Nice and Digne-les-Bains. Accessible in English, it gives times, fares, history and a few pretty pictures.

www.gites-de-france.fr

A website giving details of thousands of holiday properties all over France. Choose and book on-line – or, to give yourself more time for consideration, order the regional brochure.

www.provenceweb.fr

The official website of the region Provence/Côte d'Azur, accessible in English. Everything you can think of (with the exception of walking.) is here – gastronomy, forthcoming events, accommodation, transport, sport, etc. – and there are hundreds of photographs to whet your appetite. Guaranteed to keep you happy for hours.

1. Flamingos of the Camargue

The delta of the Rhône is a place of space and light, a galaxy of shimmering lakes held between the arms of the great river. The Camargue is magical and this walk guarantees not only flamingos, but herons, egrets, various seabirds and a wealth of flora and fauna.

Grade: Easy

Distance: 7km (4½ miles). A shorter circuit of 3km is also possible.

Time: 2 hours

Map: The whole area of the Camargue is best seen on the IGN Plein-Air map *Parc Naturel Régional de Camargue* (82004). But for this walk, the sketch map here will be quite sufficient.

Start and finish: The reception centre at the Domaine de la Palissade

How to get there: South of Arles, take the D36 running on the east side of the Étang de Vaccarès. After Salin-de-Giraud, continue for a further 4km in the direction of the Plage de Piémanson (a beautiful sandy beach) and the Domaine de la Palissade is on your left.

Refreshment: No refreshments are on sale, but there are picnic tables under the trees at the reception centre.

Notes: Short circular walks are not easily come by on the marshlands of the Camargue. The best trails are under the care of the various conservation bodies involved in the Park – the Domaine de la Palissade belongs to the Conservatoire de l'Espace Littoral et des Rivages Lacustres. Consequently, you will need to pay an extremely modest fee to go through the reception centre to begin the walk. Much of the route is on hard-surfaced track, with a centre section over rough grassland. It should not be boggy unless there has been recent heavy rainfall. There is no shade at all on the Camargue, so on a hot day this short level walk will be surprisingly demanding – cover yourself with sun-cream, wear a hat, and carry plenty of fluid. Another extra you will need here is insect repellent – mosquitoes thrive on the Camargue.

Waymarking: Yellow and then orange (backwards) arrows mark the way.

Introduction

White horses, black bulls and pink flamingos characterise the Camargue – along with rice fields, brackish lakes, salt pans, wide sandy beaches, endless space and an unbelievable intensity of light. Here you are at the interface between the land and the sea. In years gone by the area was alternately flooded by the fresh waters of the Rhône and salty waters of the Mediterranean. With the building of sea and river dykes in the middle of the 19th century the land became useful to man, and at least the northern part now yields cereals and rice. The whole area is quite unique and since the 1970s has been protected as the Parc Naturel Régional de la Camargue.

This region can hardly be said to be ideal for walking. In winter and spring it is periodically scoured by the Mistral, a relentless bone-chilling wind that, according to the local lore, can blow the tail (or the ears) off a donkey. In summer the sun scorches down from a cloudless blue Mediterranean sky. There is no shelter or shade in this low landscape, and no change of relief, with nothing higher than a lighthouse or a salt pile to break the horizon. Nevertheless this is an environment that simply must be experienced on foot – lakes glitter beside you, seabirds wheel in the air, coypu scurry across the path and 'plop' quietly into the water, flamingos stalk across the marshlands and take-off on bright pink wings. The car should have no part in this scene – this is nature getting on with its business and you feel privileged to walk through it.

The heart of the Camargue is a large round lake, the Étang de Vaccarès, itself a nature reserve. Roads run to the east and west of the lake, and it is the western road, ending in the seaside town of Saintes-Maries-de-la-Mer that seems to attract all the attention. Near the coast, lines of patient white horses wait to take visitors out onto the marsh. At Pont de Gau there is an excellent information centre and a superb *Parc Ornithologique* where you will see more flamingos than anywhere else in the Camargue. But somehow it's not the same as coming across them yourself on the marshes.

The walk here is on the other side of the Camargue, far away in its south-eastern corner – the Domaine de la Palissade sits on a lake-strewn triangle of land where the Grand Rhône meets the sea. Unlike the rest of the Camargue, the land here is not protected by the sea-dykes and so is very close to its original condition. The area is in the care of the Conservatoire du Littoral who maintain this natural state and have provided hides for visitors to observe the diversity of wildlife. Flamingos are here all the year round (although the majority are still summer visitors), but seasonal migrations bring in hoopoes and bee-eaters as well as a variety of wildfowl. The centre can offer you lots of information on flora and fauna before you set off. But above all, it is good to be able to get out into the wild, yet know you are on a secure track. Take your time on this well-marked walk and move silently – there is a lot to be seen.

Walking in the Camargue

The Walk

1. Leaving the reception centre, turn right on the gravelled track. Going through a gate you will see coloured arrows pointing you ahead. At the first junction, keep straight ahead (an orange arrow points to the right – you follow the yellow). A landscape of shrubs and low deciduous trees stretches ahead and the Grand Rhône flows silently to the left.

2. At the next junction, keep ahead again. (A right turn will take you to Point 4 in about 5 minutes if you need a short cut here). The path leads on with no variation in the terrain, but somehow it is quite beautiful. Depending on recent rainfall, there are swamps on either side of the path (noisy with the croaks of mating frogs when we were here in springtime!).

3. At a third junction, reached in something like 50 minutes, depending on your lingering time, you turn to the right towards a hide on the marsh. Now the path is rougher across the grassland. At the hide, take time to look across the lake, the Baisse Sableuse. When leaving, come down the steps and turn right on a sandy track with the lake on your right. Soon you are on a narrow strip of land between two lakes – the Grande Palun is on your left, its farther shore swallowed up in the distance. There are few landmarks on the horizon and you have a feeling of being well off-piste. Coming up to another lake ahead (oddly named the Trou de l'Oie – the Hole of the Goose), an arrow directs you right – evidence that you are still in touch with the world of man. By this time you should be well acquainted with the world of birds, with herons and flamingos sticking their heads up from every little lake around. In front of yet another large lake (Baisse Claire) you again bear right and now closely follow the path around its shores.

4. Reaching a junction with a gravelled track, turn left (there is an orange arrow pointing right – ignore it). The track follows the banks of the lake and, at a corner to the right, you can turn left to reach another hide. Returning from it, keep straight ahead to arrive at a junction with the main track you set out on at the beginning of the walk. Turn left to return to the reception centre.

More Walks in the Area

The Domaine de la Palissade was very happy for its walks to be included in this book. A possible extension to this walk, adding another kilometre, is to continue ahead at Point 3 to reach a viewpoint on the edge of the Grande Palun. On the opposite side of the reception centre, there is also a 1km discovery trail (boards in French only) taking you alongside the Grand Rhône to an observation tower. The return includes yet another hide beside a lake.

Walking in the Camargue is best undertaken in the conservation areas – see the Places of Interest section for more details. At La Capelière on the east of the Étang de Vaccarès there is a 1.5km trail, and at the Musée Camarguais there is another of 3.5km (there is no need to go through the museum to access this one). At the Parc Ornithologique du Pont du Gau, a trail of around 1½ hours will take you through lakes and marshes teeming with birdlife.

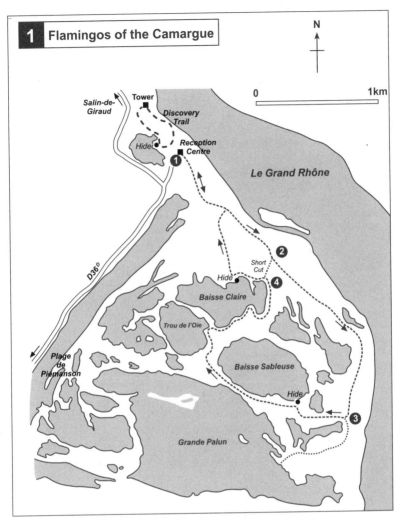

Between Saintes-Maries-de-la-Mer and la Gachole lighthouse, 12km of sea dyke (*Digue à la Mer*) holds back the blue Mediterranean. It is possible to walk out on this – although under the hot southern sun the whole there-and-back-distance is far too great. Instead you can hire bikes from Saintes-Maries-de-la-Mer – but note that cars are definitely forbidden.

On the eastern side, cars are allowed on the dyke as far as the lighthouse – although it is a very bumpy road. If you stop at the pumping station (4km away) where there is parking, you can walk out in the direction of the lighthouse. In the opposite direction from the lighthouse is the Étang de Fangassier, an important flamingo breeding site – another dyke-top path runs between this and the Étang de Galabert. The IGN map (82004) will best help you to sort it all out.

Places of Interest nearby

The Musée Camarguais is situated beside the D570, about 8km south-west of Arles. It is housed in one of the typical low thick-walled farmhouses (*mas*) of this region, the Mas de Rousty. This is the place to learn about the history of the Camargue, about the bulls and horses with their *gardians*, about the *Course Camarguaise* (a bull sport without the cruelty), and about the flocks of sheep and the traditional practice of transhumance. After the visit you can amble off alongside the drainage canal to reach an observatory on the marshes, following a waymarked trail of 3.5km The Musée Camarguais is open daily except winter Tuesdays.

The Parc Ornithologique du Pont de Gau is a lively place – flamingos, egrets, sea-birds and wildfowl compete noisily for food and water space on the lagoons, their activities observed by not an inconsiderable number of humans in season. The park is situated just north of Saintes-Maries-de-la-Mer, alongside the Étang de Ginès, and you can find more birdlife – and more solitude – by leaving the centre and taking the marked path along its shores. The park is open daily

Next door to the ornithological park is the Centre d'Information de Ginès – a modern building with wide picture windows giving superb views over the lake and its wildlife. Exhibitions, videos, and lots of literature are to be found inside. The centre is open daily except Fridays.

For yet more information, go along to la Capelière on the eastern side of the Étang de Vaccarès. This is the information centre of the Réserve Nationale de Camargue and as such has exhibitions, observatories and a discovery trail through the marshes. The centre is open daily throughout the year (afternoons only in winter).

Saintes-Maries-de-la-Mer is a cheerful little holiday resort, hiding behind the obligatory sea-wall. The Saintes-Maries were Mary Magdalene and others whose boat landed here when escaping persecution in the Holy Land – for the whole story, see Walk 13. This particular event gives rise to huge celebrations in both May and October – especially colourful as it seems all the gypsies in France and beyond arrive to extol their very own saint from the boat, Saint Sarah. When not being fêted, you can see a statue of the black Saint Sarah in the crypt of the fortified church above the town – from its roof a 'watchpath' offers wide views of marshes and sea.

Arles, the gateway to the Camargue, is chiefly renowned for its Roman antiquities – the Amphitheatre, Théatre Antique and cemetery of the Alyscamps among others. Walkers will be delighted to find the pavements inlaid with ceramic waymarks taking you on four separate themed tours.

2. With Van Gogh in the Alpilles

The limestone ridge known as the Alpilles contains some bizarre rock formations much loved by Van Gogh and frequently painted by him during his stay here. On this walk you climb to his favourite Rocher des Deux Trous through a landscape that is typically Provençal – and some very impressive Roman remains are thrown in for good measure.

Grade: Moderate

Distance: 7km (4½ miles)

Time: 2½ hours

Map: The IGN Plein-Air map 82065, *Provence – Les Alpilles* (scale 1:50,000) covers the whole area and is useful if you want to do more walks.

Start and finish: Les Antiques (the Roman arch and mausoleum) at St Rémy-de-Provence

How to get there: From St Rémy, follow the D5 south (SP Les Baux) for about 1km Les Antiques are on the right hand side.

Refreshment: None on the walk, but there are eating houses of all kinds in St Rémy

Notes: This walk is all on good tracks – for which trainers would be suitable in dry weather. There is a sustained but not too steep climb to reach the Rocher des Deux Trous. For the return from this rock, three routes of varying difficulty are possible – see the text. Although this is not a long walk, it would be advisable to carry fluid – and remember the sun-cream on a hot day. This path will be closed in summer (approx. mid-June to mid-September) due to fire risk.

Waymarking: Yellow flashes – but only intermittently. The section on the Grande Randonnée (GR) has white on red flashes. Just follow the text.

Introduction

The Alpilles are geologically speaking the last western outpost of the Luberon. But these hills are very different in appearance. On the lower slopes the scene is characteristically Provençal – olive groves, pointed cypress trees and colourful farmhouses. Above it all the glaring white limestone peaks emerge in a variety of strange shapes. Immortalised by Van Gogh, a huge rock with two holes – the Rocher des Deux Trous – looks down over the town of St Rémy-de-Provence.

Vincent Van Gogh arrived in St Rémy from Arles in May 1889. His bouts of madness had resulted in the people of Arles raising a petition against him, and he came here to admit himself voluntarily to an asylum in the old monastery, the Mas St Paul de Mausole. Here diagnosed as an epileptic, he stayed for what was to be the last year of his life – discharging himself in May 1890, he committed suicide two months later. During his time in St Rémy, Van Gogh continued painting as prodigiously as ever in the countryside around the asylum. The Poppyfield (*Le Champ de Coquelicots*), The Olive Grove (*les Oliviers*) and the Mas de St Paul come from this time. In *Les Oliviers – le Rocher des Deux Trous* (July 1889) the olive grove is surmounted by the huge rock with its two holes.

This walk starts out beside *les Antiques* – two very well preserved

19

Roman edifices dating from around 2000 years ago. Across the road are the excavations of the Roman town of Glanum, and very close to its entrance is the spot from which *Les Oliviers* was painted. Not far away is the Mas St Paul de Mausole and several other nearby sites painted by Van Gogh are marked by plaques. There is plenty to explore here – but the walk itself is a gem. The rich peaceful Provençal countryside gives way to a climb through a wooded valley and then a plateau below the Rocher des Deux Trous. There are views on all sides, wonderful scents of rosemary and thyme on the final winding path – and the rock itself is a splendid spot for a picnic. One of the loveliest paths in the Alpilles is on offer for the return – the plains beyond St Rémy and some of the strangest rock formations are seen from a hill smothered with herbs and wild flowers.

The Walk

1. From the parking area beside les Antiques, cross the road and take a path crossing the field opposite. Passing some industrial relics in the field, you arrive on the road beside the Mas St Paul de Mausole. Turn right, keeping the building on your left. On the right, just past the grounds of the old asylum, you pass on the right the spot from where *Le Champ de Coquelicots* was painted. Continue along the road to a fork before some quarries. Bear left here on to a gravelled track, following yellow waymarks (the right hand track has a yellow cross). Keep ahead to reach a cross-tracks with a signpost.

2. Turn right, following the GR6 in the direction of Eygalières. Continue climbing gently, passing many fine properties and keeping to the main track. Passing a farm called the Mas de Seraillet on the left, bear right into the woodland. The track now enters the Vallon de Valrugues, a valley ringed with pinnacles of limestone. Keep to the main track (ignore all lesser ones on the side) and the climbing becomes steeper as you go. Winding up to the head of the valley you have views of the Rocher des Deux Trous on the right. In around an hour (from the start) you arrive at a tarmacked road on the top of the hill. There are now views ahead to the south and to the left is the radio mast on the peak of la Caume

3. Turn right on the road (leaving the GR to go left here). After about 200m, a track doubles back on the right, its start marked by a pole with orange and yellow waymarks. This lovely wide track with splendid views takes you around the hillside to the Rocher des Deux Trous.

4. When you are ready to leave there are have three choices:

   a: The English version of this walk (described on a photocopied leaflet from the Office de Tourisme) directs you down a 'goat path' marked by a yellow flash on a pole about 20m from the rock itself – but even a goat might look for an alternative to this precipitous descent. Nevertheless, it is shown on the sketch map (though not on the corresponding IGN)

   b: Take the scenic route – and it really is! Retrace your steps from the rock (passing the yellow-flashed pole) and branch off after about 40m to take the obvious path to the top of the hill. The descent from this is much easier to negotiate, the views are magnificent and you can enjoy the heady scent of the garrigue with every step.

c: If you want to avoid more climbing, return along the track on which you came. Arriving at the tarmacked road, turn right and follow it to a sharp corner where you join the path of choice b – Point 5 on the map. There are splendid views on this route, too.

5. If you chose b or c, turn right here on a broad descending track. After a few minutes walking you may be able to see where the goat path joins. Continue walking through the woods on the main broad track, ignoring all waymarks. After the valley narrows, you arrive suddenly above the site of Glanum and have a very good view of the excavations. Far-

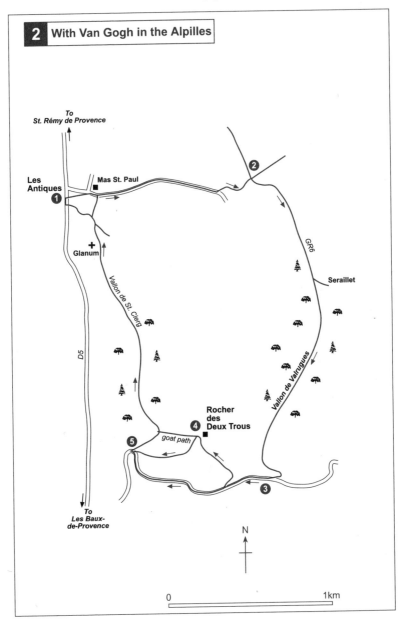

2 With Van Gogh in the Alpilles

To
St. Rémy de Provence

Les
Antiques
1

Mas St. Paul

2

✝
Glanum

GR6

Seraillet

Vallon de St. Clerg

D5

Vallon de Vairugues

Rocher
des
Deux Trous
4

5
goat path

3

To
Les Baux-
de-Provence

N

0   1km

ther on, a broad track joins from the right and you bear left downhill. On the right are the quarries painted by Van Gogh (*La Carrière de St Rémy*), and on the left, the entrance gate of Glanum, again with more painting sites, including that of *Les Deux Trous* and *La Montagne de St Rémy. Continue straight ahead now, taking a track along the edge of a field to reach the road, the D5. On its opposite side are the arch and mausoleum from where you started.*

More Walks in the Area

The Office de Tourisme at St Rémy can offer you a photocopied sheet with text in English entitled *The Footpaths of Les Alpilles*. Five routes are suggested – and described very scantily by British standards. If you aim to follow any of these, first get the relevant IGN map and make sure you know exactly where you are going. Each route is said to have yellow waymarking – but you can see from the one described here that you cannot completely rely on it.

One route whose waymarking can be relied on is that of the GR6. You could follow it to Les Baux (see Places of Interest), a distance of around 8km – being fairly demanding, it will take around 3 hours. The Office de Tourisme could advise you about transport for the return.

For other well-waymarked routes, ask at an Office de Tourisme for leaflets in the series *Topo Randonnée* produced by the *Comité Départemental du Tourisme des Bouches-du-Rhône* – for some reason, these excellent leaflets never seem to be on display. The maps in this series are first-class, so an understanding of the French text is not absolutely necessary. Nevertheless, it is worth persevering with this as the directions are for once comprehensive, and there is lots of interesting historical and geographical detail. The only detail lacking in these leaflets is an estimate of the difficulty of the walk – that must come from regarding the contours. One of the nearest routes to be described in this series is that starting from Orgon, a few kilometres south of Cavaillon. There's lots of interest on this one, but there are also a few steep slopes.

For less ambitious local walking in a classically Provençal landscape, ask for a series of leaflets entitled *Découvrez les Chemins de Randonnée (entre Alpilles et Durance)*. These walks are based on the villages north of St Rémy and are well mapped and well waymarked. The village of Maillane offers 9km of completely level walking (rare in these parts), although the interest level is not that high. Following the 12km *Chemin de la Transhumance* at Eyragues may be more exciting, with its olive groves, vineyards, oratories and views of the Alpilles.

Places of Interest nearby

Pursuing the Van Gogh theme, the Office de Tourisme in St Rémy can sell you a photocopied leaflet *Promenades sur les lieux peints par Van Gogh*. The leaflet is in French and scarcely does justice to so great an artist. The seven painting sites shown are all in the vicinity of les Antiques so could be visited at leisure after the walk. The Office de Tourisme offers guided tours of the sites in summertime.

The Mas St Paul de Mausole now functions as a medical clinic, but it offers a cool dark room (welcome on a hot day) with a continuously showing video of Van Gogh's life and work in St Rémy – French and English versions alternate. Inside the old monastery itself, a room has been

Arc de Triomphe, St Rémy de Provence

reconstructed as it was in Van Gogh's time, with a window looking out on what is said to have been his view over the Alpilles.

Reproductions of Van Gogh's work can be seen in the Centre d'Art Présence Vincent Van Gogh, housed in the Hotel Estrine. Exhibitions change every year.

St Rémy's other claim to fame is its superb Roman remains. The 'triumphal arch' was once the entrance gate to Glanum and dates from around AD 20. The mausoleum is around 50 years older. Glanum itself can be visited – although you get quite a good view on the walk. Finds from Glanum have been taken into St Rémy and displayed in the Hotel de Sade – a joint ticket will give you admission to both. All the attractions of St Rémy are open throughout the year.

South of St Rémy is the spectacular old hilltop village of Les Baux. Sadly, its old houses are now all souvenir shops and swarms of tourists throng its ancient streets. It is well worth visiting, but get here very early or at the end of the day – and preferably in January!

3. The Calanques of Cassis

South of Marseille, the limestone peaks tumble to the sea in a rugged shoreline of steep-sided coves known as *les Calanques*. This walk takes you to the three most easterly of these – where the shining white rocks, the turquoise sea and the deep greens of the vegetation make for some particularly stunning scenery.

Grade: Easy / moderate. There are several options for the return – see the Notes section below.

Distance: 8km (5 miles) approx., whichever way you go

Time: 3½ hours – but allow least another hour for exploration.

Map: The best is the IGN Plein-Air map no. 82011 (scale 1: 15,000) entitled *Les Calanques*.

Start and finish: The parking place at the Plage du Bestouan, Cassis

How to get there: The Plage du Bestouan is on the west side of Cassis beyond the port. From the town, follow prominent signs to Les Calanques, which take you around the outskirts of the town and then down to this large car park opposite the beach. There is a small charge for parking here in high season.

Refreshment: Just down the road in Cassis there are bars and restaurants of all kinds, but you will find none on the route.

Notes: This walk has little shade, so, in summer, make sure you take plenty of fluid with you, wear a hat and apply the sun-cream. The outward path is well-used, and includes a short rocky descent to the very pretty Calanque of Port-Pin and then a rather longer climb out of it. Neither could be classed as difficult, and trainers would be quite suitable footwear. The return from the Calanque d'En Vau can be made entirely on broad gravely tracks – but for wilder walking, you could choose instead a waymarked path crossing the garrigue and then descending into a deep valley. Those who can't get enough of a good thing can enjoy a final steep rocky scramble to leave this point – but others will be happy to know there are much easier ways home.

Waymarking: The route first follows the Grande Randonnée of the Calanques (GR 98) and so is waymarked in white on red. After leaving En Vau you can stick with broad but un-waymarked tracks all the way. The optional garrigue path is waymarked in yellow and brown.

Introduction

Calanque is an old Provençal word for a deep cove, and you will find it used all along the south coast of France. But the region of *les Calanques* – the 20km of indented shoreline between Marseille and Cassis – is something very special. Here two mountain massifs of glaring white limestone, their flanks thinly sprinkled with green pines and multi-coloured flowers, break into a crystal-clear sea with a cascade of islands, rocky peaks and coves of deep blue water. The calanques range from simply awe-inspiring to staggeringly beautiful.

Way back in time, the scenery here was very different. These mountains were covered in dense forest and the coves you now see are river valleys that were flooded when sea-levels last rose, around 12,000 years ago. Man was here well before that time. Deep beneath the sea in the rocky

Calanque of En Vau

sides of the Calanque of Sormiou, 1991 saw the discovery of a cave with wall paintings dating from around 20,000 years ago – predating even the caves of Lascaux by one or two thousand years. The paintings have been proved authentic, but they remain in their sub-marine world away from public gaze.

Today the Calanques enjoy legal protection as an historic monument. They are rich in wildlife – Bonelli's Eagle, the large ocellar lizard and Europe's longest snake live here (for snake-o-phobes, it's only a grass-snake – on the positive side, the area is completely free of adders). The vegetation is equally rich – more than 900 species are claimed, some being unique to the area. Botanists can look out for the Marseille astragalus and an even rarer asphodel. The creeks and valleys enjoy their own micro-climate – facing south, they are protected from all winds (and particularly the Mistral) and winter temperatures may reach 10ºC higher than those in Marseille, just around the corner.

Car access to the calanques is restricted, and fitness, stamina and sure-footedness are needed to undertake the demanding 28km path from Callelongue all the way to Cassis. The walk here gives you just a taste, taking in the three calanques at the eastern end of the chain. Each is very pretty in its own right – Port-Miou is the longest of the calanques and shelters a harbour of white boats, Port-Pin is much smaller with a sandy pine-shaded beach and turquoise water, and the calanque of En-Vau is undoubtedly the deepest and most dramatic of them all. The accessibility of these calanques means that, at least for the first part of this walk, you are unlikely to find yourself alone – but nothing can detract from the magnificence of these views. And whatever you do, don't forget the camera! One of the less obvious gems on this walk is the *trou souffleur*, a tiny 'whistling hole' in the rock above the Calanque of Port-Pin. Connecting with a sea-level passage below, its narrow bore produces a breathy hoot as each wave sucks out the air – if you go looking for it, ears are more useful than eyes.

For the return route, you have a choice of paths over the hillside with sweet-smelling garrigue at your feet and views of the pinkish steep cliffs of Cap Canaille across the bay. And if this short walk tempts you to see more of the Calanques, there are plenty of suggestions for further exploration in the **More Walks** section.

The Walk

1. Leaving the car park at the Plage du Bestouan, turn right and continue on the road uphill. After about 100m, follow the white on red waymarks taking you to the right on the Traverse du Soleil, a narrow road climbing steeply uphill. At the T-junction at the top, turn right on the Ave. du Révérend Père Jayne. As you descend on this road, a white limestone face can be seen ahead and you reach a wooden sign-post.

2. Turn left here following the GR98. After just a few paces on this path, look out for a waymarked right turn, taking you down a steepish path to the head of the Calanque de Port-Miou (before you turn down here, it's probably worth continuing on the top path for a couple of minutes to get the very best view of this calanque). Cross the head of the calanque and continue on the path alongside the moored boats on the far side. About half way along the calanque – and before it opens out – keep your eyes open for a waymarked path climbing the slope beside you to reach the quarries above. Walk ahead to join a shingly broad path running high on the side of the calanque, with some splendid views over the water. Coming to a rockface ahead, bear right up the slope beside you to reach the top of the cliff.

3. You are now only about 5 minutes from the *trou souffleur*. To find it, bear left here and follow the central path under the trees to where a deep calanque comes in below you on the left. Here, make your way to the left (not as far as the edge) and keep your eyes and, more importantly, your ears wide open – the hole is a mere 3 – 4 cm. in diameter. At this point the next calanque, the very pretty Calanque de Port-Pin, is below you to the right. Cross the isthmus of land and find a descending path that will take you along the side of the calanque. After crossing some rocks you arrive on a lovely little sandy beach with a few pine trees. On the far side of the beach an obvious path leads up the valley ahead. This is not the one you want! Go to the left of it and look for the white on red waymarks leading you up the rocky flank between the shrubs and flowers. Follow these to the top of the hill (they seem to disappear at one point, but all routes lead to the same place) and keep ahead to arrive at a cross-tracks with a stone signpost.

4. Continue ahead here, following the GR waymarks to the edge of the amazing Calanque d'En Vau where it begins the descent. Now you have a glimpse of how demanding this path can be. Follow it no far-ther, but take your time to explore the magnificent scenery of this calanque. To your left is the huge rocky finger known as the Doigt-de-Dieu, but there are many lesser *aiguilles*. Continue to the right and peer into the depths to see the tiny beach at the head of the calanque. White trip boats come and go on the cobalt-blue water, some allowing passengers to stop and bathe in summer – this

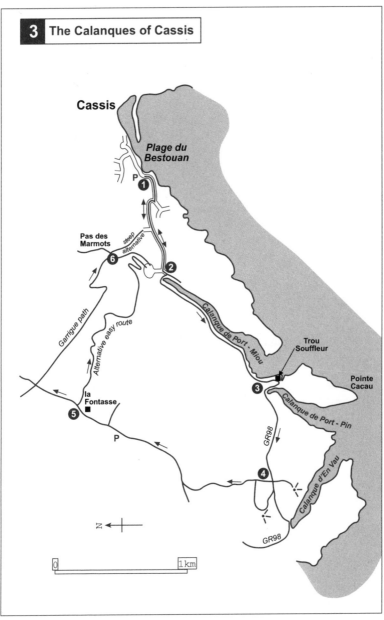

3 The Calanques of Cassis

calanque is one of the most spectacular sights on the coast of Provence, visited by around 800,000 people a year. When you have looked long and hard and taken all your photographs, return to the cross-tracks at Point 4. Now take the track that heads uphill (standing on the path on which you first arrived at this point, it's the track on the right). Continue on this, the main track, as it climbs, dips and climbs again with fine views of the cliffs of Cap Canaille across the bay. Reaching a small concrete area, bear right keeping to the main track, which now climbs steadily to arrive at a parking area. Continuing ahead, you now pass the yellow buildings of the Youth Hostel, la Fontasse, on the right.

5. Here a choice must be made:

The easiest option for the return is the rough access road that descends on the right immediately after la Fontasse. This road wiggles its way down the hillside and eventually arrives at the parking area behind the Calanque de Port-Miou. A couple of minutes walking uphill on the road from here returns you to Point 2.

For a wilder return, keep on the wide track passing la Fontasse and continue to the top of the hill. At a cross-tracks marked by a large stone, take the track crossing the garrigue on the right – there are yellow waymarks on this one. As you descend the hill, the path divides. Here take the left-hand option – a narrower path, now waymarked in yellow and brown. The path takes you down the flank of a slope to a narrow valley and you continue the descent along its stony floor. At length you emerge on a wide level track in another steeper valley at a place known as the Pas des Marmots.

6. The yellow and brown waymarks now direct you straight up the opposite side of this valley. But you don't have to follow them – you can simply turn right and walk through the valley to the car park behind the Calanque de Port-Miou. Turning uphill on the road here, you soon pass the signpost at Point 2 and can return along the road on which you set out. At the top of the hill you will pass the Impasse Calendal on your left – those who chose to follow the yellow and brown waymarks out of the valley at Point 6 will rejoin you here to complete the return to the Plage du Bestouan.

More Walks in the Area

The key to walking in the Calanques is the IGN 82011 map. This shows all possible paths and assigns a degree of difficulty to each. Do not even consider a 3-star route (they are the domain of the rock-climbers) and even a 2-star (the GR 98 is one of these) is only for more experienced walkers. The 1-star routes should cause little trouble and you could compose your own itineraries from these. One such possible circuit in the western part of the massif starts by following the GR 98 along the coast from Callelongue to the Callanque de Marseilleveyre. It continues on a green-waymarked path up the Grand Malvallon, crosses the slopes to la Madrague on a path waymarked in black, after which more black waymarks (or the coast road) will return you to Callelongue. The total distance is around 12km – but it will probably take you at least 6 hours.

If you are still keen to walk more of the GR 98 coastal path, but can't manage 28km of it in one day (who can?), there are various possibilities hinging on the car park at la Cayolle, about 2km from the Calanque de Sormiou, and approximately the mid-point of the whole route. Just along the road from here you can catch a no.23 bus taking you to the Gare de Prado bus station in Marseille. From here pick up a no. 20 bus to Callelongue if you want to walk the western half of the calanques, or a no. 13 bus to Cassis if you want to walk in the east. Life will be much easier if you have a friend who can drop you off in his car and pick you up at the end of the day. In all cases, an early start is recommended.

You may well like to visit the western end of the calanques just for comparison after you have completed the walk described. The west is more bare, the harsh white rocks and islands quite stark against that brilliant sea. But the vegetation is superb and some of the rarest plants are found here. For just a simple walk you could follow the GR 98 from Callelongue as far as the Calanque de Marseilleveyre (three-quarters of an hour approx.) and return by the same route. This does involve a rocky scramble around the headland at the outset (we watched a young man tackle this with a baby on his back and a toddler held by the hand!) – but the excellent informal restaurant beside the beach at the calanque can only be reached on foot, and should provide extra incentive.

Getting right away from the calanques, an impressive walking route known as the Route des Crêtes clambers along the summits of Cap Canaille (the sheer cliffs you could see across the bay on this walk). Well-waymarked in yellow, the route is a simple out-and-back taking around 2½ hours and the Office de Tourisme in Cassis can provide you with a free leaflet describing it. The sea cliffs of Cap Canaille are some of the highest in France and the coastal views are breath-taking. If you have a head for heights, give it a chance to prove itself – and if you haven't time for the walk, take a drive (see below)

Places of interest nearby

If walking is not possible, the best way to see the calanques is by boat. All year round (weather permitting) several boats a day leave from the Quai St Pierre in Cassis and you can choose how many calanques you want to visit – although the Cassis boats stop short of the western calanques. Some trips allow you to disembark for an hour or two at the Calanque d'En Vau and then catch a later boat home. To see all the calanques you will need to take a 4-hour trip starting from le Vieux Port in Marseille.

The coastline to the east of Cassis is almost as spectacular as that to the west – Cap Canaille appears to have been cut out with a giant spade, its sheer vertical cliffs rising to an impressive 394m.. Again, if you are unable to walk, there is an alternative (but by no means soft) option. Leaving Cassis by the D559, turn right where signed to the Route des Crêtes. The road climbs steeply and executes an amazing series of hairpin bends as it conducts you to all the best viewpoints with views from Marseille to Toulon.

Other delights in Cassis are the twice weekly (Wed. and Fri.) Provençal market, and the opportunity to experience the most palatable AOC Cassis wines. The white is apparently particularly good with the local delicacy sea-urchins (*oursins*) – and if you do consider trying the latter, you might like to know that it is actually their sexual organs and seminal fluid that you are eating – raw!

4. Climbing the Ste Victoire

The impressive limestone bulk of the Ste Victoire provided inspiration for Cézanne, who painted it many times. From the huge iron cross on its summit, there is perhaps the most awe-inspiring view in all Provence.

Grade: Moderate / strenuous

Distance: About 10km (6¼ miles) – but it's not distance that matters here.

Time: Around 2½ hours to the top – and it takes almost as long again to get down.

Map: IGN Top 25 3244 ET

Start and finish: The hamlet of les Cabassols, east of Aix-en-Provence

How to get there: From Aix, take the D10 east for 12km. Les Cabassols is just before the village of Vauvenargues and there is a small car parking area beside the road at the bus stop.

Refreshment: Take all you need with you. Vauvenargues can offer resuscitation at the end of the walk – or otherwise return to Aix.

Notes: There are many routes up the Ste Victoire (see the **More Walks** section), but this is the simplest, the most popular, and the only one that stays open throughout the summer. It is a straightforward there-and-back, following the GR9 all the way. The only difficulty is the steepness of the climb for the first hour or so – and coming down isn't any easier as the track, though wide, has many loose stones. Walking boots are the order of the day. Notices at the foot advise you to carry two litres of fluid per person (a couple at the top with us had their ration in red wine – it can't be recommended!). Above the forest line, the mountain is very exposed – according to weather conditions, you may need extra warm clothing or a large bottle of sun-cream. Do not even think of going in heavy rain, mist or high winds.

Waymarking: The white on red flashes of the Grande Randonnée are with you all the way to the top

Introduction

The almost vertical south face of the Ste Victoire makes it the most recognisable mountain in Provence. The north side is a little gentler – but it is the view from the west, a gigantic triangle of white rock, that inspired Cézanne to paint it more than sixty times during his lifetime in these parts.

The highest point of the Ste Victoire is the 1011m. Pic des Mouches at its eastern end – nevertheless, it is the western summit (945m) that attracts all the attention. At the apex of Cézanne's triangle is an iron cross 17m. high, lit up at night and visible for miles around. Below the cross an old priory is tucked into the mountain side. Abandoned by the monks in 1879, it has now been restored – services are again held in the chapel and some of the old buildings have found use as a mountain refuge. Across the courtyard of the priory is a well, and behind it a gap in the rock (Monks Gap) gives you a staggering view of the drop on the south side. Most people take it lying down – if you choose to stand, you will appreciate the support of the rope let into the rock face.

There is no 'easy' route, but the one described here ascends the north side and probably presents the fewest difficulties. It is marked on the map as the *Chemin des Venturiers*. The early part of this route is a steep

The priory and Croix de Provence

lung-bursting climb through the forest – surprisingly, the true inclination seems to strike you more on the return. Just when the priory is directly above you and you think the path can only get steeper the reverse happens – the forest ends and the strain is reduced by a series of zigzags across the open garrigue. The views increase with every step you take and your eye is drawn to the turquoise Lac de Bimont gleaming in the north-west.

The priory offers a welcome pause before the real objective, the huge Croix de Provence on the summit. Around 10 minutes of rocky scrambling will take you there – and it makes you wonder however that cross got up here, let alone how it was erected. The gentle breeze at the bottom is transformed to a howling gale up here (three previous crosses have been blown off) and you quickly dive for the relative shelter of a low-sided viewing platform. If you can bear to look, all Provence is laid before you, from Mont Ventoux to the Ste Baume, from the Alpilles to the Maures, and, on a fine day, even to the distant Alps.

The Walk

1. From the parking area beside the D10, an earthen path (SP Prieuré de Ste Victoire) leads on to a gravelled track. Turn right on this to head for the mountain – which, at this point, looks a little daunting. Walking downhill on this track you pick up the first, rather faded, white on red waymarks of the GR9. At an early fork, keep right, and soon you are crossing a stream. Now keep to the main track, following the occasional waymarks, and at another fork keep right around a metal gate (a slightly optimistic signpost here predicts your time to the priory and cross). Now you begin the ascent and after a slight dip, the rough stony track climbs in earnest – concrete has been laid on the very steepest parts. At around 1¼ hours from the start you reach a clearing with a metal seat – the hardest part is over.

2. To the left of the seat the much narrower path now climbs across rocky ground – the waymarks confirm your route. The cross towers above you, but the slope is definitely less steep and at last you have a view. Coming up the valley under the priory the path swings suddenly to the right and from thereon makes its way across the slope in a series

5. The Dentelles de Montmirail

To the west of Mont Ventoux, a lacy fringe of white limestone pinnacles breaks the horizon – the beautiful Dentelles de Montmirail. On this fairly adventurous walk you enjoy some stunning views from the rocky peaks – and on the return, a ruined castle and an orientation table are thrown in for good measure.

Grade: Moderate, occasionally strenuous

Distance: 5km (3 miles). A short cut will reduce this by about 1km

Time: 2½ hours

Map: IGN Top 25 3040 ET

Start and finish: Parking area at the Col du Cayron, east of Gigondas

How to get there: From Carpentras, head north on the D7, and in approx. 12km bear right on the D70 to Gigondas. Do not turn up into the village but continue ahead, soon climbing fairly steeply to the Col du Cayron.

Refreshment: You will need to take your own

Notes: This walk starts with a brief steep climb, followed by a winding balcony path tucked into woodland at the base of the rocks. The subsequent descent is fairly abrupt in parts. Walking boots have to be the order of the day for all this. The latter half of the walk is almost entirely on wide shingly tracks, the only difficulty here being one short sharp ascent. Although a 'short' walk, you won't find yourself moving very quickly, at least in the early part. Carry plenty of fluid and chocolate or other snacks. Much of the route is exposed, so make sure you have protection from the sun on a hot day.

Waymarking: Mostly blue splashes – just follow the text.

Introduction

The Dentelles de Montmirail represent the farthest extension of the Alps towards the Rhône valley. Here the sharp folding of the earth caused it to crack, so bringing to the surface a layer of Jurassic limestone. Many millennia of erosion have produced the landscape of today – three low green ridges topped by huge shards of gleaming white rock piercing the blue Mediterranean sky. From a distance the hills appear to have a scalloped fringe of white, hence their name (dentelle = lace).

Although quite northern hills, the vegetation here is definitely Mediterranean – the slopes are dotted with fragrant rosemary, holm oaks and Aleppo pines. In the valleys between the ridges are the vineyards of Gigondas, producing some of the very finest of the Côte-du-Rhône wines. The bonus on this walk is the opportunity to do a little sampling in the village before you go home.

The Dentelles de Montmirail occupy only a small area – it is about 15km from one end of the ridges to the other – but nevertheless they offer plenty of opportunity for outdoor activity. The rocks clearly are a climber's heaven – their south faces are accessible all the year round, being sheltered even when the dreaded Mistral is in spate. The hills themselves are criss-crossed by paths demanding varying degrees of agility while broader tracks running through the valleys below are ideal for cyclists and those looking for gentler walks. Both sorts of terrain are included in the route described here, but if you would like something easier or more adventurous, simply look at the **More Walks** section below.

At the heart of the Dentelles is the Col du Cayron, a convenient place to park your car for the start of this walk. From here a path heads straight up to the Dentelles Sarrazines, the central ridge and the most beautiful of the three. Fairly vertiginous paths now thread their way along the base of the rocks themselves – the route chosen is the gentlest option, taking you beneath the Rocher de Turc, a rock with a 'window', and at 627m., the highest point of the

Summit path through the Dentelles

Dentelles. There are splendid views south to the ridge of the Grand Montmirail and beyond. When at length you descend to the valley there are more views to be had from the Tour Sarrazine, a 12th century signalling post overlooking the Rhône valley to the west. And you can complete the full Provençal panorama on the way home when you pass the Belvédère du Midi, a viewing table identifying Mont Ventoux in the east and the arc of more distant peaks to the north.

The Walk

1. Across the road from the parking area, take a path signed *Sentier d'accès aux Dentelles* and marked with blue flashes. The path climbs quite steeply through the woods and after about 15 minutes, reaches a junction. Here another blue-flashed path goes off on the right, but you continue ahead, still climbing and following blue dots (and an occasional white 2 inside the blue circle). Arriving at the top of the slope you are in a photogenic location – a gap between two splendid limestone ridges. Here the path forks.

2. To the left is a path labelled as no. 3, a route for the footsure and fancy-free (see **More Walks**) – instead, turn right and climb the stony path (no. 2) to the base of the Rocher du Turc with its two holes. Here you will need to scramble up a rocky slope to the left (waymarked) to

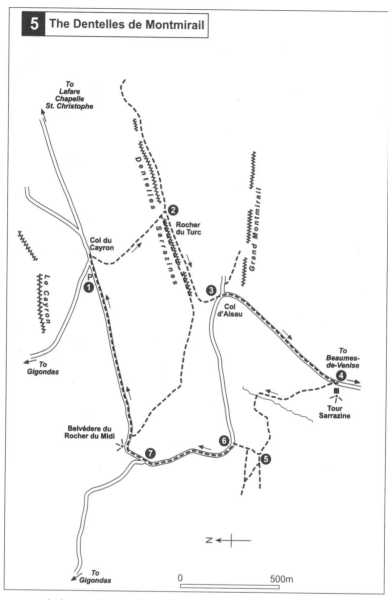

5 The Dentelles de Montmirail

reach the south side of the limestone teeth. An obvious path leads you on beneath the rocks. In a few minutes a path on the right leads to the Chambre du Turc, but is labelled *accès difficile*. At a gap in the rocks beside you, the stout-hearted can take a breath-snatching glimpse of the drop to the north. The path now begins to descend the south face. Ignore any path to the right (heading over the rocks) and keep to the main path left, looking for blue waymarks bearing the nos. 2 and 8. After a steep passage you arrive on the broad gravelled track at the Col d'Alsau

3. If you would like to shorten the walk a little (omitting the tower), turn right here and reach Point 6 in about 10 minutes. Otherwise, turn left

at this junction, and at the track junction in about 50m, keep right in the direction of Beaumes-de-Venise. 10 minutes downhill walking will bring you to the ruined Tour Sarrazine. A little more rocky scrambling is needed to get the view, but it's worth the trouble. To the south-east is the giant's back of the Luberon, succeeded by the jagged Alpilles and then the plains of the Rhône valley.

4. To continue you need to be a bit careful. Do not take the path descending into the valley (confusing – there's a blue waymark) but take the slightly wider path to its right, parallel to but below the very broad gravelled track on which you arrived. This track too has the occasional blue waymark (sometimes including a no. 4), and is obviously making for the head of the valley, with some vineyards on the far side. After crossing the stream the path skirts vineyards on the left and you can look back to the Tour Sarrazine on its hill. Soon you arrive at a clearing – and, as they do, all waymarks have disappeared. Turn left through the gap in the bank here and cross between the vineyards. On the far side, bear right around the red-roofed building and climb on a broad track beside a third vineyard to reach a multiple junction.

5. Take the track on the right here, climbing steeply uphill – you soon pass another 'blue 4' waymark. In a few minutes another track leaves on the left, but you continue with the climb ahead, now following yellow waymarks. At the top you arrive at a wide gravelled road.

6. Turn left on this road and enjoy the open views to the south-west as you go. Reaching the junction, ignore the road ahead to Gigondas (unless you fancy a little wine-tasting – the village is about 20 minutes away) and turn right in the direction of the Belvédère du Rocher du Midi. Just a couple more minutes along the road and you will reach it – except that there's a bit more climbing to do first. A series of log and then stone steps lead up a further 100m to the *table d'orientation* with its splendid panorama of the distant hills. When you have taken it all in, descend to the road and continue heading east. Fine views of the towering Dentelles Sarrazine, glowing in the evening light, accompany you on this last kilometre to the Col du Cayron.

More Walks in the Area

If you are thinking of more walking in this area, get hold of the leaflet *Chemins et Sentiers du Massif des Dentelles*, stocked by the Offices de Tourisme of Gigondas, Malaucène and possibly other places nearby. All the waymarked paths are shown on this leaflet – but be a little wary as they are not all strictly accurate (the area around the Tour Sarrazine, for example). It would perhaps be advisable before setting out to locate the routes on the appropriate IGN map (3040 ET). Note also that these paths vary greatly in difficulty, although there is no indication on the leaflet. Perhaps a couple of suggestions are in order:

For those looking for just a short ramble on good hard-surfaced tracks, start from the village of Gigondas, climb to the Belvédère du Rocher du Midi and continue on the track beneath the Dentelles Sarrazine as far as the Col du Cayron. Here turn downhill past les Florets and complete the circuit on the GRP *Tour des Dentelles de Montmirail* (yellow on red waymarks), shown on the IGN map. The total distance is around 4.5km

Anyone seeking a good rocky scramble could turn left instead of right at Point 2 on this walk. The path is not dangerous, but you will certainly be using 'all fours' much of the time. After a long up and down section beneath the sheer rock faces, the path suddenly begins an earnest descent to a vineyard and a hard-surfaced road. Turn left on this to return to the Col du Cayron. This is a short walk (just over 3km), but it is likely to take you at least an hour and a half.

An extension to the walk described, and a route of only moderate difficulty, could begin by turning left instead of right at the junction 50m after Point 3 on this walk. Almost immediately, ascend the yellow-waymarked path on the right, leading you along the slopes of the Grand Montmirail. This path eventually reaches the wide dusty track near the Chapelle St Christophe, and you can turn left for the Col du Cayron. Check out the route on the IGN map before you set off.

Places of interest nearby

In the pretty village of Gigondas are several caves where you can taste the delicious product of the vineyards seen on this walk. The village also boasts a walking trail dotted with modern sculptures.

Gigondas is one of the most prestigious wines of the Cotes-du-Rhône region. Even more exalted is Châteauneuf-du-Pape – the village is just south of Orange, about 20km from Gigondas. And a completely different treat from the vineyards can be sampled at the village of Beaumes-de-Venise, just south of the Dentelles, where the 'Muscat' grapes produce a mellow fortified dessert wine.

Aside from its superb wines, this region of Haut Vaucluse is fascinating. This is the Comtat Venaissin, in the 13th century ruled by the Popes who preferred the area to Italy and had their Papal Palace built in Avignon. In summer they moved out of town to Châteauneuf-du-Pape – you can combine the wine-tasting with a visit to the ruined Château du Papes.

In the south of the region two other places are worth a mention in connection with the River Sorgue. The river arises from a deep blue pool in a rocky enclave above Fontaine-de-Vaucluse. It was not until 1985 that an unmanned submarine probed its depths and declared them to be around 315m. The waters of the Sorgue arise from an extensive underground system draining the slopes of Mont Ventoux. The village of Fontaine-de-Vaucluse was much loved by the poet Petrarch and there is a monument to him at its centre. From here a long path lined by souvenir shops and stalls of all kinds leads you up to the bottomless pool. An intriguing place it is, but if you go along in the holiday season (which seems to extend from about April to November) you will find that not only Petrarch but about half the population of Europe appear to love Fontaine-de-Vaucluse. Perhaps give it a try in January – when in any case, the torrent arising from the pool is at its most impressive.

The Sorgue soon begins to divide, and by the time it reaches Isle-sur-la-Sorgue (5km) there are many branches. This 'little Venice' is blessed with many waterside walks. On Sundays these streets are the scene of the biggest antique market in Provence and again the visitors swarm around the honey-pots, making it difficult to drive through the town let alone park. Love it or hate it – it has to be worth a look.

6. At the foot of Mont Ventoux

For those travelling down the Rhône valley, the first glimpse of Provence is the white stony cap of Mont Ventoux. This giant is both high and wide, and from its bare summit to the forested lower slopes there are many fine rambles. Here is a walk for all the family, heading for a little-known viewpoint over the gorges of the River Nesque.

Grade: Easy

Distance: 5km (3 miles)

Time: 1½ hours

Map: IGN Top 25 3140 ET

Start and finish: The farm of Saint-Hubert

How to get there: Starting from Sault, head south to St Jean-de-Sault and pick up the D5 heading west. The attractive farm and gîte d'étape of Saint-Hubert stands beside that road in about 5km, and parking is possible on the roadside verges, close to the farm

Refreshment: None at all. Take your own for a picnic in front of the farm or en route.

Notes: This walk is on good tracks all the way and is almost entirely on the level – unless the weather has been very wet, walking boots are not necessary. The path ends rather abruptly at the viewpoint, where you will need to keep a close eye on children. Although the distance is only very short, it is still worth carrying fluids on a hot day – and, of course, put on the sun-cream.

Waymarking: Most of the route is on a Grande Randonnée (GR9) with white on red waymarks.

Introduction

Mont Ventoux is a mountain standing alone, the last far-flung western peak of the Alpine chain. Its name derives from the winds that constantly batter its bare stony summit – so white are the flakes of limestone here that from a distance the mountain appears snow-capped all year round. To the south-west, the next high ground is the Pyrenees – and from the summit on a clear day you can see the Pic du Canigou some 300km away near Perpignan.

Ventoux is 1910m in height and the first recorded ascent of the mountain was, surprisingly, made by Petrarch in 1336. Setting out from nearby Malaucène one May dawn, he was accompanied on this purportedly crazy venture by his brother and a couple of donkeys. When he arrived at the summit (and how long must it have taken him?), he described himself as 'stunned' by the panorama. That same peak can now be reached by car and is occupied by a radar station and a TV mast, a café and a souvenir shop – but it all makes no difference to the view, it's as overpowering as ever it was.

The whole massif of Mont Ventoux extends for about 25km in an east-west direction and is around 15km from north to south. Fortunately, all is not as bare of vegetation as the summit. Descending its flanks, you first reach a region of green alpine pastures and beyond them, the pine and oak forests and the deep gorges of its lower slopes. The best time to visit the mountain is in late spring when the high meadows are scattered

Rocher du Cire

with bright alpine flowers – or perhaps later in the year, when the colours of autumn touch the forests below.

The many differing terrains of Mont Ventoux provide excellent walking country. The short walk here is on the Plateau of Sault some distance from the mountain itself, but it has been chosen for three reasons – firstly, because it starts from the handsome pink-walled *mas* of Saint-Hubert with its splendid lavender-dotted meadow and view of the white-topped mountain; secondly, because the route ends at a unique viewpoint facing the towering pink-coloured Rocher du Cire and looking into the rocky-sided Gorges de la Nesque; and thirdly, because, unusually for these parts, the route is virtually on the level, making this particularly beautiful stretch of countryside accessible to everyone.

The Walk

1. Facing Mont Ventoux with Saint-Hubert behind you, turn left on the road (in the direction of Méthamis). The road first bends to the right (where it is joined by the Grande Randonnée) and then to the left. At this latter bend, leave the road and keep straight ahead on a track, following the white on red waymarks of the GR. At the fork in about 150m, continue ahead again, and a couple of minutes later, at another fork, keep to the right on the main path, which is climbing ever so gently. This truly lovely path winds its way through scattered woodland of oak and box, pines and juniper, with an abundance of wild flowers. Ahead you have glimpses of distant Mont Ventoux, while to the right the land falls into a valley with a smattering of farms. After around 15 minutes of walking you reach a clearing.

2. A few metres to the left you can see a wide earthen track. Walk over to it and turn to the right – you are still on the Grande Randonnée and there is a sign to the Jas de Barbéris. After following this wide track for about 500m, you arrive at a junction with a signpost. Bear right here, heading downhill in the direction of Monieux and Champ de Sicaude. You are still following the Grande Randonnée, which at this point is

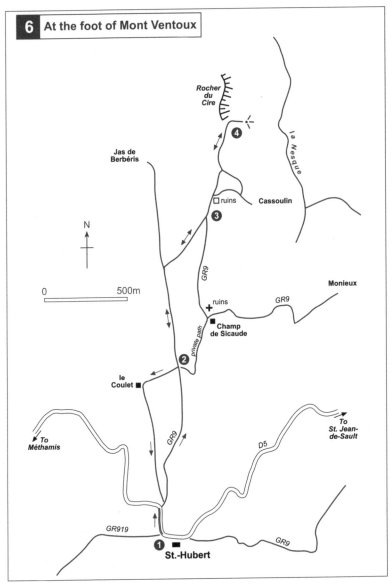

6 At the foot of Mont Ventoux

incorrectly marked on the IGN map. A few minutes farther on the Grande Randonnée buckles sharply back to the right to descend to Champ de Sicaude, a farm and ruined chapel in the valley below.

3. At this point, leave the Grande Randonnée and instead go through the gate directly ahead. A sign warns you that the track leads to the Domaine de Cassoulin, private property. Don't worry – you are not going down to the farm. To your right below the path here are the ruins of a shelter once used by shepherds and their flocks. Where the farm track bends right in about 100m, keep straight on along a lesser path between the trees. Arriving at a lovely clearing with rocks and wild flowers, bear left uphill. There are old-looking white on red waymarks – the GR obviously went this way once upon a time. Now

you are heading straight for a wall of rock, the Rocher du Cire (the translation is Rock of Wax – apparently bees have nested here). Just before the edge of the precipice the path swings right and descends – ahead of you is a rock painted with the words *Fin de Sentier*. It certainly is! You are on a sort of balcony high on the rocky walls of the gorge, with the pink-tinged cliffs of the Rocher du Cire towering on your left. Looking down you can see the river deep in its canyon and, way below you, the viewpoint on the road (D942) on the opposite side.

4. The return must be made by the same route as far as Point 2. Here you can vary things a little by continuing ahead on the broad track, which soon swings to the left as it passes the farm of le Coulet. Just before reaching the road, the track joins the track on which you set out, and you can retrace your steps to Saint-Hubert.

More Walks in the Area

There is unfortunately no topoguide covering the circular walks in this area. Instead, anyone with a working knowledge of French will enjoy the small book *30 balades en famille autour de Ventoux*. Don't be misled by the title – families in France must be more adventurous than in England because a few of these walks are technically quite difficult. But there is scope here for everyone and the difficulties, times, lengths, etc. are clearly stated with each walk. The maps however, though informative, are not too helpful for route-finding. You would need to locate each route on the relevant IGN map (most of them are on 3140 ET) before setting out. One particular route of interest from this collection starts from the Parking du Groseau on the D974 about 2km south-east of Malaucène. From this beautiful site a yellow-waymarked path leads you on a *circuit de découverte* which climbs to the top of the cliffs above the valley of les Gipières with some splendid views. The whole walk takes around 2½ hours – and you should also be able to get details of it from the Office de Tourisme at Malaucène.

The summit of Ventoux is not a particularly attractive location for walking – covered in loose stone with virtually no vegetation, there is no more windswept place in Provence. Nevertheless, it seems almost sacrilegious to arrive there by car. If you want just a short walk to the summit, start from the Chalet Reynard, 5km to the east on the D 974. Beside the chalet, take the path that climbs up the side of the little valley to reach the summit ridge and the GR4. Turn left on this path to the top – the whole ascent will take around 2 hours.

Those who want none of this quick dash stuff could consider starting from Sault on the eastern side of the mountain and following the GR4 all the way – a distance of 17km (each way) with an ascent of around 1200m. Anyone wishing to climb Ventoux *à la Petrarch* should climb the western flank from Malaucène. The GR4 is again your best bet – a distance of 22km with an ascent of 1550m should take around 10 hours allowing for pauses (and what with brother, donkeys and 14th century walking boots, it probably took Petrarch a lot longer than this). And don't forget you have to get back again. All the main routes up the mountain are clearly marked on the IGN map 3140 ET.

Places of interest nearby

Walk or drive, the summit of Mont Ventoux is a must. But there is another way up the mountain and you may well be amazed at the number of people taking it – cycling. Mont Ventoux is one of the classic climbs of the Tour de France and the ascending roads are painted with the names of its heroes – in particular France's beloved Virenque. Between Chalet Reynard and the summit is a memorial to the British cyclist Tommy Simpson, who died of heat exhaustion here on the Tour of 1967 when temperatures reached a record high. The many caps, water bottles and other cycling paraphernalia surrounding the memorial are tokens of respect left by passing cyclists.

As for the summit itself – to say the least, it's cluttered. In addition to the antennae of radio communications, there are cafés, car parks, a chapel, a souvenir shop and stalls selling everything from boiled sweets to sausages. Getting away from all this, there is the view – and no words can do justice to what is spread before you. Standing at the wind-scoured *table d'orientation* to the east you look to the Alps and the Vercors. From the *table* to the south of the summit the panorama extends over all the ranges of Provence to the Étang de Berre near Marseille. On the clearest of days, it is just possible to see the Pyrenees.

The attractive little town of Sault, on the D974 about 24km east of Mont Ventoux, is famous for its Wednesday Provençal market and for its annual Lavender Fair. Fine lavender (as opposed to the hybrid *lavandin*) thrives best at altitudes above 800m and the fields around Sault are ablaze with it in July and August. During these months, visit the Jardin des Lavandes, a lavender botanical conservatory with a collection of over 160 species. If you're here outside the season, visit instead the shop of the Jardin des Lavandes in the main street for lavender products to take home, including the plants themselves (although not much of Britain is above 800m). In Sault you can also visit the Vallon Lavender Distillery and exercise your legs again on a 4km lavender trail. The Office de Tourisme in Sault can give you details. And for lavender visits further afield, ask for the free booklet The Lavender Roads (in English)

7. The Gorges de Régalon – a walk for the slim!

The Gorges de Régalon are spectacular – at times the walls are less than a metre apart. Climbing out of this rocky chasm, you reach a lovely sunny plateau dotted with pine and broom, with fine views over the Durance valley

Grade: Moderate with one or two brief strenuous sections

Distance: 9.5km (6 miles)

Time: 3 hours

Map: IGN Top 25 3142 OT

Start and finish: Parking for the Gorges de Régalon

How to get there: The parking area is signed off the D973 Cavaillon – Pertuis road, about 4km west of Mérindol.

Refreshment: None – take your own picnic. There are a couple of bar/restaurants in Mérindol.

Notes: This walk is only possible after a spell of dry weather and should not even be attempted if rain is forecast. After a downpour the narrow gorge quickly becomes filled with rushing water draining from the hills above. But if the weather is fine, there is no reason why you should not go. The path through the gorges is at times very narrow (you're not really likely to get stuck) and there are one or two short 'hands-on' rocky scrambles, but nothing difficult or dangerous. Beyond the gorges, the tracks are wide and easy, with the exception of a steepish section of descent near the end. Trainers would be quite suitable footwear. The plateau at the top is exposed and you might appreciate protection from the sun here on a hot day.

Waymarking: None in the gorge (you can't get lost). Thereafter the white on red flashes of the GR6-97 will take you to Point 4. After Point 4, the waymarking is yellow all the way. There are also first-class signposts at every junction.

Introduction

On the edge of the Petit Luberon, the Gorges de Régalon claim to be the narrowest gorges in Provence. You can't really get much narrower – the path through one section is no more than 80 cm. wide, the width of an average household doorway. Beside you the near-vertical rock-faces rise some 30m, while above, huge boulders have become wedged in the narrow crack. Every gorge has its river, and after a heavy storm, torrents can rise suddenly in this restricted passage, so choose your day for this walk carefully. The path you follow is simply the bed of the river, with one or two scrambles up 'waterfalls' as you go.

Although all this might sound a bit alarming, for most of the year the bed is dry and the Gorges de Régalon make a very popular outing for families. On a fine summer weekend everyone is out enjoying the adventure – and the welcome shelter from the blazing Provençal sun. The gorges have their own micro-climate, cool and damp, in which species like box, ivy and butcher's broom obviously thrive and grow to enormous proportions.

At the end of the narrow rocky section the path emerges into woodland – and here most of the families stop for a picnic under the trees

Walking into the gorges

before the return passage. On this walk you go on, and climb to a fine open sun-baked plateau scattered with pine trees. From its edge there are views across the Durance to the plains with the ragged silhouette of the Alpilles rising in the west. The path takes you down across the Crau Mayorques, (*crau* (Occitan) = a stony plateau) where an old farmstead has been taken over by the Luberon park authorities. Its orchards now house the national apricot collection. The courtyard and old stone barns offer pleasant shade for a picnic. To return home, the path descends the south-facing slope with its splendid Mediterranean vegetation, while below you the plains of Provence stretch out to a distant horizon.

The Walk

1. The walk starts from the parking area on the right hand side of the road where there is a toilet block. Several paths lead out of this area and all eventually lead to the gorges – the best choice is probably the farthest path to the right, initially a stony track under the trees. After a few minutes walking you are joined by tracks from the left. Farther on another track arrives from the left and you bear right towards the rock faces. The path skirts an olive grove on the left and then joins a track coming from the right before entering the gorge itself. Soon the walls are towering above you and trees overhang. After scrambling over a rocky chaos of boulders you can look up to see a big rock wedged in the narrow crack above your head. A little farther on the path enters a cave. Don't be lured by the wide path on the left – it just returns you to the entrance. Instead squeeze yourself through the narrow fissure at the far end of the cave and just carry on climbing. After a rather tricky rocky section the path improves and after about 45 minutes (from the start) you emerge into woodland of holm oaks, laurels and box. Continuing on the obvious path, another 5 minutes or so will bring you to a fork of paths.

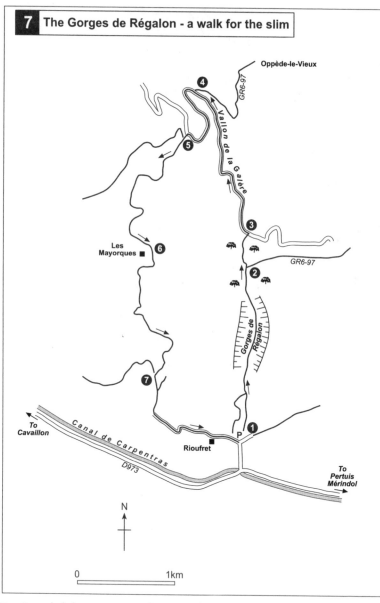

| 7 | The Gorges de Régalon - a walk for the slim |

Oppède-le-Vieux

Vallon de la Galère

GR6-97

Les Mayorques

GR6-97

Gorges de Régalon

To Cavaillon

Canal de Carpentras

D973

Rioufret

To Pertuis Mérindol

N

0   1km

2. Bear left here, now picking up the white on red waymarks of the GR6-97, and also the yellow waymarks of one of the Luberon walks (no. 23). A post tells you that you are heading for Les Mayorques and Trou du Rat. After a few minutes walking you reach a clearing and continue straight ahead, now on a much wider track. A few minutes more, still following the waymarks, and you are at a junction with a very wide stony track.

3. Turn left here in the direction of the Vallon de la Galère (galère = galley, a reference to the many Vaudois (see Places of Interest) who passed this way on their way to slavery). This wide track now climbs

between rocky outcrops to arrive at another junction graced by one of those excellent yellow signposts.

4. To the right the GR doubles back to head for Oppède-le-Vieux. Leave it to go, and continue ahead in the direction of Régalon (4.8km). Soon you round the head of the valley and continue climbing, with views back into the gorges. As the track bends again you reach a junction on a stony plateau.

5. Turn left here, and immediately left again in the direction of Ferme de Mayorques. The track here is crossing a high plateau dotted with pines and holm oaks and scented by rosemary and juniper. At a fork you can choose to go left around the small hill or ahead straight over it – the latter gives better views. Ahead the Alpilles rise jaggedly from the plain. The track now descends to the Ferme des Mayorques where along with olives and almonds, 48 ancient varieties of apricots are grown.

6. Walk around the wall of the farm (you can go in if you wish) and cross the field of almond trees in front of it. A signpost in the fence tells you that Régalon is now one hour away. The path ahead was once marked only by cairns, but you now have yellow waymarks to guide you. Over the crest of the ridge the path begins to descend quite steeply, and there are views of the blue River Durance below. Once that river was a wild torrent, but now it has been so tamed to provide hydro-electric power that its bed seems much too wide for it and there are many lakes and side arms. The path continues its rocky descent, always clearly marked – and the abundant colourful vegetation more than compensates for the one or two moments of difficulty. At the bottom of the slope you reach a junction with a wide track.

7. Turn left here, signposted to Régalon. The track is at first dazzling white and stony, but as you descend it becomes tarmacked. At the hamlet of Rioufret you pass a wayside spring as you continue on the road to regain the parking area.

More Walks in the Area

For those with a couple of days to spare, it is possible to enjoy a magnificent (if fairly demanding) extension to this walk, crossing to the north side of the Petit Luberon. After following this walk to Point 3, continue on the GR6 as far as the forest cabin of Bastidon du Pradon and on to the summit road (superb views). Here leave the GR6 and head west along the road for just over a kilometre to where a signpost directs you right to les Taillades. Descend the Vallon de la Sapine as far as la Citerne (just before la Bergerie), turn right in the direction of Robion and climb the slope. At its summit, keep right in the direction of le Quillot and descend the valley to the village of Maubec. Here there is a Gîte d'Étape (Gîte des Royères du Prieuré, tel. 04 90 76 50 34) where it is possible to spend the night. From here the return can be made on the GR6, passing Oppède-le-Vieux and Bastidon du Pradon and continuing to Point 4 to complete the circuit via Mayorques as in the walk described. All this will not make much sense until you have before you the appropriate IGN map (3142 OT) where all these paths are clearly marked in red – and be reassured, your navigation skills will be boosted by the excellent signposting at every junction. The distance from the Gorges de Régalon to Maubec is around 15km, for which you should allow at least 6 hours. The return route is just a fraction longer. If you can't make the whole round trip, perhaps you can persuade a friend to drive around via Cavaillon to meet you – this is truly one of the best hikes in the Luberon.

Yet another extension to this walk can be found in the Topoguide *Le Parc naturel régional du Luberon à pied* (Ref. PN01)– an excellent book describing 24 of the best walks in the Luberon (a very good investment if you are spending time here). Walk no. 23 in this book is a circuit of 18km starting from Mérindol and looking particularly at some of the history of the Vaudois in these parts (for more of this, see the Places of interest section). The route of this circuit joins our route at Point 2 – on our walk you then followed its yellow waymarks all the way back to the car park. The Luberon topoguide is published in French only, but with first-class maps and excellent waymarking on the ground, no-one should have difficulty following any of these routes.

In the topoguide referred to above, one other short circuit is described starting from Mérindol (actually from the car park in the forest on the south side of the D973). This very easy 3km circuit crosses the garrigue to the banks of the Durance above the Mallemort dam. Take it as a botany lesson – many Mediterranean species are named on the way – or just enjoy the ramble and spend a few minutes in the bird observation hide overlooking the swollen waters of the Durance.

Places of interest nearby

In the mid-16th century, the villages of the Luberon, and in particular Mérindol, were a stronghold of the Vaudois (or Waldensians). These early dissenters from the Catholic Church preached poverty and pacifism and later came to reject many of the established doctrines. Pursued by the Inquisition, the Vaudois were responsible for the sacking of the Abbey of Sénanque in 1544. The next year brought reprisal – an outstanding warrant for the arrest of 19 Vaudois from Mérindol was authorised and in the bloody conflict that followed, 3000 Vaudois lost their lives, hundreds more were sent to the galleys and many villages were burnt to the ground. Following the GR6 north out of Mérindol you will pass information panels relating to these events and climb to a memorial on a viewpoint above the village. In the surrounding hills are caves that were once Vaudois hide-outs, and also many isolated and unmarked graves, since these heretics were excluded from the Catholic cemeteries. For those interested in further pursuit of the story of the Vaudois, the Office de Tourisme in Mérindol can give you details of a themed itinerary, the *Route Historique des Vaudois en Luberon*.

A few kilometres west of Mérindol is the town of Cavaillon. At the western end of the main street is a Roman arch dating from the 1st century and nearby are the Romanesque cathedral and an architecturally superb synagogue. Above them all towers the rocky Colline St Jacques, with its chapel and splendid viewpoint. Cavaillon dubs itself the 'Melon Capital' of the world. In early summer the Monday market is teeming with them, July sees a 'melon festival' and throughout the season, the Office de Tourisme offers guided trips to the melon fields. Special – and extremely expensive – delicacies are melon liqueur and melon chocolate.

8. In the Shade of the Cedar Tree

Retreat from the heat to the breezy heights of the Petit Luberon where a forest of cedars offers welcome shade. Here are two short walks that could be combined, each offering magnificent views across the Durance valley.

Grade: Easy / moderate

Distance: 3km (2 miles) and 5km (3 miles). Combined walk 7.5km (4¾ miles)

Time: 1¼ hours for the shorter, 1½ hours for the longer (2½ hours combined)

Map: IGN Top 25 3142 OT

Start and finish: Car park for the Forest of Cedars

How to get there: From Bonnieux, take the D36 east for 1.5km and turn where signed to the *Forêt des Cèdres*. After about 5km on this climbing winding road you reach a barrier. A small fee is payable, after which you continue for another 2km or so to the car park.

Refreshment: None in the cedar forest – but you have plenty of choice in Bonnieux

Notes: Both these walks are on good tracks suitable for trainers. The shorter *sentier botanique* descends into a valley and then climbs again, but there is no real difficulty. The second walk around the Roque des Bancs is virtually flat. Take water and sun-screen with you, and perhaps binoculars for the view.

Waymarking: The *sentier botanique* is marked with yellow flashes – and there are information panels. The track along the Roque des Bancs is waymarked in blue.

Introduction

The widely spreading branches of the cedar tree create beneath them a cool fresh micro-climate of their own. Sitting down to rest in the shade of the cedar trees is not just a Biblical notion, but a very practical solution to an over-warm day!

The cedar forest here was sown by the local villagers in the 1860s using seed gathered from the Atlas Mountains in North Africa. It was a long-term policy – cedars take more than 50 years to reach maturity and begin to reproduce themselves. But cedar wood is valuable, its great density and impermeability making it very useful for carpentry and joinery. In 1952 a large part of this forest was destroyed by fire. Only its heart was spared, but cedars have tremendous powers of regeneration, and now a third generation is growing between and around the old. These young trees have pointed tops – the classically rounded shape of the stately cedar develops only as the years go by. Cedars have been venerated from ancient times, and their great age has, in some religions, made them a symbol of immortality.

The first walk here is a *sentier botanique*, taking you down into a valley and then up to a plateau overlooking the valley of the Durance. Eight display boards along the way tell you (in French only) about the natural forest and how it has been changed by man. At the viewpoint on the plateau, the last of the boards points out the more distant features of the landscape. If you feel like extending the walk there are plenty of opportunities. A

Roque des Bancs

narrow tarmacked forest road continues for several miles along the crest of the ridge, ideal for bikes, pushchairs and wheelchairs. The second walk described here takes you on a beautifully scenic path a little below the crest, a path flanked by buttresses of limestone known as the Roque des Bancs, and returns on the forest road. And for those who want something more ambitious, there is a longer waymarked circuit through the forest – see the **More Walks** section for details.

The Walk

1. From the parking area, walk around the road barrier and continue for about 200m At a signpost, turn left for the *sentier botanique* – there are also yellow flashes bearing the no. 11 (the waymarks of the long forest circuit). The wide gravely path winds down to the bottom of the valley through woodland where cedars give way to holm oaks (*chênes verts*) and downy oaks (*chênes pubescents*). On the way you pass the scene of old charcoal burnings (*le rond des charbonniers*).

2. At the bottom of the hill the path bears around to the right. Now you begin to ascend the rocky slope. If in any doubt about the path, look for the yellow flashes (there are old blue ones and a few orange dots scattered around as well, but they are less reliable). A few minutes after panel no. 6, look out for a small blue post with a yellow arrow beside the path. Turn sharp left here and ascend the slope – there are yellow waymarks on a tree and you pass to its right. Maintaining the same direction, you reach information panel no. 7, explaining that sheep no longer graze here and that box is taking over the plateau. Continue ahead to the concrete circle on the ground, and bear right to find the eighth panel at the viewpoint. Before you spreads the Durance valley, over to the left the Ste Victoire raises its rocky head, and to the right, the irregular outline of the Alpilles graces the horizon.

3. Turn your back on the Durance valley, and walk away, bearing slightly to the left. Now you reach an arrow telling you to bear right to reach a

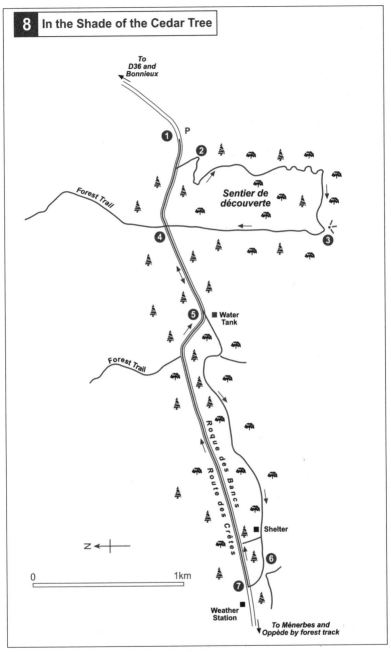

8 **In the Shade of the Cedar Tree**

To
D36 and
Bonnieux

P

*Sentier de
découverte*

Forest Trail

Forest Trail

■ Water
Tank

Route des Bancs

Route des Crêtes

N

0   1km

■ Shelter

■
Weather
Station

To Ménerbes and
Oppède by forest track

broad track. Continue on this for about 10 minutes to reach the main forest track, the Route des Crêtes

4. Turning right here, you will quickly return to the car park. To take the second walk, turn left here and continue for a further 10 minutes or so, to where the road takes a bend to the right – there is a water tank on the left hand side.

5. Take the narrow blue-flashed track to the left of the road here. After a couple of minutes, you reach a fork and bear left, still following blue flashes. The narrow path cuts through the vegetation. At another fork about 5 minutes later, keep right and continue descending gently. Ahead you can see the white rock bulging from the side of the slope, and soon you are walking along below it. The path winds through flowering shrubs and there are more wild flowers at your feet. The Durance valley falls away to your left giving some splendid views. The path meanders on beneath the billowing rocks until after 20 minutes or so you reach a stone wall probably built as a shelter, beneath the overhanging rockface. Here the blue waymarks direct you up the slope behind the rock. Do not follow them, but continue ahead on the clear path (ignore the blue cross). After a couple more minutes walking, you reach a fork just before the head of the valley.

6. Surprisingly, there are more blue waymarks here. Follow them up the slope to the right to arrive at the edge of a stony plateau. On the far side of the plateau are some cedar trees and, beyond them, the road. The path across the plateau is indistinct (and the blue waymarks seem to have disappeared again) – the best you can do is to look for the most used route, as indicated by the browner earth and turned stones. This will lead you across to the right and in a couple of minutes you reach the belt of cedars. Once in them, a clear short path takes you to the road.

7. Turn right on the road. After about 1km, you pass a yellow-flashed track heading into the forest on the left. This is the forest circuit (no. 11) and following it, you will extend your walk by about 9km (see below). For the less energetic, a further 15 minutes or so along the road will see you back at the car park.

More Walks in the Area

If you are spending any time in this area it is well worth getting hold of the Topoguide *Le parc naturel régional du Luberon à pied (Ref. PN01)*. The Luberon is prime walking country and 24 of its best walks are described in this slim volume – including among them the *Circuit des Cèdres*., the yellow-flashed circuit no. 11 that you met on this walk. This Topoguide is produced in French only, but its excellent maps combined with the first-class waymarking on the ground should ensure that you have no problem with any of the routes.

Route no. 12 in the topoguide (*Le vallon de Combrès et la Sautadou du Bausset*) is a more ambitious forest hike, this time on the north face of the Luberon. This fairly demanding 12km walk starts from the medieval village of Oppède-le-Vieux, perched on one of the ridges that characterise this north slope. After a hard climb up the wild valley of Combrès, where Atlas Cedars offer shade, you again reach the forest road along the summit (*Route des Crêtes*). The descent is at times steep, but there are splendid views to Mont Ventoux in the north. While at Oppède, visit the landscaped terraces of Sainte-Cécile with their collection of local species.

Another route of interest is no. 22 from this topoguide, the *Grande Tour de Mange-Tian* (8km). The starting point this time is the delightful village of Goult – famed for its terraces of olive trees. At first descending to the Imergue River, the path climbs steeply to encircle the stony plateau of

Mange-Tian, where there is evidence of ancient habitation. Unfortunately at the time of writing, the yellow waymarking on this route was in need of renewal – this will almost certainly be done, but in any case, the topoguide map is quite good enough to get you round.

And finally, Walk 10 in this book starts just a few kilometres to the east, near Buoux in the valley of the Aiguebrun. It is also possible to walk between the villages of Bonnieux and Buoux on a well-marked Grande Randonnée du Pays (GRP *Sentier de la Pierre* – see under Walk 10) – all you need is the appropriate map (3242 OT) and someone to pick you up.

Places of interest nearby

Bonnieux is a classic hillside village, a photographer's dream. Unfortunately it is teeming with people in season (which seems to be most of the year) and it is difficult enough to drive through it, let alone find a parking place. But if you do, you can wander through terraces of old streets and admire views to both north and south. The *Musée de la Boulangerie* (open in high season) attracts visitors with its wide range of traditional breads.

Just a few kilometres west, Ménerbes is yet another old *village perchée*. Its fame grew to astronomic proportions when Peter Mayle settled here and wrote about it in his best-selling book, *A Year in Provence*. His old farmhouse (he now lives in Lourmarin) is on the D3, on the right just after the playing field – there are usually a few (or many) fans in the vicinity. Forgetting Mayle – the curious Corkscrew Museum (*Musée du Tire-Bouchon*) is well worth a visit.

The most photographed of all the *villages perchées* is surely Gordes (15km north-west of Bonnieux, across the N100). The best viewpoint is on the D15 west of the village. 3km to the north of Gordes is the Abbey of Sénanque, set among the lavender fields and beautiful in its Cistercian simplicity. It is open for visits throughout the year.

Coustellet (on the N100 north-west of Ménerbes) is home to the *Musée de la Lavande* – the museum is owned by a family who farm the Château du Bois north of Apt in the Monts de Vaucluse. Just a few minutes here and you will be in no doubt of the superiority of fine lavender over the hybrid lavandin. A 10-minute film will give you a good idea of the farming year, after which you can browse through the collection of old stills and other equipment and finally leave with your supply of fine lavender essence and probably a lot more. In July and August, when the lavender is in flower, it is possible to visit the Château du Bois and take a 2km signposted path around the purple fields.

9. The colours of ochre

The ochre quarries of the north Luberon are no longer in use – but the brilliant colours remain and the rocks have been weathered into a miscellany of curious shapes. Choose a sunny day for this walk, which contrasts the lush green vegetation of the hills with the blazing colours of the quarries below.

Grade: Moderate

Distance: 11km (7 miles)

Time: 4 hours

Map: IGN Top 25 3242 OT. The snack bar in the car park will sell you a (rather confusing) map of the quarries.

Start and finish: The car park for the quarries, near Rustrel

How to get there: From Apt, take the D22 north. At the junction in 10km, keep ahead on the D22 (do not follow Rustrel). After a further kilometre or so, the car park is signed on the right hand side.

Refreshment: A hut in the car park sells light snacks, drinks and ice-cream. For anything more substantial, you will be very well served at the auberge in Rustrel.

Notes: This walk is all on reasonable tracks and could be undertaken in light shoes or trainers in dry weather, although boots would probably be preferable. At the beginning of the walk there is a steady climb on a good broad track – the corresponding descent near the end is on a lesser track, but presents no particular difficulty provided you stick to the waymarked route. Make sure you have protection from the sun and carry water with you.

Waymarking: Up to point 7 the route is waymarked in yellow. After that – just follow the directions.

Introduction

According to one text there are 17 colours of ochre. In another it is 25 – but goodness knows how anyone can count them. Standing in the quarries here in Rustrel you can run your eye over the whole spectrum from deepest red through radiant yellow to almost white. The area has adopted the title 'Colorado Provençal'.

A rather gruesome local story goes that way back in time, the lord of the lands around Apt had a beautiful wife, who fell in love with a troubadour visiting his castle. When the husband discovered what was happening he took the young man out hunting – and stabbed him to death. His heart was cooked and duly served for dinner the next day. At the end of the meal the wife was told what she had just eaten – at which she promptly rushed outside and threw herself off the nearest cliff. It is her blood that has stained the earth so deeply.

If you prefer a geological explanation, this area lay under the sea for over a hundred million years. When the waters retreated, green sands were left behind on a bed of clay. Heavy acidic rains fell on the earth and the iron in the sands was oxidised, thus producing a brown pigment. This natural ochre was known to Neolithic man and used by him to paint on the walls of his cave. The Romans were probably the first to quarry for the pigment, but the present quarries here in Rustrel were opened only towards the end of the 19th century. The ochre was extracted by washing and filtering away the impurities, after which the residue was taken off for drying. This was sometimes followed by baking in high-temperature ovens. The quarries here closed in 1956, by which time a synthetic ochre could be produced more cheaply.

Today traditional values are returning. Though many quarries have fallen into disuse, a few are still able to continue production. Houses in this area are now only coloured using natural products – if you have time at the end of this walk, take a few miles drive to the village of Roussillon to see how splendid these colours are in the light of the setting sun.

The walk at Rustrel first takes you out on to the hills behind the quarries. There are fine views of the hump-backed Luberon before you dip into the pine forest on the flanks of the 'Colorado Provençal' where there are glimpses of orange and gold between the trees. Eventually you enter the quarries themselves. The area known as the Sahara is dazzlingly red under the hot sun. Where the sands are covered by iron and clay deposits, erosion has left many strange pinnacles of rock, known as *Cheminées des Fées* (fairy chimneys). At one point there is a tunnel through the cliffs, in another, the path is a 'river of sand'. There will probably be plenty of visitors in the quarry – most of them getting lost on account of the discrepancies between the maps issued in the car park and the signs on the ground! Just follow the directions here to take you past all the most interesting sights.

The Walk

1. Leave the parking area and walk down to the road below it. Follow the road to the left, and where it bears right, continue ahead on a descending track marked with both yellow flashes and the white on red flashes of a Grande Randonnée (and also signed to Barriès). At the bottom of the hill cross the stream (the Doa) and bear to the left, passing the ruins of an old cabin. Now keep on the main track, which is well waymarked. The track passes lavender fields and then climbs to a fine viewpoint over the quarries. The whiteness of some of the rock is due to the removal of ochre pigments. The path continues to climb quite steeply.

2. Here the GR leaves you and continues across the rocky slope to the left. You continue on the main track, now following signs to the Croix de Cristol. Below you on the right is the ravine of Barriès, named after a brave woman who lost her life fighting for the Vaudois. At the top of the slope, the track meets a tarmacked road – turn left here, following yellow waymarks. At the junction in about 300m, turn right and continue as far as a ruined farm surrounded by cypress trees at the top of the hill.

3. Now take a broad gravelled track curving around the edge of a field on the right. To the left now is the village of Caseneuve, and beyond, the dark green hills of the Grand Luberon. Over to the right there are distant glimpses of the Lure mountains and below you is the deep valley of the Doa. The path continues along the edge of the plateau and then descends to a junction.

4. Turn right here and descend quite sharply. Soon you again come to

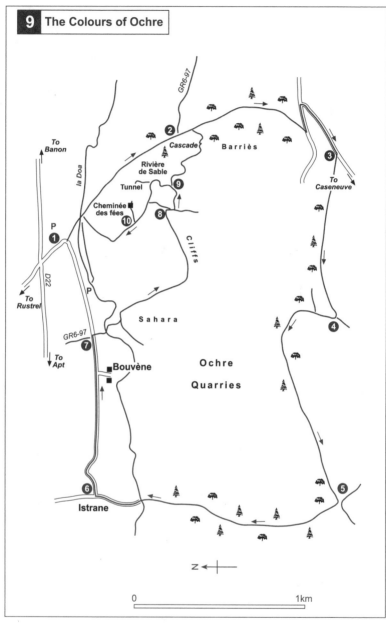

9 The Colours of Ochre

the edge of the ravine and follow a lovely path through the woods with views over the colourful quarries below. The path meets a wide track and continues beside a cultivated field, and then yet more lavender. Ahead of you is the hill of St Cristol, but at its foot you reach a junction with a signpost

5. Turn right here in the direction of Istrane. The terrain falls away quite steeply and 'gravestones' warn you of the dangers of straying from the path. Soon you reach the edge of the quarry, where once again you are asked to keep on the marked route. There are quarries to the left

table indicates the northern ranges of Provence. From another viewpoint beyond the Place Pignotte you can look more locally to the ochre-stained *Aiguilles du Val des Fées*. More brilliant red cliffs are in view from the road beside the Office de Tourisme – if you walk towards them you will find yourself at the start of the *Sentier des Ocres*. There is a small fee for this short walk (45 mins approx.) but the extraordinary formations and their range of colours are well worth seeing. The path is open every day, the hours varying with the season – outside July and August, aim to arrive before 5pm

When you have finished touring the village, you might like to consider a visit to the *Conservatoire des Ocres et pigments appliqués* in the old Usine Mathieu (1km south of Roussillon, on the D104 to Apt). It is open in the afternoons between July and October but only occasionally outside those dates. On a guided tour you can learn something of the history of extracting ochre and even buy a few kilograms of the pigment to take home (a face-lift for the house, perhaps?)

10. Buoux and the valley of the Aiguebrun

On a rocky spur above the gorges of the Aiguebrun, the ruins of the medieval village and fort at Buoux are some of the most impressive you will find in Provence. Before or after a visit, take this ramble around the valley, passing through Sivergues, said to be 'the village at the end of the world'.

Grade: Moderate

Distance: 12km (7½ miles), with optional 5km extension

Time: 4½ hours (taking the extension will add almost another 2 hours)

Map: The route of this walk (or virtually all of it) can be found on two different IGN Top 25 maps – 3242 OT and 3243 OT

Start and finish: Car park on the D113 south of Buoux

How to get there: Buoux is in the heart of the Luberon, just east of the D943 Apt – Cadenet road. Leave that road on the D113, but at the fork (2km), do not turn left for Buoux, but continue ahead, signed to the Fort de Buoux. There is a car park on the left hand side in about 200m.

Refreshment: There is a very pleasant auberge in the village of Buoux, but no other refreshment possibilities en route.

Notes: This walk is all on good well-waymarked tracks and minor roads. There are just two notable sections of ascent (to the hamlet of Chantebelle and out of the Aiguebrun valley) but both are short and not too severe. In dry summer weather, trainers would suffice – otherwise go for stouter footwear. And much of the route is exposed, so if the day is hot, think of protection from the sun.

Waymarking: Most of the route is waymarked in yellow. But in places you will also see white on red and yellow on red waymarks – just follow the text.

Introduction

The Aiguebrun is the one and only permanently-flowing river of the Luberon and its deep valley represents the great divide – to the west are the gentle shoulders of the Petit Luberon, to the east, the more severe slopes and higher peaks of the Grand. The valley is a very special site. Deep, cool and humid, the vegetation here is that of more temperate climates. At the base of its cliffs are many caves, once the home of Neanderthal man who hunted the deer, wolves and bears that roamed the valley some 50,000 years ago. Later, when man could create his own shelter, he moved to the slopes above, and it was probably in the Bronze Age that the spur on which the Fort of Buoux now stands was first occupied. From that time until the 17th century the promontory high above the river provided a place of security, a site easy to defend, a point with a clear view along the length of the valley. At the time of the Wars of Religion the fortified village became a haven for the dissenting Vaudois of the Luberon. Subsequently taken by the Catholics, the fort had again become a Protestant stronghold when Louis XIV ordered its destruction in 1660.

This walk starts near the fort and you will probably want to have a look around before you set out. The little flower-decked house where you pay a modest entrance fee gives no hint of the fascinating place that lies up the stone steps beyond. It would be easy to spend a couple of hours here. Equipped with a leaflet in English, you can explore every detail of this medieval citadel – trenches, watchtower, guardrooms, church, houses, cisterns for water, silos for food and all the rest. In springtime the whole site is scattered with wild flowers – and there are always superb views into the valley.

When you are ready to leave (the more footsure could exit via the 'hidden' staircase from the postern gate), the route here takes you on up the valley. Deep caves can be seen in the cliffs as you climb up to Chantebelle – the farm built into the rock here is all that remains of a one-time *bastide*. Farther on is the pretty hamlet of Sivergues, again perched above a ravine. This place, too, was a stronghold of the Vaudois, and in its turn was almost entirely destroyed by the Catholics. Over the last two centuries Sivergues has been restored to its former glory. Unfortunately it has also been supplied with a car park – its epithet 'the end of the world' seems much more apt outside the months of July and August. Beyond Sivergues the route descends to the river, and then climbs to a plateau dotted with loose stone where fields of lavender line the track. Eventually you reach the village of Buoux itself – its auberge (Auberge de la Loube) was apparently a favourite of Peter Mayle in *A Year in Provence*. And for those with a real surplus of energy, a further loop will take you past the 17th-century Château de Buoux and along a woodland trail with a splendid stone *borie* before returning down the valley of the Loube.

The Walk

1. Leaving the car park, turn left (east) along the road. In a couple of minutes you will pass a second car park, this time on the right of the road. At the back of this car park, steps lead to a waymarked path into the woods, a path that shortly emerges on a wide hard-surfaced track that is the access road to the fort. If you want to visit it now, turn uphill to the right – otherwise (or after the visit), walk downhill on the track, passing another car park as you return to the same road you left earlier.

2. Turn right on the road and continue up the valley. The sheer cliffs on its opposite side are very popular with rock-climbers. After about 10 minutes walking, a track to the left leads down to the pretty Auberge des Seguins, tucked under the base of the rocks. Ignore it and keep ahead (right) here, following the yellow on red waymarks of a Grand Randonnée du Pays. At a fork in about 200m, bear right, now leaving the waymarks. The path climbs, and soon you will pass a path on the left (bearing the white on red flashes of a GR) dipping down into the valley. Continue on the main track uphill to reach a wider open area.

3. Here the GR turns away to the right, but you continue uphill, following yellow waymarks. The wide path you are on was once a well-used mule track in the days when salt was a valuable commodity and was transported this way from the coast. Where the path reaches the valley of an entrant stream it bears to the right – there are huge caves in the base of the cliff ahead. The cobbled track continues and curls left around the head of the valley. A few moments after this, where

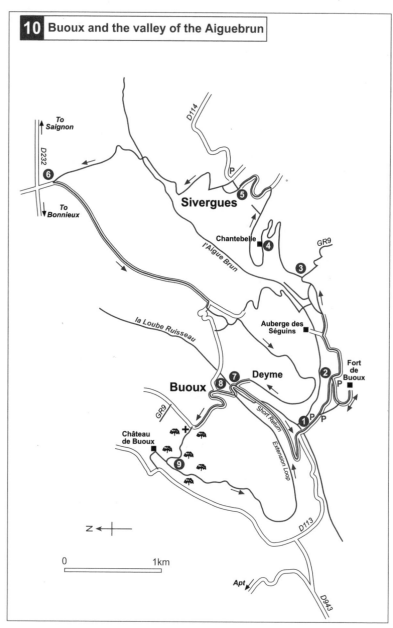

10 **Buoux and the valley of the Aiguebrun**

the track hairpins back to the right, the yellow waymarks invite you to leave the main track for a narrow track into the trees on the left. No-one seems to have done this (the path is very overgrown), so it seems best to keep to the mule track which zigzags up the slope to the buildings of Chantebelle, jammed into the rock.

4. Bear around to the left on a balcony path, and at some big rocks, follow the yellow waymarks to the right. There are views of the terraces on the opposite side of the gorge and you can also see a cave in the cliffs. Continue ahead on this track (ignoring a track crossing a wall on the left) to reach the head of another valley. At the track junction here, turn left and then keep to the main track as it winds its way up to Sivergues where more houses are built into the rock.

5. Turn up the ramp in front of the big stone building (this was the old fort, now converted to a gîte d'étape). The cobbled track leads you right through the pretty hamlet, past the chapel and on to a junction with the car park on your right. Turn left (a signpost indicates Apt and Barbe Blanche this way) and walk down past the cemetery wall. At a junction where Chantebelle is signed to the left, keep ahead, now again following the yellow on red waymarks of the GRP down into the valley of the Aiguebrun. Reaching the river, you cross on stepping stones, and in a further 20m or so you arrive at a path junction. Keep left here to begin the climb out of the valley. This pleasant path now zigzags gently up the stony slope – there are several junctions, but at each you keep to the main waymarked track. At the top of the slope the waymarks lead you ahead beside a wall to reach a track junction. Continue ahead and walk between lines of trees to reach a narrow tarmacked road.

6. Turn to the left here in the direction of Buoux. You now have an easy walk of around 2km on this road on the edge of the stony Plateau of Claparèdes. On either side are fields with walls, piles of stone (*clapiers*), and the occasional broken-down *borie*. Some of the fields have been planted with lavender. To the right is the valley of the Loube, and looking behind you can see Mont Ventoux – often enough with its head in the clouds. After around half an hour of walking the road swings sharply to the right. About 40m farther on, take a track on the left signposted to *les Ramades*. This gravely track soon brings you to another junction where you swing left, briefly joining the GR9. The broad track you are on now veers right and you keep to it, leaving the GR9, which dips into the valley of the Aiguebrun again. The track winds its way around the border of the plateau and becomes tarmacked when it reaches the hamlet of Deyme. Shortly afterwards you descend to the D113 near the village of Buoux.

7. If you want a quick return from here, simply turn left on this road. It drops down through the high-sided rocky gorge of the Loube to a road junction near where that stream joins the Aiguebrun. Turn to the left for about 200m to reach the car park.

    If you would like an extra loop to the walk (around 1¾ hours), or would just like to see Buoux itself, turn to the right here The road climbs to the renowned Auberge de la Loube (closed on Wednesday and Thursday) and you then continue on a track on its right hand side. Turn right on the road into the village.

8. Keeping the *Mairie* on your left, turn left on a road that climbs and swings back to the right. You are again on the GR9, which is now taking you past an oratory to the 11th-century Chapel of Sainte-Marie at the top of the hill. In front of the chapel, leave the GR9 and bear left (SP Bonnieux), now following yellow on red waymarks once more. This delightful path descends through woodland of oak and box. To the right there are glimpses of the château through the trees. Reaching a track junction at the bottom, the château is to your right –

Ruins of the Fort of Buoux

and it looks a lot less attractive from here. The intact part dates from the 17th century, but one wing is simply a shell – the Revolution prevented its completion. The château is now used as a study centre.

9. Go along for a look at the château if you wish, but your homeward route turns left at this junction. The track is waymarked in yellow, and leads you first through oak woodland. Later you reach more open terrain and pass a magnificently constructed *borie* on your right. Farther on you pass newly-planted lavender fields and there are views across to the fort on the opposite side of the valley. Finally you reach the D113, just south of Buoux. Turn right here and return through the gorge of the Loube to the car park (see Point 7)

More Walks in the Area

To the east of Buoux rises the Mourre Nègre, at 1125m the highest peak in the Luberon. From its summit on a clear day there are views from the Massif Central and the Alps to the sea near Marseille. The shortest ascent of the Mourre Nègre starts from a car park just off the D48, south of Auribeau, and should take around 1½ hours. Other routes start from the village of Cucuron, to the south of the mountain. The topoguide *Le Parc naturel régional du Luberon à pied* describes an 18km (7 hour) circular hike from that village, including a section along the crest track. You will not need a knowledge of French to follow this route – both the map in the topoguide and the waymarking (*balisage*) are excellent.

The yellow on red flashes you met on this walk were the waymarks of the local Grande Randonnée du Pays, known as the *Sentier de la Pierre* (Stone Trail). The circuit skirts the Plateau of Claparèdes with its many dry-stone walls, terraces, agricultural buildings and ancient villages. The whole length is 45km, and as it is so well waymarked, any section could be followed with ease. Locally, you could walk from Bonnieux to Buoux, a distance of 7.5km, but you might consider the whole circuit (two longish days), staying overnight at Bonnieux, Apt or Saignon. The complete itinerary of the *Sentier de la Pierre* is shown schematically at the back of the booklet *Balades en Luberon – Apt*, obtainable inexpensively from the Office de Tourisme in Apt. From this, the route should be translated to the appropriate IGN map (3242 OT) before setting off – altogether not a simple task, but patience should give results (and the waymarking is there to confirm them).

And finally, Walk 8 in the cedar forest is very close by. It offers a choice (or combination) of two short routes in an attractive woodland setting – and might be particularly appealing on a hot day.

Places of interest nearby

Buoux is at the very heart of the Luberon, one of the most distinctive and traditional areas of Provence. The entire region was given the status of Natural Regional Park in 1977. If you are staying for any length of time, begin your exploration by visiting the *Maison du Parc* in Apt. Here you can get information on flora and fauna, find maps for cycle routes (very popular) and purchase walking maps and the regional topoguides. The building also houses a small museum of palaeontology – the northern part of the Luberon is a geological reserve and you can get details of 28 sites of significance to be visited. In addition to the *bories* and other dry-stone buildings in the north, the Luberon is also famed for its ochre quarries (see Walk 11), its lavender fields (see Walk 8 for an interesting museum), its olive oil (the *Maison du Parc* can give you details of several oil mills that can be visited) and its wine (the Luberon has its own AOC)

Following the Aiguebrun south through the divide known as the Combe de Lourmarin, you will first reach Lourmarin itself, a town dominated by its impressive château (visits possible throughout the year). Further on is Cadenet, where the *Musée de Vannerie* (Basket-making and Wickerwork) is worth a visit. A few kilometres farther south, on the banks of the Durance, stands the Abbey of Silvacane. Clean and unpretentious in style, it embodies the Cistercian belief in simplicity, poverty and closeness to the earth. Silvacane Abbey has suffered the usual catalogue of wars and destruction (including Cistercians at war with Benedictines at one point). But since 1949 it has been under restoration and can be visited throughout the year, except for Tuesdays in winter.

11. Bories on the Plateau de Vaucluse

The old hilltop village of Viens is the starting point for two delightful short walks with splendid views. On each of them you will come across *bories*, the traditionally built stone huts that are particularly found in this area.

Grade: Easy

Distance: Northern circuit 4km (2½ miles), southern circuit 3km (2 miles)

Time: About 1½ hours for each circuit

Map: IGN Top 25 3242OT

Start and finish: Both circuits start at the archway entrance to Viens on the west side.

How to get there. Viens is about 16km east of Apt on the D209. Arriving on that road, there is roadside parking facing the bell-tower and archway. Otherwise turn left at the bell- tower and park at the viewpoint at the top of the hill.

Refreshment: There is a bar/restaurant opposite the bell-tower.

Notes: These two circuits can easily be joined to make a longer walk – you might do one in the morning and one in the afternoon with a leisurely lunch in the village between. The tracks for both are good and you would be quite happy in trainers unless the weather had been particularly wet. There is not a lot of shade, so take appropriate precautions on a hot day. Both walks are short, so you could give your rucksack the day off – leave water in the car or visit the bar/restaurant. And take the camera – bories are very photogenic.

Waymarking: Both circuits are waymarked in yellow

Introduction

The sun is blazing down from a clear sky, you have been working out in the fields all morning and now it's time for a spot of lunch and a rest. But where to go to escape the heat? Well, there's that stone hut in the corner!

That's just one theory for the use of these bories – they offered refuge from the weather, be it scorching sun or drenching rain. They were also a good place to store a labourer's tools. Larger bories could give shelter to animals, even to whole flocks of sheep. And no doubt some of the largest were temporary dwellings for shepherds and perhaps their families when the sheep were on high pastures in summertime. In places whole villages of bories have been found – huts grouped behind stone walls, accompanied by stone outbuildings and even a communal stone bread-oven

There are bories all over Provence (and elsewhere), but the greatest concentration of them is to be found in the Luberon and on the Vaucluse plateau, where the underlying rock is limestone. Whole areas are scattered with loose stone, used by previous generations for building their farmhouses and cowsheds and for constructing walls to enclose the flocks of animals. In the fields and more remote places were built the little dry-stone huts called bories. Round, square or even ovoid in shape, they were given a double wall and a door that always faced south or south-east. The roof had no supporting beams but was formed from flattish stones known as lauzes – these were set at an angle to shed the rain and laid in ever-decreasing circles until the whole hut was finished with just one stone on the top. It is thought that the earliest bories were built around

2000 BC – although the ones you see today are not likely to be more than three or four hundred years old.

To learn more about bories, you can take a trip to the Village des Bories near Gordes, where around twenty of them have been preserved. On both circuits of this walk near Viens, you will find bories 'in the wild' – no longer in use, but on their natural sites, where they were originally constructed for agricultural purposes. On the northern circuit there are two bories to investigate, while on the southern circuit you will return up a valley where one slope is entirely covered with ancient stone dwellings. But both these circuits are also splendid walks in their own right, with hilltop paths, marvellous views of the Calavon valley to the north-east and a wealth of wild flowers springing from the limestone grassland at your feet. And between the two routes is the tiny walled village of Viens with its tall houses, narrow streets and hilltop château.

The Walk

Northern circuit

1. Facing the entrance to Viens beneath the clock-tower, turn left up the D33 in the direction of Simiane. Reaching the viewpoint with its stone seats, look left to find stone steps up the bank opposite. Continue with the wall on your left and almost immediately bear left following yellow waymarks. These then lead you across stony ground with views on either side – to the left is the north face of the Luberon, to the right, the land falls away to the valley of the Calavon. On the left you soon pass the first borie, crumbling a little with age – go around to the other side to find its door. Continue on this splendid path lined by pines, broom, juniper, heather, and, in spring, the lovely blue *aphyllanthes*.

2. Emerging at a junction with a field ahead, the waymarks direct you to the right. They are leading you to a spot (a clearing) that was once a viewpoint looking out to the southern slopes of the Monts de Vaucluse – unfortunately the Scots pines have now grown up and you can only catch a glimpse of it. Beyond this clearing the path is suddenly marked with a yellow cross and you can go no more – retrace your steps to Point 2 and now continue ahead (if you don't want to bother with the viewpoint, you will need to turn left here). After passing a lavender field on the right the path swings to the right (ignore the track ahead). There are now lavender fields on your left, and between them, a few almond trees. You arrive at a junction with a wide cross-track

3. On the other side of the track there is a borie with an enclosing wall. When you have looked around, turn left on this track and follow it past lavender fields and various ensembles of stone. Reaching the village of Viens, the track bears left to meet the road on which you set out. Turn right to return to the clock-tower.

Southern circuit

1. Facing the clock-tower, turn to the right and walk downhill. At the bottom, in front of the Post Office, turn sharply right (there is a yellow waymark and the no. 16B – the number refers to a circuit in the

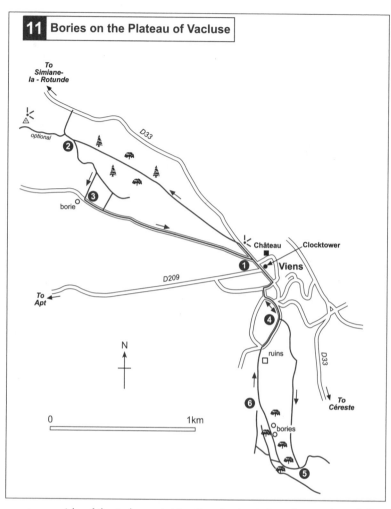

11 Bories on the Plateau of Vacluse

topoguide of the Luberon). Meeting the 'main' road, turn downhill to the left and continue around the bend. Two roads now leave on the right – take the most right of the two.

4. After about 150m on this road, take a track on the left, curving round alongside a fence. The track is waymarked, but there are also waymarks on the road ahead as the circuit returns that way. The track passes between stone walls and emerges as a balcony path along an edge with splendid views across the valley below. Holm oaks shade your path and the rocks are covered in red sedum. The path descends gently, and soon there are olive groves below you – this is just about as far north as you will find them. Soon you arrive at a path junction with yellow waymarks on both paths.

5. Turn right here on a lovely path under mixed oaks. In a few minutes you reach a fork where the yellow marks direct you to the left. Instead take the path on the right, running around the flank of the hill – it is this one that will lead you to the bories. You reach them very soon – first, one with a fine stone lintel, and then, set back from the path, one

with a curious vaulted arch. The path continues past the bories (there are still yellow waymarks here) and then bends to the left. In an area of stone walls you reach a track junction with a field ahead.

6. Walking to the left a little here you can get a glimpse over the wall – there is a very fine more recently constructed borie in this field. But your way home is to the right, climbing uphill between the walls. In a few minutes you pass the ruins of what was once a splendid stone house with outbuildings. Continuing uphill, you soon reach a tarmacked road at a junction. Turn right here to return to Point 4, from where you can simply retrace your steps to Viens.

A borie near Viens

More Walks in the Area

If instead of turning right at the Post Office in Viens you turned left, you would find yourself on the GR6-97 with white on red waymarks. Following this trail for about 4km would bring you to the bridge over the spectacular Gorges d'Oppedette. From this point on the Grande Randonnée takes an exciting route above the gorge on its eastern side, after about 3km reaching the medieval fortified village of Oppedette itself. It is possible from there to return to the bridge on a route marked with yellow flashes along the western side of the gorge. The whole circuit is described in the topoguide *Le Parc naturel régional du Luberon à pied* (Ref. PN01) – the text is in French, but the map and waymarking are together quite adequate to get you round. It must be said that this route is physically quite demanding and also requires a head for heights – it is definitely not for children.

Starting from Oppedette, another excellent route is described in the Luberon topoguide. The 15km circuit at first continues along the GR6, but then heads east to include the Belvédère de Vachères, yet again a splendid viewpoint – except that this is possibly more splendid than most. To the north are Mont Ventoux, the Lure and the Pre-Alps, to the south, the Luberon and the ever-visible Ste Victoire.

Finally, two other walks in this book are not too far away – Walk 9, visiting the ochre quarries of Rustrel, and Walk 10, touring the Aiguebrun valley and the Fort of Buoux.

Places of interest nearby

If you can't walk the Gorges d'Oppedette, it is well worth taking a drive to see them – park near the bridge at the south end or farther on where the road comes close to the edge of the gorge. From Oppedette you can walk south on the Grande Randonnée for just a few hundred metres to a viewpoint overlooking both gorge and town – from the entrance to the village, turn left before the *lavoir* and follow the white on red waymarks.

To learn more about bories and other stone constructions, visit the Village des Bories on the D2, about 4km south-west of Gordes. Here about twenty bories, each more than 200 years old, are now restored and put on show – some were apparently human dwellings; others were animal houses, toolsheds and more. The village is open daily throughout the year.

Back in Apt, all you could ever want to know about the Luberon is housed in the Maison du Parc in the Place Jean-Jaurès. Books, maps and advice on walking and cycling are on offer, along with a free exhibition of all things typical of the Luberon. For a few euros, you can also visit the Museum of Palaeontology and see some of its very distant past. The Maison du Parc is open every day except Sunday all year round.

12. The legend of the Ste Baume

High in the Ste Baume mountains, the Grotte de Sainte Marie-Madeleine is a place of pilgrimage, a site blending faith, history and legend. A not-too-difficult walk takes you from the cave to a chapel on the summit of the cliff above, from where there are views over all Provence.

Grade: Moderate. Not technically difficult, but there is a sustained climb

Distance: 6km (3¾ miles) – 2km less if you decide not to climb to the summit after visiting the cave

Time: 3 hours allowing for a visit to the cave and time at the summit. Around 2 hours to the cave and back.

Map: IGN Top 25 3345 OT

Start and finish: Hôtellerie de la Ste Baume

How to get there: The massif of the Ste Baume is just to the east of Marseille. The Hôtellerie stands beside the D80 between Nans-les-Pins and Plan-d'Aups, close to that road's junction with the D95. There is plenty of parking space on the grassy plateau beside the road.

Refreshment: The Hôtellerie de Ste Baume is a religious institution offering accommodation, good food and even packed lunches. The nearby souvenir shop doubles as a bar and restaurant serving light meals.

Notes: This walk involves a steady but never-too-steep climb of around 280m to the cave, followed by a descent and an optional further 100m or so of ascent to the summit. Only the final section along the hill is exposed – elsewhere you are in shady forest. The paths are well-surfaced, and in reasonable weather you would not need more than trainers or stout shoes on your feet. Even though the walk is short, it is wise to carry fluid and perhaps chocolate. The usual mountain rules apply, at least for the final section – in mist or very high wind, don't go.

Waymarking: The route to the summit is on a Grande Randonnée, and thus is well-waymarked in white on red. The path of the return is obvious, with occasional yellow waymarks.

Introduction

The massif of the Ste Baume is a 12km limestone ridge, running from east to west in the typical manner of Provence's mountain ranges. But this particular range is a geological curiosity. Formed by the folding of the earth's crust in the tertiary era, the fold here split and turned over, leaving the older rock to cover more recent deposits. The Ste Baume's northern face is a sheer cliff; the south side is covered in Mediterranean garrigue and slopes much more gently.

Beneath the cliff on the north side is a forest of oaks, beeches, limes, yew and holly, the sort of forest you might find in much more northern latitudes. The overhanging rock offers shade and creates its own cool micro-climate. The woodland here is 'ancient', a curious survivor from the tertiary era, when all Provence was covered in forest and temperatures were much like those in Britain today. Most probably on account of this different vegetation, the forest has been considered sacred from pre-Christian times – but lying so silently beneath the massive cliffs it easily lends itself to suggestions of a mystical nature.

High in the cliff face above the forest is a huge cave (*baoumo* = cave in Provençal, hence the name of the range) – a cave that is associated with one of the most famous legends of Provence. It is said that after the Crucifixion, Mary Magdalene, Mary the sister of the Virgin Mary, Lazarus, St Maximinus and others escaped persecution in the holy land and crossed the Mediterranean, landing at the place that is now Saintes Maries-de-la-Mer on the edge of the Camargue. St Maximinus and Mary Magdalene travelled inland, he to found a priory and she to preach and then to live in retreat in this cave for 30 years. When she died, she was buried by St Maximinus in his priory, on the site of the Abbey of St Maximin-de-la-Ste Baume today. A skull said to be that of Mary Magdalene rests in a reliquary in the crypt. The cave in the cliff was inhabited by monks from the 5th century onwards and over time has become a place of pilgrimage, with special celebrations both on Whit Monday and on Mary Magdalene's feast day, the 22nd of July. On Christmas Eve, Midnight Mass is held in the cave after a procession through the forest.

From the 12th century onwards, this sacred site has been under the care of the Dominicans. The walk starts from their hostelry, the Hôtellerie de la Ste Baume, from where you can look up to the buildings around the cave in the cliff and to the little speck that is the chapel on the peak you are heading for. Don't be put off – it is nowhere near as difficult as it may look. A steady climb through the forest takes you to the oratory below the cave – from here you climb 150 steps (matching the 150 Psalms of David and 150 Ave Marias of the Rosary) to reach the cave itself. It contains a shrine and an altar – and of course, there is a splendid view from the terrace. Sadly a rock-fall forced the cave's closure in 1998, but at the time of writing, it was scheduled to re-open at Easter 2002.

Returning from the cave to the oratory, you can continue to the summit of the cliff, a height known as St Pilon after a column which has long since fallen down and been replaced by the chapel. Beside the chapel is an orientation table (and quite possibly a flock of mountain goats). The views encompass all Provence from Mont Ventoux and the

At the orientation table

Luberon in the north to the massif of the Maures and the distant south coast at la Ciotat. From here the descent is easy, and you can vary the route to take in the Chemin des Roys, the traditional pilgrim road to the shrine, taken by many kings both French and English over the centuries.

The Walk

1. Standing on the road, take the track to the left of the hostelry and shop – it soon turns to head for the forest and cliff, and is waymarked as a Grande Randonnée (white on red). On reaching the forest, turn right on the broad track, and after about 50m, bear round to the left, following the waymarks. Now just continue along the obvious track, which climbs steadily through the oaks and, later, beeches. Do you feel at home in this forest? After something like half an hour, you reach a cross-track and bear left. After another 5 minutes or so, you arrive at a junction known as the Carrefour de l'Oratoire (Crossroads of the Oratory). The oratory represents Mary Magdalene at the Holy Sepulchre.

2. Turning right on the concrete road here, you can climb and then take the 150 steps to reach the cave. After the visit, retrace your steps to the oratory. If you now want to return directly, continue on the downhill path ahead (the Chemin des Roys), and read the directions under Point 2*. Those who want first to climb to the summit should instead bear right, taking the broad path climbing uphill below the rockface. At this point you wonder how you are ever going to get up there. The path is not too steep, but continues its relentless ascent. Soon you pass the Chapelle des Parisiens, dated 1636, and then another oratory representing Mary Magdalene at the feet of Jesus. Eventually the path makes a little rocky climb and bears right to go over the Col de St Pilon.

3. Turn to the right and follow the white on red waymarks carefully. The path crosses rocky slabs and keeps well below the crest of the ridge. It is in no way difficult or dangerous, but you should note the way you came, as it seems less easy to find it on the way back. After a few minutes walking you see the chapel above you on the right – legend has it that seven times a day, angels lifted Mary Magdalene to this spot so that she might hear the music of Paradise. You probably won't hear more than goat bells, but climb up and take in the views from the excellent *table d'orientation*. Every feature is identified, from mountain ranges to islands off the south coast. When you have seen it all, return to the Col de St Pilon and retrace your steps down to the Carrefour de l'Oratoire (Point 2).

2* *This time take the track to the right, continuing the descent. You are now on the Chemin des Roys, the ancient pilgrim route. Soon you pass a fountain on the right that is the 'Source of the Nans' and further down there is another oratory. When finally you can see the road ahead, do not go down to it, but turn left on a yellow-waymarked track along the edge of the wood. After a few pleasant minutes of level walking, you reach the point at which you entered the wood earlier, and can turn right to return to the hostelry.*

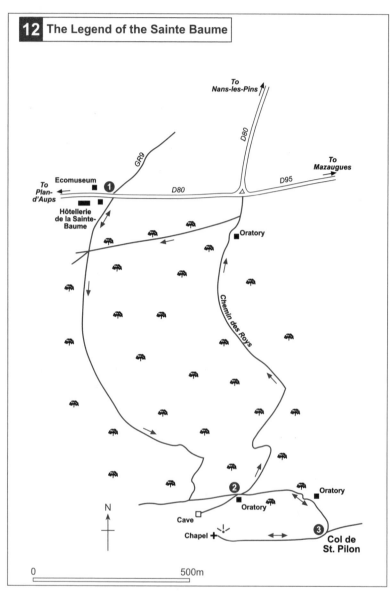

12 The Legend of the Sainte Baume

To Nans-les-Pins

D80

GR9

Ecomuseum ❶

To Plan-d'Aups

D80

To Mazaugues

D95

Hôtellerie de la Sainte-Baume

Oratory

Chemin des Roys

❷ Oratory

Oratory

Cave

Chapel

❸ Col de St. Pilon

N

0   500m

More Walks in the Area

The Chemin des Roys continues from the foot of the mountain all the way to Nans-les-Pins – the place where the kings took lodging before making their pilgrimage. There are three more oratories along the way. The route is actually that of the GR9 – the white on red waymarks are easy to follow and you would reach Nans in a further 2 hours or so. The GR9 is marked on the relevant IGN map (3345 OT) – but you can also find details of it among the leaflets described below.

    The Office de Tourisme at Nans-les-Pins (in the town square) has produced a series of seven waymarked walking routes, on sale for a few euros. Printed on A4 sheets and bundled into a brown envelope, you wonder what you are getting – but these walks are full of interest, the English translation is delightful and much appreciated, the maps (photocopies of the IGN) are clear, and the routes are well-waymarked. A walk for everyone is the 2-hour ramble entitled The Nans Way – it passes the old village and takes you along a botanical trail produced by the local school to reach the hilltop ruins of the old castle. On the way you can divert to climb up to a cross known as the Sainte-Croix, from which there are some splendid views of the Sainte-Baume and further afield. Other longer walks take you to the viewpoint at the Chapel of Notre Dame d'Orgnon, to the source of the Huveaune river and through the vale of Castelette. It is the latter route that includes a return on the Chemin des Roys.

Another source of walks in the region is a little booklet entitled *Guide Promenades – La Provence Verte*. You should be able to find it in the Offices de Tourisme at Nans-les-Pins, Plan-d'Aups, St Maximin de la Ste Baume and many other places. This guide is entirely in French, but you get some reasonable maps, all relating to waymarked routes, and a wide area is covered.

Places of interest nearby

Across the road from the Hôtellerie is a rather dilapidated building housing the Ecomusée de la Ste Baume. Inside is lots of information relating to this fascinating area, from the Christian traditions surrounding it to the ecology, flora and fauna of the ancient forest itself. There are permanent and temporary exhibitions, a video room with a variety of programmes and a wealth of literature is on offer, including details of walks. The ecomuseum is open daily throughout the year, but in afternoons only out of season.

Following the story of Mary Magdalene, a visit to the Basilica of Ste Maximin de la Ste Baume is the next step. It is said that her remains were originally kept in a sarcophagus, and then secretly buried in the 8th century to escape the clutches of marauding Saracens. In 1279, they were re-discovered by Charles II of Anjou, and he together with the Pope of the time decided to build a Basilica worthy of being their resting place. A monastery was built next door, and the relics were put in the care of the Dominicans. Today only Mary Magdalene's skull remains, housed in the crypt of the basilica, where it can be visited. Beside it are the sarcophagi of St Maximinus and other saints. The basilica has other points of interest. A milestone with Roman inscriptions, dating from the 1st century AD stands in the cloisters and the organ is one of the finest in France. The latter was lucky to escape destruction in the Revolution. The basilica was converted to a food store at the time, and the organist cunningly protected his instrument by giving a fine rendering of the Marseillaise at the approach of any Revolutionary officer. The organ can be heard in a series of summer concerts in July and August.

13. A tour of Cap Sicié

Just west of Toulon, the green headland of Cap Sicié thrusts deep into the blue Mediterranean. Colourful shrubs, wild flowers, butterflies and cicadas enjoy its surprising tranquillity – all are there on this walk, which starts by visiting the chapel on the highest cliff above the sea.

Grade: Easy – with optional moderate sections

Distance: 7km (4½ miles)

Time: 3 hours allowing browsing time

Map: IGN Top 25 3346 OT

Start and finish: Aire des Mascs in the Forêt de Six-Fours

How to get there: From the town of Six-Fours-les-Plages, head east on the D16 in the direction of Mandrier-sur-Mer. Approaching les Sablettes, turn right at a roundabout, following signs to *Notre Dame du Mai* (and the *Corniche Merveilleuse*). The road winds uphill with some fine coastal views and eventually arrives at the parking area known as les Mascs, in the heart of the forest, and not too far from the chapel.

Refreshment: None on the walk – although you do pass a large picnic area. There are plenty of bars and restaurants in Six-Fours

Notes: This is a walk you can easily take in trainers. Virtually all of the time you are on good tracks – although in places a rougher but perhaps more interesting path through the garrigue has been suggested. Even though this is 'forest', you are often exposed to the sun and appropriate precautions are recommended. It would also be sensible to carry fluid. Many tracks cross this lovely forest and all sorts of extensions are possible for those who want a longer walk – see the **More Walks** section. As with all woodland in this area, the paths will be closed at times of high fire risk (most probably from 15th June to 15th September)

Waymarking: There are lots of waymarks in the forest, but at the time of writing, all the colours were being changed! The only reliable waymarks are the yellow flashes of the *Sentier du Littoral* (Coastal Path). Elsewhere, just follow the text.

Introduction

This is a walk for simply wallowing in splendid vegetation and fine sea views. Here you are on the south coast in the heart of holiday country – Six-Fours, Sanary and Bandol are some of the most popular resorts – and you can escape to this delightfully green forest with mimosa, eucalyptus and umbrella pines set above the sparkling sea. The flowers are even more remarkable. This headland is slate, as opposed to the limestone found farther west, and in spring and early summer the coastal slopes display the bright purple French Lavender (*Lavandula Stoechas*, known in France as the *Lavande des Maures*). Other flowers to be found here depend on the season – spring is no doubt best with the rosemary in flower and the rock roses beginning to show their colours. On the slopes facing the sea, the cliffs are spectacularly covered from February to April in the pink flowers of Sea Mallow (*Lavatera Maritima*) – if you are here at the right time, it is worth a diversion.

The walk starts with a climb to the Chapel of Notre Dame du Mai. Perched at the top of the cliff, it is not perhaps as beautiful an edifice as it might be – but it does have a story. Once upon a time there was a lighthouse here on Cap Sicié. In a terrible gale one night in 1625 it was completely destroyed – yet somehow the lighthouse keeper survived. In recognition of this miracle, first a cross and then a chapel were erected on this spot. It became a chapel for mariners, a place where they could pray for calm weather or bring their ex-votos, tokens of thanks for safe delivery from storms. This latter custom died with the 19th century, but many ex-votos remain in the chapel. Unfortunately it is only open at certain times – throughout the month of May, when there are pilgrimages and on some other Sundays and Feast-days. Outside the chapel is an orientation table on which you can pick out features of the coast from the Calanques near Marseille to the islands of Port-Cros and Porquerolles. The walk continues from here to an old signalling station and after descending a slope with some fine views across the harbour of Toulon, dips into the valleys and hills of the forest. At one point you can choose to follow a *Sentier Botanique* and the walk returns along the route of the annual pilgrimages, a road flanked by oratories.

The Walk

1. From the parking area, walk uphill. After 200m or so, a road joins you from the right, but you continue uphill, where the Chapel of Notre Dame du Mai is now signed. Coming to a junction below the chapel, continue on the road to the right, which seems to be heading for a transmitting station, but instead curves round to the chapel itself. Take time here to admire the sea views and check out the *table d'orientation*.

2. When you are ready to go on again, you have a choice. Just below the steps of the chapel a yellow-flashed path heads off downhill to the right. This cuts across the garrigue to join a broad main track. The same point can be reached by returning from the chapel to the road-junction, and then taking a broad track behind a barrier on the right. This broad track continues to a junction below the old *sémaphore* (signalling station), from where you can walk up to take a look at the crumbling buildings with their view. (another 'short-cut' is possible on the way – just look at the map)

3. From the *sémaphore*, again the yellow-flashed *Sentier du Littoral* heads off on the right and sweeps downhill – you can easily see where it is heading. If you prefer a wider track, return to the junction below the *sémaphore* and now take the track on the right. This track descends and, at a bend, is joined by the yellow-flashed track from the *sémaphore*. Continue downhill to a junction at a bend, from where there are views across the Rade de Toulon. Here the yellow track turns right, but you go left, winding downhill into woodland with many cork oaks. Soon you reach the main road

4. Cross the road to the picnic area opposite. Bear left to leave by the main track, passing behind the barrier and heading away from the road. The track goes on between pines and cork oaks to arrive at a major track-junction.

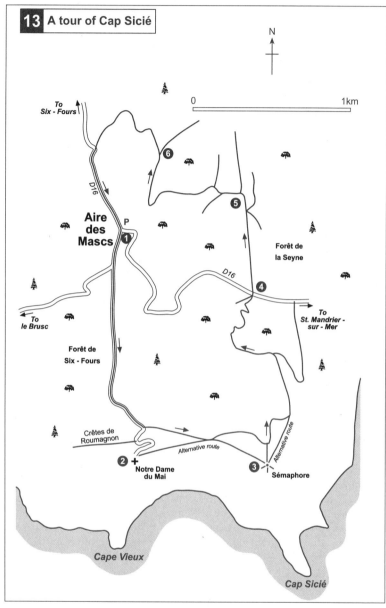

13 A tour of Cap Sicié

N

To
Six - Fours

0   1km

D16

6

5

Aire
des
Mascs
P
1

Forêt de
la Seyne

D16

4

To
le Brusc

To
St. Mandrier -
sur - Mer

Forêt de
Six - Fours

Crêtes de
Roumagnon

Alternative route

Alternative route

2 ✛
Notre Dame
du Mai

3
Sémaphore

Cape Vieux

Cap Sicié

5. Turn left here, to climb on a wide rutted track. (At the side of this track is an information board for the *Sentier de Découverte* – you can access it via a path on the left). At the junction at the top of the slope, bear right and then immediately left, sticking to the main track. As you continue climbing, you can look back over the lovely deep-green velvety tops of the *pins parasols* (umbrella pines) from slopes scattered with asphodels in spring. The path bears left and then negotiates a sharp hairpin bend to the right, after which it begins to descend.

6. At a fork, keep to the left. The path climbs again, now lined by euca-

lyptus trees, and there are distant views of the sea. On reaching the tarmacked road, turn left uphill. An oratory is passed on the right and the road begins to flatten out. Eventually you come to another oratory on the left, and arrive again at the parking area.

The forest of Cap Sicié

More Walks in the Area

The forest on Cap Sicié is crossed by many paths, and the tourist office at Six-Fours-les-Plages (on the sea front) has produced a folder suggesting 5 separate walking routes. The routes are all waymarked in different colours, but unfortunately, at the time of writing, the colours on the ground did not match those in the folder, thus causing chaos! It is promised that order will soon be restored. Nevertheless, the folder is backed by an overall plan of the forest routes, and it is not too difficult to devise your own circuit, or to take one of the recommended ones, if you are not too bothered about waymarking. One of the suggested routes (one which should eventually be waymarked in purple) offers some fantastic views as it crosses a crest of rock known as the Crêtes de Roumagnon. These are the rocky slopes that are covered with Sea Mallow in springtime, while later in the year you can enjoy the silver foliage of Senecio. The path following these crests leaves the road on the bend below the Chapel of Notre Dame du Mai. You can see where it is heading from here – and that it is a little more *sportif* than the other forest tracks. If you decide to take this whole circuit (as in the folder) it will take around 2½ hours.

Moving west from Six-Fours, there is another lovely stretch of coastline unspoilt by development between the resorts of Bandol and St Cyr-sur-Mer. The distance between the two is around 11km and a well-waymarked yellow-flashed coastal path runs all the way. If you go to the Office de Tourisme in Bandol, they will find you a leaflet about the walk (sadly with only the scantiest of directions), but included with it there should be a timetable for buses between the towns. Yo-yoing between clifftop and shoreline, the path is a fairly energetic one, but the harbour of la Madrague, the beautiful Bay of Nations and the Calanque of

Port d'Alan are highlights and there are plenty of opportunities for a swim. The whole journey is optimistically scheduled to take around 3½ hours. A map is not strictly necessary, but the coastal path is shown on IGN 3245 ET. For more coastal walking, get hold of the topoguide *La Côte Varoise et les îles à pied (Ref. P831)* – it is possible to walk virtually all the way from St Cyr to Fréjus.

Places of interest nearby

This walk will have given you views of the Îles des Embiez, off the western point of the peninsula. The main island can be visited by taking a few minutes boat trip from the port of le Brusc. This is an island largely devoted to the under-sea world. Divers can take advantage of the *Centre de Plongée*, those less ambitious can take a ride on the aquascope, an extraordinary vessel with sub-marine viewing chambers. At the *Institut Océanographic Paul-Ricard* (open throughout the year with the exception of Saturday mornings out of season) there are many huge aquaria of Mediterranean sea-life. And if your feet need a rest, there is also a small tourist train to take you round the island.

Heading directly north from Six-Fours and crossing the coastal autoroute, the road begins to climb abruptly. Ollioules is a busy little Provençal town of coloured houses, and beyond it, the N8 will lead you into the hills passing through some fairly spectacular gorges on the way. If you turn right in Ste Anne d'Evenos, another dramatic gorge climb will take you to the old village of Evenos perched very high on a hilltop. Amid the narrow streets of collapsing houses the strains of plainsong waft from the chapel (unfortunately it's a recording), and at the end of the village an old castle is crumbling quietly on a spur that once saw life as a volcano. The view is again superb – from a newly installed *table d'orientation* you can see the Ollioules and Destel gorges, the rocky limestone ridges of the Gros Cerveau, the mountains of the Ste Baume and the coast around Cap Sicié.

14. Port-Cros – an island paradise

One of France's seven national parks, Port-Cros thrives as nature intended – an island of green Mediterranean vegetation set in an emerald sea. A choice of footpaths is on offer – this route takes you around the lovely bays on the eastern side of the island, from one of which you can even follow a waymarked trail under the sea.

Grade: Easy / moderate

Distance: 9km (5½ miles)

Time: 4 hours

Map: IGN Top 25 3446 ET

Start and finish: The port at Port-Cros

How to get there: There are daily crossings throughout the year from the Port of Hyères (crossing time 1 hour) and from the port at Le Lavandou (crossing time around 45 minutes, depending on whether the boat first calls at the island of Levant). Between October and April, this amounts (for day trippers) to one boat out from each port in the morning, returning late afternoon. In summer, there may be several boats a day and some faster crossings. Check with the Office de Tourisme at Hyères or le Lavandou.

Refreshment: A couple of bars and restaurants beside the port should cater for all needs.

Notes: This walk is entirely on well-surfaced tracks – a pair of trainers should suffice unless it has been exceptionally wet. The only real gradients are on the last part of the walk – in particular, the climb to the Fort de l'Estissac. You can make this ascent either on the main path or on the slightly more demanding but interesting *Sentier des Plantes*. The vegetation of Port-Cros offers good shade on a hot day, but even so, you should carry fluids and put on the sun-cream. And note that at times of increased fire risk in summer, only the tracks leading to the beaches – that is, the north coast track between Port-Man and Plage du Sud – will remain open. If in doubt, enquire at the port or the Office de Tourisme before you leave. And when you arrive on the island it is worth calling in at the Maison du Parc (the *Capitainerie* on the quayside) for a map and all information about the park before you set off.

Waymarking: Signposts at all junctions.

Introduction

Once upon a time three beautiful princesses were enjoying a morning swim in the blue Mediterranean. A gang of pirates appeared on the scene and the gods, fearing for their safety, changed the girls into a group of islands. So were born the Îles d'Hyères, or to give them their more evocative name, the Îles d'Or, the Golden Islands.

The three main islands form an arc following the curve of the mainland shore. To the west is Porquerolles, the largest and most popular. It receives over a million visitors a year – an alarming thought, but then most of them come in July and August. Out of season there is plenty of space for everybody and, in addition to the attractions of many footpaths and fine bathing beaches, touring Porquerolles by bike is a splendid way of passing the day. The most easterly island is the Île du Levant, which although equally beautiful, is almost entirely given over to a military camp. The

Walking along the coastal path

remaining 10% or so is home to a nudist colony – so, although a surprising number of people get off the boat at Levant, it doesn't offer a lot in the way of walks. The third island, Port-Cros, smaller and hillier than the others, is the brightest jewel among them.

In an effort to preserve at least one little corner of heaven from the rapid development of this coast, Port-Cros was made a National Park in 1963. Not only the land needed protection – the vegetation and creatures under the sea were at risk from pollution and the constant churning of the bed by increasing water traffic. The park boundaries were set to encompass not just the island itself, but a much larger zone of water around it. Off the shores of Port-Cros, a densely-growing weed known as posidonia acts as the 'lungs' of the sea, and, besides oxygenation, offers shelter and food for many marine creatures. A thick forest of Mediterranean vegetation covers the land – holm oak, Aleppo pine, lentisc (mastic), strawberry tree, myrtle, juniper and olive. The island fauna include a variety of birds, their numbers swelled by annual migrations, and a few mammals and reptiles. The most interesting of these is the rare Tyrrhenian painted frog (*Discoglossus sardus* – sage green with darker blotches). Its presence here and in Sardinia and Corsica proves that these islands were once part of the same land mass.

The island of Port-Cros measures around 4km by 2.5km, and is crossed by something like 30 km of footpaths taking visitors out to the various bays, to the highest point of Mont Vinaigre (194m), and to a scattering of forts built here over the centuries for coastal defence. On the west side, a ridge walk along the *Sentier des Crêtes* gives some fine views of cliffs and ocean. This walk around the eastern shores is gentler and includes a visit to the forts of Port-Man and l'Estissac. The very beautiful bay of Port-Man makes an idyllic spot to stop for lunch and in the afternoon you can go on to a beach more suited to swimming, the Plage de Palud. From here you can conclude the day by following the Sentier des Plantes, a botanical trail winding up the cliffside, or, if you can use a snorkel and flippers, opt for something quite unique. A waymarked underwater trail, complete with submarine information panels, leads out to the Rocher du Rascas in the bay – see the Places of interest section for more information.

The Walk

1. Leave the harbour via the Route des Forts – the narrow road opposite the landing stage, on the left hand side of the harbour, beneath the 'château' (the Fort du Moulin). The track climbs uphill and you keep ahead (ignoring a left turn to the château), enjoying increasing views across the bay to the little Île de Bagaud with its forts. This island is a conservation area and only a couple of points on its coast are accessible for diving activities.

2. Where the main track doubles back to the left, leave it and continue ahead under the holm oaks on a path signed to the Barrage. At the fork in about 5 minutes, bear right and soon reach a multiple path junction. Take the upper path on the left, in the direction of the Barrage and the Vallon de la Solitude. At another fork 3 or 4 minutes later, ignore the Barrage and bear left, now following signs to the Col des Quatre Chemins.

3. Reaching a gravelled road you are at the Col des Quatre Chemins. Turn left on the road for about 20 metres, then leave it for a path on the right, signed to la Sardinière and Port-Man. The path continues through deep forest to the junction beside the ruined building at la Sardinière. Here you disregard the left path to la Palud and follow the direction of Port-Man – as you do just a few minutes later when you pass a left track leading to the Plateau de la Marma. The path now begins the descent to the Bay of Port Man. On the way you pass a sign pointing right to the Pointe du Tuf. This possible diversion involves a steep descent (and of course you have to get back again), but you may think the curious yellow rock of the Pointe de Tuf merits the effort. The rock is not tufa at all, but rather a conglomerate of sand and tiny organisms, a fossilised dune from more than 10,000 years ago. When you return to the main track there is soon another track on the left to ignore (even if it does say Baie de Port Man), after which it is all downhill on a path lined by holm oaks and strawberry trees to reach a path junction overlooking the bay.

4. The main track to the right here leads out to the Fort de Port Man. The fort itself dates from the 16th century and is not open to the public – but there are some splendid views across to Levant. On returning, take the path descending to the beach at Port Man. In the winter months this beach may be covered in a thick layer of something that looks like wood-shavings but is actually the dried leaves of posidonia, shed in the autumn – this covering stabilises the sand and protects the beach from rough seas. Walk right across the beach to the far side where a little hut stands beside the start of another path. Bear right here to follow the coastal path with some lovely views across the bay. The path curves around the headland of la Mitre and descends to the little beach at the very beautiful Calanque Longue. From here it's a climb again to the Pointe de la Galère with its sea views and rocky inlet where a path on the left climbs to the Mont de la Galère. Disregard this one, and continue on the coastal path to reach a 4-way junction

5. Take the path to the right that descends to the coast and in around 20

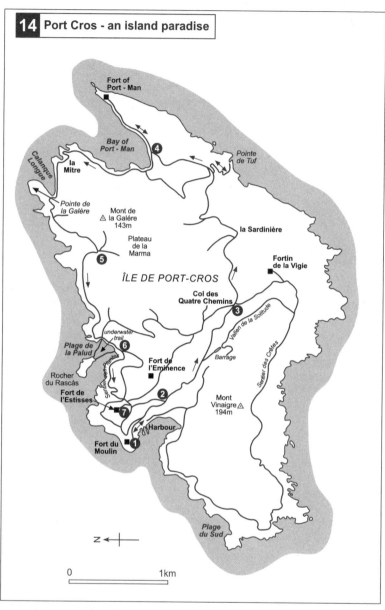

14 **Port Cros - an island paradise**

ÎLE DE PORT-CROS

Fort of Port - Man

Bay of Port - Man

4

Pointe de Tuf

la Mitre

Calanque Longue

Pointe de la Galère

Mont de △ la Galére 143m

Plateau de la Marma

la Sardinière

5

Fortin de la Vigie

Col des Quatre Chemins

3

Vallei de la Solitude

underwater trail

Plage de la Palud

6

Sentier des Crêtes

Fort de l'Eminence

Barrage

Rocher du Rascàs

Fort de l'Estisses

Mont Vinaigre △ 194m

7

2

Harbour

1

Fort du Moulin

Plage du Sud

Z ←┼─

0   1km

minutes reaches the Plage de la Palud. The buoys of the underwater trail stretch across to the Rocher du Rascas and an information panel tells you all about it. Cross the beach, climbing the rocks on the far side to pick up the main path again.

6. Almost immediately a path on the right is signed to the *Sentier des Plantes* and you have a choice. The path ahead climbs directly up the hillside to the Fort d'Estissac. The *Sentier des Plantes* arrives at the same place, but, with lots of bends and twists, plentiful sea views and quite a lot of French to read (if you have bought the leaflet from the Maison du Parc – there are only numbers on the trail), it will take a little longer. Whichever way you go, the paths join again, after which it is only a short stride to the junction where the Fort de l'Estissac is signed to the left. Turn up here and then right on the hard-surfaced road to reach the fort, which has exhibitions in summer time.

7. Leave the fort on the hard-surfaced road and very soon turn right on a track signed to the Village. Reaching a junction, bear left to the Fort du Moulin, the 'château' dominating the harbour. Descending on the concrete road you reach again the road on which you set out – turn right to return to the harbour.

More Walks in the Area

If you have bought the information package from the Maison du Parc you will have a map of all the footpaths on Port-Cros. The other popular circuit is the one heading down the Vallon de la Solitude and then along the Sentier des Crêtes, returning on a path skirting the beaches facing the Île de Bagaud. The tiny Plage du Sud is the only one (other than la Palud) suitable for swimming. This western circuit takes about 3 hours – or it could be combined with the route described for a complete circular tour of the island.

Porquerolles is similarly blessed with footpaths. But this island is bigger (approx. 7km x 3km) and you will have to hire a bike (from the quayside) to see it all in a day. If you intend to remain on foot, again get a map from the quayside and head west or east – the circuits are larger on Porquerolles, but the island is less hilly. There are splendid views from the cliffs at the south of the island and several fine bathing beaches on the north.

On the mainland, it is possible to follow the coastal path from le Lavandou all the way out to Cap Blanc (the peninsula pointing to the islands) – a distance of about 10km On the coast near Hyères, there is an excellent walk around the Giens peninsula. Starting from la Tour Fondue (where the boats for Porquerolles leave) around 15km of coastal footpath to the west are waymarked in yellow. All these paths (and those on Port-Cros and Porquerolles) are included in the topoguide *La côte varoise et les îles à pied* (Ref.P831). This topoguide is (as usual) entirely in French, but the maps are excellent – a worthwhile investment if you are spending any time in this area.

Places of interest nearby

The undisturbed waters off Port-Cros are a Mecca for divers, most especially around the tiny Îlot de la Gabinière off the south coast of the island. If this is for you, the Office de Tourisme at le Lavandou will give you all the details you need to enrol. But there is no need for the complications of diving equipment to see at least something of the splendid underwater life. If you can manage a snorkel, mask and flippers, the underwater trail off the Plage de Palud will introduce you to reefs of sponges, anemones and algae and a veritable submerged forest of posidonia sheltering fish of all kinds. Free guided tours take about 30 minutes and leave the beach every half hour or so in high season (mid-June to mid-September) – you can enrol at the port office, where some of the shops also offer hire of snorkels etc. Or you can do it yourself, reading the information panels on the buoys. In either case, invest in the plastic card (Guide de Sentier Sous-Marin) from the port office as an aid to identification.

The other way of seeing the underwater world is to take a trip in a glass-bottomed boat. Equipped with a sort of glass cage below the water line, these boats leave frequently from both the harbour at Port-Cros and the harbour at le Lavandou. The boats generally operate between April and October, but will not venture out if the sea is particularly rough.

Much of the island of Porquerolles is also under the protection of the Parc National de Port-Cros. At the centre of this island is the *Conservatoire Botanique National Mediteranéen* where, between May and September, you can learn all about the island flora and walk a botanical trail. Porquerolles claims the sunshine record for France – and has some magnificent beaches where you can take advantage of it. If you don't mind a walk (or bike ride) of around 3 km, head for the very beautiful pine-fringed Plage Notre-Dame, near the north-east corner, but much nearer are the silver-sands of the Plage d'Argent, on the west side of the port.

15. The umbrella pines of Cap Lardier

Close to St Tropez, Cap Lardier remains completely unspoilt, an unexpected haven of peace in a busy holiday area. Umbrella pines shade your path, at your feet are colourful wild flowers and there are plenty of opportunities for a swim as you take this ramble around the headland.

Grade: Moderate

Distance: Gigaro – Cap Taillat and return 12km (7½ miles); Gigaro – Cap Lardier and return 8km (5 miles)

Time: Gigaro – Cap Taillat and return, 5 hours; Gigaro – Cap Lardier and return 3 hours

Map: IGN Top 25 3545 OT

Start and finish: The seafront at Gigaro

How to get there: At the cross-roads at la Croix Valmer (on the D559 between Port Grimaud and Cavalaire) turn east and follow signs to Gigaro. There is roadside parking on the seafront and a car park near its eastern end.

Refreshment: Restaurants in la Croix Valmer and Gigaro, but none en route

Notes: This walk follows the coastal path from Gigaro around Cap Lardier and on to Cap Taillat. Before Cap Lardier the path is easy apart from one stiff climb up log steps. Between Cap Lardier and Cap Taillat, the path is more tortuous with many ascents and descents. A possible variation on the return follows wide forest roads. Trainers would be quite suitable footwear for this path in all but the wettest of weathers. Particularly on the east side of the peninsula, the path is exposed – protection from the sun is essential. Take binoculars for the views and if the weather is right, don't forget your bathing costume. Remember that at the height of summer the headland just may be closed due to increased fire risk – check with the Office de Tourisme at la Croix Valmer before you go.

Waymarking: The coastal path is waymarked in yellow throughout. Inland paths are not waymarked, but there is clear signposting.

Introduction

This is an outstandingly beautiful section of coastal path, all the more surprising as it is so close to St Tropez. Umbrella pines, shrubs, wild flowers and cacti crowd the path as you head around the peninsula to Cap Taillat, thrusting deep into the turquoise sea. In an area of rapid development (St Tropez's current popularity largely stems from the arrival of the film stars of the 50s) the coastline between Gigaro and Cap Taillat is under the auspices of the Conservatoire de l'Espace Littoral and this splendid walk is protected for all time.

The centrepiece of the walk is the rocky headland of Cap Lardier. Jutting to the south, it was once the site of one of Napoleon's batteries. On the first part of the walk, between Gigaro and Cap Lardier, the path is wide and fairly well frequented. Superb stands of umbrella pines offer shade and the path dips to two beaches – the pretty little cove of Jovat and the wider sandier Plage du Brouis. From this latter there is a steepish climb to reach the wooded plateau of the headland, at its highest point, 144m above the sea.

The Bay of Briande

After taking in the views from the ruined walls of the battery at the tip of the peninsula, most people opt to return – and so miss the very best of this coast. The path becomes narrower, climbing and dipping along the cliffside amid lush vegetation and multi-coloured flowers. The purples and yellows of the cactus-like Hottentot Figs give an exotic springtime display and there are stunning views across the brilliant blue sea to Cap Taillat, a rocky island connected to the coast by a growing sandbar. Eventually the path descends to the white sandy beach at its foot – an irresistible invitation for a swim on a hot day.

From Cap Taillat there are several possibilities. Continuing on the coastal path for another three-quarters of an hour or so will bring you to Plage de l'Escalet, where there is a car park – you could perhaps persuade a friend to pick you up. Cap Lardier being a headland, many have attempted to cut across it to return – a track is quite clearly visible on the IGN map. But not a chance of it – those paths are all the private roads of a wine-growing domain, and they make it quite clear that they don't want visitors. Instead retrace your steps around the coast at least as far as the clifftop above the Plage du Brouis (a spot known as les Pins Blancs). Here you can opt for the inland forest track with some excellent views over the bay. And for those with stamina at the end of the day, a final diversion will take you to the top of the hill for a yet wider panorama – and possibly a glorious sunset.

The Walk

1. Starting at the east end of the coast road at Gigaro, the coastal path sets off between fencing behind a lovely sandy beach. Bearing to the right, a sign for the Sentier du Littoral points you up some steps under the trees and along a path bearing yellow waymarks. Across the bay is Cavalaire and out to sea are the Îles d'Hyères – Levant, Port Cros and far away, Porquerolles. The path takes you past a fine cluster of umbrella pines (*les Pins Parasols*). At a fork, bear right down some steps to reach an attractive little sandy cove – the Plage de Jovat.

2. Across the beach, you again pick up the waymarked coastal path, which continues around the Pointe du Brouis and then descends to a much wider beach, the Plage du Brouis. A signpost informs you it is

2.1km to Cap Lardier. After crossing the back of the beach, the path now takes you steeply uphill through a woodland of cork oaks, mastic and butcher's broom – you may be grateful for the shade. At the top of the incline you emerge at the path junction at les Pins Blancs.

3. Bear right here in the direction of Cap Lardier. Soon you can see ahead another contour-crossing path to the old signalling station, but this one isn't for you (unless you feel like the diversion). Instead, bear right on a path soon flanked by high vegetation, but brightened by pink rock roses (*cistus albidus*, known as *cotonneux* in France, owing to its furry leaves). At the next junction, again bear right, heading towards the cape. At a clearing with a stone wall, continue ahead through the bushes to arrive at a sheltered spot among the ruined walls of the battery. Still walking south from here, you descend to reach the farthest point – a rocky perch battered by the wind, high above the glistening blue sea.

4. The path now turns left, cutting through the vegetation and affording fine views of Cap Taillat across the sparkling waters of the Bay of Briande. Steps take you steeply downhill on a path between mastic and yellow spurge and bright Hottentot figs cling to the rocks facing the sea. Eventually you reach the rocky shore.

5. After touching down at a little beach, the path heads off between the bushes and again climbs. Passing a small house on your right the waymarks seem to have vanished – keep ahead on the broad track beside the vineyard at the top of the hill. After about 30m a sign directs you to the right on a narrow path through the bushes. This path now weaves its way through lush vegetation, soon dipping to the shore before climbing again. The waymarks are infrequent, but if in any doubt, keep to the wider track – it is impossible to get lost, but you may find yourself doing a little extra climbing if you go wrong. At length the path comes down to the lovely bay of white sand, the Plage de Briande. On the far side of the beach, the path crosses the rocks to arrive at the sandbar leading to Cap Taillat. It is possible to walk out to its tip (Cap Cartaya) if you are prepared for one or two rocky scrambles.

6. For those fortunate enough to have transport arranged, the coastal path continues around the bay and over a rocky outcrop beside an old customs house. Around three-quarters of an hour of walking will bring you to the car park at the Plage de l'Escalet. But to return to Gigaro, it is necessary to retrace your steps past Cap Lardier and on as far as les Pins Blancs (Point 3). Here you can choose the inland track, S.P. Gigaro par l'Intérieur, 2.2km. The broad track initially descends quite steeply with splendid views of the velvety umbrella pines clothing the hillside. At the bottom of the hill a track to the left leads to the Plage du Brouis you passed earlier. If you keep straight ahead here, the track climbs again. In about 10 minutes (just after passing on the left the track to Jovat) you reach a track junction with a signpost. Keeping straight ahead from here (marked 'Short Cut' on the map), you will be back in Gigaro in about 20 minutes. If you have an extra half hour and remaining energy, turn instead on a track to the right (S.P. Piste des Crêtes). Climb around the head of the valley and after a bend to the left, take a broad track doubling back to the left. This good track is crossed by a barrier (keeping out motor vehicles) and then continues to climb taking you high above the bay with magnificent

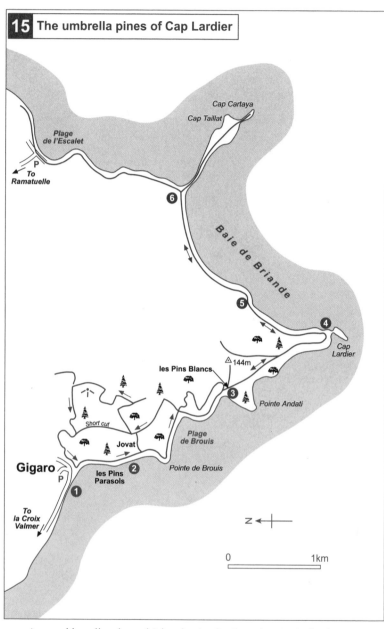

15 The umbrella pines of Cap Lardier

Cap Cartaya

Cap Taillat

Plage de l'Escalet

P

← *To Ramatuelle*

6

Baie de Briande

5

4

Cap Lardier

les Pins Blancs

△ 144m

3

Pointe Andati

Short cut

Jovat

Plage de Brouis

Gigaro

P

les Pins Parasols **2**

Pointe de Brouis

1

To la Croix Valmer

z ←

0   1km

views of headlands and islands. At the junction at its highest point, leave the Piste des Crêtes to go right and instead bear left to descend again to the main track. On reaching it, turn right to return to Gigaro.

More Walks in the Area

The waymarked coastal path continues to the north of Cap Taillat as far as St Tropez. At Plage de l'Escalet (three-quarters of an hour) a signpost tells you that St Tropez is a mere 6 hours 45 minutes away – a rather ambitious estimate, as you can see from the predicted time to Gigaro! Nevertheless it is a splendid long day's walk, first rounding Cap Camarat with its lighthouse, then skirting the long beautiful Plage de Pampelonne, followed by the fashionable Plage de Tahiti. Beyond the Pointe de Capon (Brigitte Bardot has her villa here), you arrive at another popular beach, the Plage des Salins, from where there are bus connections to St Tropez. A section of rocks, cliffs and creeks follows, and then the Pointe de Rabiou, the Baie des Cannebiers and ultimately the harbour in St Tropez – where suddenly your boots and rucksack may make you feel slightly out of place! The only practicable public transport for the return is a bus from St Tropez to Ramatuelle, which takes the D93, parallel to but about a kilometre inland from the coast (giving reasonable access to the Plage de Pampelonne). From Ramatuelle, it is a further 4km walk to Plage de l'Escalet. Things are easier if you have a friend to pick you up – or if you can afford a taxi.

West of Gigaro, the waymarked coastal path continues a further 4km around the bay to Cavalaire. If you are thinking of doing either of these walks it would be advisable to get hold of the appropriate IGN map, 3545 OT. Only a little more expensive is the Topoguide *La côte varoise et les îles à pied (Ref. P831)*. In this excellent publication, all waymarked coastal paths between Bandol and St Raphaël (including the islands of Porquerolles and Port-Cros) are clearly marked on the relevant sections of IGN maps – and if you can understand some of the French text, so much the better. North of St Tropez, the coastal path between les Issambres and St Aygulf appears in this Topoguide, and would make a good choice as it is well-served by public transport all the way. Enquire at the Office de Tourisme at les Issambres for more information.

The Office de Tourisme in la Croix Valmer (and others in the region) can find you a free leaflet (with English version) showing all the waymarked footpaths in the Gulf of St Tropez and the region of the Maures. Several such circuits are possible starting from la Croix Valmer – ask for their leaflet *Guide Randonnées*. Other circuits are marked starting from Cogolin and Grimaud – the appropriate Offices de Tourisme will have the details.

Places of interest nearby

St Tropez is a 'must', even though it is an incredibly busy place for most of the year. Its show-piece is its harbour, where the yachts of the rich and famous can be viewed from the pavement cafés and you can always hope for a glimpse of the stars themselves. St Tropez was merely a fishing village until around a hundred years ago, when it was 'discovered' by the artist Paul Signac. Others (including Matisse and Utrillo) soon joined him. Their work can be seen in the Musée de St Tropez in the old chapel of the Annonciade, while present-day artists set out their easels on the quayside opposite. Other attractions in St Tropez are a stroll along the long jetty (Môle Jean Réveille) for classic views of the town and harbour, and a climb to the hilltop *Citadelle*, from whose ramparts there is a wide panorama across the bay to the distant mountains.

At Rayol-Canadel (just a few miles west along the Corniche des Maures), the exotic gardens of the Domaine du Rayol are well worth a visit. Initially the private gardens of a banking magnate in the early part of the 20th century, they passed from hand to hand and were eventually rescued by the Conservatoire du Littoral in 1989. Now there are spectacular displays of plants from Mediterranean-type climates all over the world, all the more stunning in their splendid location above the azure sea. The gardens extend to the sea itself – in summertime there are conducted tours of the underwater gardens, and possibilities for diving.

16. The forests of the Massif des Maures

The Massif des Maures is a splendid range of forested hills where cork oaks thrive in abundance and chestnuts are grown to produce a variety of local delicacies. From the lovely old Provençal village of Collobrières, this walk begins with a botanical trail introducing you to the shrubs of the maquis.

Grade: Easy

Distance: 6km (3¾ miles). An optional short cut can reduce this to 2km, while for those wanting more, an extension is detailed in the **More Walks** section.

Time: 2 hrs. – and allow extra time to linger over the plants of the botanical trail.

Map: IGN Top 25 3445 OT. You can get a leaflet of this walk from the Office de Tourisme in Collobrières, but beware of the map – it is 'upside down' (north at the bottom)

Start and finish: The Office de Tourisme at Collobrières

How to get there: Collobrières is in the heart of the Maures mountains, on the D14, about 20km east of Cuers. The Office de Tourisme is on the riverside, close to the Pont Vieux. There is some parking on both sides of the river, and more in the centre of the little town.

Refreshment: Collobrières boasts a handful of restaurants, both beside the river and in the central square.

Notes: This short walk is on good tracks and can easily be undertaken in trainers in dry weather. If the day is warm, make sure you carry water, and have appropriate protection from the sun. The botanical trail at the beginning of the walk does involve some climbing, but nothing too severe – and you can always take your time. The plants are named in French only – so consider taking a dictionary. Farther on, an optional diversion is a twenty-minute circuit around a 'working' chestnut grove, where you can see the raw product before sampling the delicacies in town.

Waymarking: The route leaves Collobrières on the GR90 (white on red waymarks) and you soon pick up the wooden signposts of the *Sentier Botanique*. Farther on, the discovery trail is marked with blue arrows and flashes.

Introduction

The Massif des Maures is an extensive range of thickly wooded hills stretching from Hyères in the west to Fréjus in the east, and from the coast for some 30km inland. The name is derived from the Provençal *mauro,* meaning dark – the hills are densely covered in evergreen oaks and maritime pines. At the coast the land falls steeply to the sea, giving a spectacular coast road known as the *Corniche des Maures*. Inland, the remote unpopulated hills are a walker's paradise, yet they are within reach of many of the famous resorts.

In the forests of the Maures, there is one tree that is particularly prevalent and easily recognised – the commercially valuable cork oak. Cork oaks (*chênes lièges* in French) grow everywhere and the younger ones can be identified by their leathery leaves and thick, deeply furrowed bark. At

The chestnut festival at Collobrières

around 25 years of age they are considered mature, and receive their first *levage* – the stripping of the bark. This first harvest is known as the 'male' bark and is commercially useless. But the stripping must be carefully performed in order to yield a further layer of bark some 10 or 12 years later. This second bark is the 'female', and it is this that is used for chipboard and matting – and for corking the bottles of Provençal wine. In 1850, there were 17 cork-making factories in Collobrières. Unfortunately plastic corks have recently become more popular, so the bark of France now goes to cork the wines of Spain and Portugal, where the industry remains more traditional. Cork oaks that have been stripped have a bizarre appearance – their bare trunks are initially bright orange-red, a colour that darkens with the passage of time.

The second important tree in the Maures is the sweet chestnut. This provides a range of local products from the rich marrons glacés to sticky chestnut purée and even an expensive chestnut liqueur. The quaint, typically Provençal village of Collobrières, where this walk starts, regards itself as the 'chestnut capital' of the Maures and offers ample opportunity for sampling, and lots of options for presents to take home. The chestnut festival in October attracts crowds from miles around.

There are plenty of wild rambles in the Maures (see the **More Walks** section), but the walk here makes an excellent introduction to the forest. The first part is a *sentier botanique* where mastic and juniper, strawberry trees and cistus, tree heather, lavender and a lot more are all beautifully labelled. Later there are choices to be made – you can wander through a chestnut grove, return directly to Collobrières, or continue through a part of the forest that is obviously home to herds of wild boar. Here you have a fair chance of spotting these normally elusive creatures – at least you won't miss their droppings! And while thinking of creatures, there is one other unusual one you might just spot in the Maures – the Hermann's Tortoise. These small tortoises still live and breed in these hills, the only such site on the French mainland.

The latter part of the walk is a *sentier découverte*, a discovery trail intended to tell you about the work of the forest. Unhappily, this area too has its vandals, and the display boards had been taken down at the time of our visit. Hopefully they will be replaced – but the path through the cork oaks is interesting enough in its own right and makes a pleasant return to Collobrières.

The Walk

1. Leaving the Office de Tourisme, walk along the riverside to the Pont Vieux, and then turn left up the Rue Camille Desmoulins, following the white on red flashes of the Grande Randonnée. Continue ahead on the narrow Rue Blanqui, and at the top, turn to the left on the Rue Buffon. The lovely little square you now enter is the Place Rouget de l'Isle. Pass under the archway and continue uphill.

2. Emerging with the ruined church of Saint-Pons on your left, bear right and immediately left on a gravelled path. A board proclaiming the *Sentier Botanique* stands beside the path, and just after it, you bear round to the right on a track climbing into the wood. Now you meet the first of the ceramic plaques naming trees and shrubs. Meeting a wider track, continue to the left, and further on, take a narrower track on the left – all is well-signposted with wooden boards and green arrows, in addition to the waymarks of the Grande Randonnée. Arriving at a plateau with a fine view, follow the arrows left on a wider track, which climbs again. Almost at the top of the hill, fork right with the GR to reach a broad track on the summit.

3. Turn right here (now leaving the Grande Randonnée) and continue to the ruined windmill. There is a picnic table here overlooking the deep valley of La Malière below. The path makes a winding descent from this point, with some splendid views of the hills both near and far. Eventually you arrive at the oratory of Saint-Pons and cross a track to a path opposite. This is the start of wild boar territory. A board advises you to stay on the path – don't be alarmed by this, the boar are very shy creatures and want no trouble. You can see the electric fences that keep the animals from straying and the ground is dotted with droppings that would do credit to a herd of elephants. Nevertheless, the biggest boar is only around 60 cm. in height. Over the winter months there are regular wild boar hunts. Eventually you reach a gravelled road at the Col du Pilon.

4. Here you have a choice. Turning right downhill will return you to Collobrières in about 20 minutes. On the way (about 5 minutes downhill on the left) you will pass the entrance to the châtaigneraie – the chestnut grove. A circular path of around 200m will take you through it. Even if you want to continue with the main walk it may well be worth a diversion to see the chestnuts.

    The main walk continues by crossing over the road to some log steps climbing the bank opposite. The path continues over an old wall and descends, soon being joined by a broader track on the right. Shortly the path bears left, and you are in the forest of cork oaks and can see the extent of the harvesting. Still following the blue arrows, you at length reach a reservoir of water where a sign directs you ahead to the *Château d'Eau*. After a long descent, a cross-track is reached

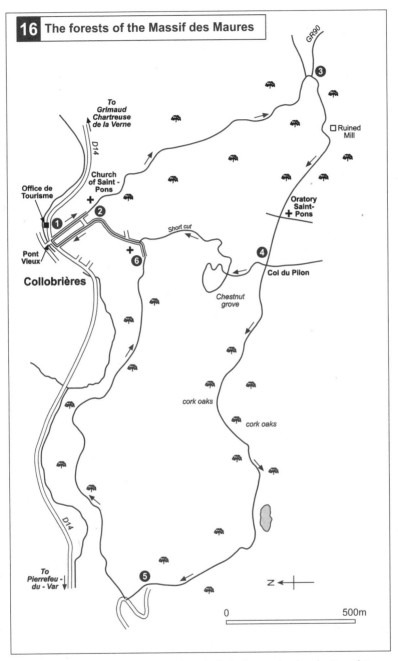

16 The forests of the Massif des Maures

To Grimaud Chartreuse de la Verne

Ruined Mill

Church of Saint - Pons

Office de Tourisme

Oratory Saint- Pons

Pont Vieux

Collobrières

Short cut

Col du Pilon

Chestnut grove

cork oaks

cork oaks

D14

To Pierrefeu - du - Var

0   500m

5. Turn right here, and immediately left down the bank. Reaching a rough road, turn to the right and then take a wide track on the right. After 20m or so, take a track on the left going down into a field – there are blue flashes on the trees. A track on the right soon joins but you continue ahead alongside a vineyard. After another track joins from the right, bear left on a stony and grassy track behind houses. The path takes you into the woods again. Reaching a wider track, turn downhill

to the left. Arriving at the sewage station, keep to the right and pass behind it, following above the river on your left.

6. Meeting a surfaced road, keep ahead to the church with its impressive guard of plane trees. Pass the church on your left and after passing the parking area, bear left to reach the Place de la République, a lovely old square with a restaurant. Leave at the opposite point from which you arrived, and walk downhill to find again the riverside and the Office de Tourisme.

More Walks in the Area

If you would like to explore farther into the forest it is possible to extend this short walk to make a circuit of around 4 hours. The Office de Tourisme in Collobrières stocks a brochure (Randonnées au Pays de Maurin des Maures – in French only) describing 5 local walks, including one by the title Circuit des Menhirs de Lambert. The map offered with this is an alarmingly poor photocopy, but the route is clearly marked, and if you purchase the appropriate IGN map (3445 OT) as well, you should have no difficulty following it. There is also waymarking to help – the first half of the walk is on the GR90 (continue ahead at Point 3), and the return route is marked with blue flashes, rejoining our walk at Point 4. This ramble has no particular difficulties, but it is a real foray into the forest, with terrain varying from scrubby upland to the deep lush valley of the Desteou. The two curious menhirs on the Plateau of Lambert are an additional point of interest.

Two other walks in the above-mentioned brochure start from the Chartreuse de la Verne, a magnificently-sited monastery deep in the forest. The shorter of these walks (4 hours) is a descent to the barrage and lake in the valley below. To follow the Circuit du Barrage de la Verne, simply head downhill on the wide track through the chestnut grove at the far end of the monastery. After about 3km (where the track widens) turn right, following signs to la Môle, and this path will bring you to the main track around the lake. Very good French directions and stone signposts will guide your return (and you can see this path on the IGN map) – or you could simply go back the way you came.

A winding 30km or so to the north-east, the delightful old town of la Garde-Freinet is likewise engulfed by the forest of the Maures. The Office de Tourisme here can offer you a really superb folder of walks, the text translated into both English and German. For just a taste of these, follow the 4km route to the Croix des Maures on its rocky bluff above the town and continue to the ruined hilltop Fort Freinet with extensive views. Another worthwhile walk is that to Les Roches Blanches, where you can admire the white quartz rocks and the panorama extending to the gulf of St Tropez.

Places of interest nearby

If you are looking for chestnut products, the Confiserie Azuréenne (across the Pont Vieux in Collobrières) has a very high quality selection – including chestnut ice-cream, which you can enjoy on their terrace. Other shops too sell 'souvenirs' – chunks of cork, bags of lavender and spices, chestnut jams and purées, santons (tiny Provençal figures) and all the rest. But Collobrières remains a completely genuine Provençal town, without the inflated prices of the south coast resorts.

Around 12km from Collobrières, up the windiest of winding roads, the impossibly remote buildings of the Chartreuse de la Verne overlook a deep green valley with hills all around. Geographically and metaphorically, this is the 'heart of the forest'. The original priory here was founded in the 12th century – abandoned after the ravages of the Revolution, the place fell into disrepair. In the late 60s, an association known as Les Amis de la Verne was founded, and refurbishment began. Now nuns of the Order of Bethlehem occupy the premises and it is possible to take a limited tour. The most interesting point is possibly the reconstructed monk's cell with its tiny walk and garden – it doesn't seem anywhere near as austere as you might have expected. The Chartreuse de la Verne is open all year except in January, and every day with the exception of Tuesdays and Holy Days.

Following the cork theme, Gonfaron (20km north on the twisting D39) has a still-thriving cork industry and is home to the Ecomusée du Liège. Here you can learn what happens to the bark after it has been cut, and watch a film showing the traditional techniques involved. The museum is open on weekdays throughout the year.

A couple of kilometres east of Gonfaron, the *Village des Tortues* makes a fascinating visit. If you didn't manage to spot a Hermann's Tortoise on the walk (and it's not easy), you can see plenty here. The centre is devoted to promoting the tortoise population of the Maures – a hospital unit cares for those brought in with injuries, a nursery hatches the eggs, while the Lilliputian young tortoises are kept for their first three years to preserve them from their natural predators. All are finally returned to the wild. The tiny Hermann's Tortoise is the only one native to France, but other 'rescue' tortoises from all over the world are here waiting re-patriation, including some real giants from Africa. The Village des Tortues is open every day from March to November.

Heading south from Collobrières, another wildly convoluted road takes you over the spectacular Col de Babaou (of Tour de France fame) to Bormes-les-Mimosas, a hillside town of palm trees, exotic flowers and pastel-shaded buildings. The Office de Tourisme can offer you a walking tour of the old medieval city – but if you want to escape the holiday throng, leave the town and take to the hills. The Office de Tourisme has produced an excellent folder of walks to guide you.

17. In the mountains of the Esterel

All the colours of Provence are here in the Esterel, where the deep-red rock is offset by the shining greens of the maquis and the brilliant hues of wild flowers and butterflies. In the heart of these mountains the walk reaches a beautiful blue lake – and there is an optional ramble with sea views to follow.

Grade: Easy / moderate

Distance: 11km (8 miles). The walk to the lake itself is about 3.5km

Time: 3 hours

Map: The best map showing the walking routes is the *Plan Guide Esterel* published by the Office National des Forêts. An alternative would be the IGN Top 25 3544 ET

Start and finish: The parking area at the Col de Belle Barbe, near Agay.

How to get there: From Agay, take the road that heads inland just north of the river bridge. After 1.5km, turn right (SP Col de Belle Barbe) – it is a further 2km to the parking area.

Refreshment: None in the mountains of the Esterel – you will have to return to Agay.

Notes: This walk is mostly on wide forest tracks and can readily be undertaken in trainers in dry weather. After the Lac de l'Ecureuil there is a steady but not over-steep climb – if you want to avoid it, you could simply return the way you came. The Esterel is closed to walkers from around 15th June to 15th September. In spring or autumn the sun can still be hot and there is little shade, so take adequate precautions – and carry water with you.

Waymarking: None – but you won't get lost.

Introduction

Provence is essentially a colourful place, but it is to the Esterel that the prize must go. These rocky hills are the oldest in Provence, the dark pink volcanic porphyry plunging in weathered and fissured outcrops to the dark blue Mediterranean below. Add to that the varied greens of the maquis, a multitude of wild flowers and butterflies and the fluffy yellow mimosa of early spring and you have a walk with every colour of the spectrum.

Successive summer fires over the last hundred years have changed the appearance of these hills. Originally they were covered in a dense forest of pine and cork oak – a forest that made them a convenient hideout for prisoners escaping from Toulon jail, and in the 18th century gave cover to a famous highwayman who dressed in scarlet robes to rob travellers on the road that is now the D7. The last fire devastated the Esterel in 1986. Now the roads through the massif are all closed to traffic, as are the footpaths over the season of high risk in summer. Some reforestation has taken place but the naturally occurring maquis of mastic, tree heather, strawberry trees and cistus is simply splendid.

The walk here takes you through an impressive ravine to the Lac de l'Ecureuil (Squirrel Lake), a blue lake ringed by various rocky peaks, and a fine place for a picnic. From here the old forest road climbs to a pink escarpment on the skyline known as the Grosse Vache. Beneath the rocks you have wonderful views of the steep green valleys below. Briefly the route follows a Grande Randonnée, the GR 51, a narrow flower-banked trail along the hillside from which there are distant views of the sparkling Mediterranean. A gentle descent into the valley completes the circuit.

The Walk

1. Leaving the car park at the Col de Belle Barbe, cross the road and take the broad track behind a barrier opposite, signposted to Lac de l'Ecureuil. On your right is the Ravin de Grenouillet and the view ahead is dominated by the rugged summit of Pic de l'Ours (496m). After about 15 minutes walking you reach a concrete ford over the stream and the track bears round to the left. Ignore a track doubling back on the right and continue ahead, climbing gently. The ravine becomes narrower as you go, and, after a right-hand bend, you reach a spot where the stream has been dammed, creating a little waterfall. The size of the blue pool behind it depends on recent rainfall. Continuing up a valley flanked by curiously shaped outcrops of the red rock, you notice the white on red waymarks of a Grande Randonnée (GR) that has joined you from the other side of the stream. With the rounded summit of Mamelon de l'Ecureuil ahead, the path eventually descends to ford the stream. Continue past the first small lake to reach a barrage and then the beautiful Lac de l'Ecureuil itself, surrounded by mimosa and eucalyptus.

2. Keep ahead passing the lake on your right-hand side. At the head of the lake the Grande Randonnée goes off to the right (to climb to the Col Notre Dame) but you leave it and continue ahead. The track climbs steadily now and there are good views of the lake behind. A valley appears on the right – the Ravin des Trois Termes – and the rounded top on your left is the Pain de Sucre. At a sharp left hand bend, keep to the main track (a path descends ahead to the Ravin des Trois Termes). To your right the pink outcrop like Ayres Rock in the sky bears the name la Grosse Vache (the Big Cow). Beneath

A mountain path in the Esterel

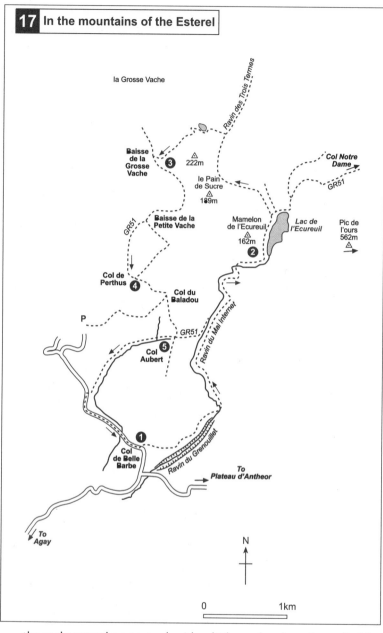

17 In the mountains of the Esterel

la Grosse Vache

Ravin des Trois Termes

Baisse de la Grosse Vache

3 △ 222m

Col Notre Dame

GR51

le Pain de Sucre △ 189m

Baisse de la Petite Vache

GR51

Mamelon de l'Ecureuil △ 162m

2

Lac de l'Ecureuil

Pic de l'ours 562m △

Col de Perthus **4**

Col du Baladou

Ravin du Mal Internet

P

GR51

Col Aubert **5**

Ravin du Grenouillet

1

Col de Belle Barbe

To Plateau d'Antheor

To Agay

N

0   1km

the rocks you take a corner beside a little pool and continue climbing to a path junction at a spot known as Baisse de la Grosse Vache.

3. Turn left here and continue on the forest road, climbing now rather more gently. There are splendid views into the valleys below. Soon the path begins to descend and you reach a left-hand bend (this point is the Baisse de la Petite Vache),. You could continue on the main track here, but the prettier route is that of the Grande Randonnée that goes to the right (rather than the left) of the hill ahead. To reach the

Grande Randonnée, take a track leaving the forest road on the right. Very soon you will pick up the white on red waymarks, and following these to the left, you will find yourself on a beautiful flower-lined track around the back of the hill, with distant views of the blue waters of the Bay of Agay and the hill of Cap Dramont. After about 15 minutes walking you reach a sign announcing the Col de Perthus. Here you follow the GR to the left and descend to join the forest road again.

4. Turn right on the forest road and follow it for a further 10 minutes or so to a sharp right hand bend (at the Col du Baladou). Here you leave the road and continue on the broad track ahead, still following the waymarks of the Grande Randonnée. This shingly track descends between pines and heather (not to mention asphodels, cistus, strawberry trees and the rest) to reach a path junction at the Col Aubert.

5. If the weather has not been too wet, the easiest return from here is the broad track to the right. This soon descends to pass a small lake and then joins – and crosses – the bed of a stream. Keep on this main track, always following the stream, until the track rises abruptly to meet a tarmacked road. Turn left on the road and continue for about 10 minutes to reach the car park.

If you think this path beside the stream bed could be boggy, turn instead to the left at the Col Aubert (Point 5) and follow the GR back into the Ravin du Mal Infernet. Once across the stream here, turn right and follow the track on which you set out back to the car park.

More Walks in the Area

If you are thinking of more walking in this area, you would do well to get hold of the *Plan Guide Esterel* published by the Office National des Forêts. Its scale (1:25,000) is the same as the IGN map (3544 ET), but its advantage is that the main hiking paths are marked in, as are possible cycle tracks and tracks suitable for equestrians. Few of the tracks in the Esterel are waymarked, but there are signposts at the main junctions and the map is more than adequate to get you round.

The Grande Randonnée of the Esterel is the GR51 – it wiggles its way across the area trying to take in as many of the sights as possible. On this walk we met it briefly at the Lac de l'Ecureuil and again at the Baisse de la Petite Vache. If at this latter point you had followed the GR to the right instead of to the left, it would have taken you (in about 11km) to the top of Mont Vinaigre, at 614m. the highest peak in the Esterel, and a panoramic viewpoint. From the summit, the GR continues down the west side of the mountain and in just a few minutes arrives at a parking area above the forest hut at Le Malpey. You could get a friend to pick you up here. (This latter track taken in reverse makes the quickest ascent of Mont Vinaigre.)

For something rather less demanding, park at the Plateau d'Anthéor (south-east of the Col de Belle Barbe) and take a half hour stroll along the car-free corniche road to the Rocher Barthélemy. The Mediterranean sparkles blue below you, and when you reach the big red rock itself, it is possible to clamber out on it for further views. Behind the Rocher Barthélemy, a waymarked path climbs around the back of the jagged peak of St Pilon and on to the summit of Cap Roux – one of the most splendid viewpoints on this coast. Yet another peak offering a magnificent vista is that of the Pic de l'Ours – park at the Col Notre Dame and follow the road uphill for about three-quarters of an hour.

From the GR51 on this walk, you had a brief glimpse of the headland of Cap Dramont, guarding the entrance to the Bay of Agay. A really delightful coastal path circles the headland and will take about 1½ hours of your time. From the coast road west of Agay, turn south for the Camp Long car park – or opt instead for the harbour at the Plage du Poussai, overlooked by the tiny tower-topped Île d'Or. The coastal path around the headland is waymarked in yellow and the short inland return is obvious. For views of the Gulf of Fréjus – and more – include a climb to the signalling station at Cap Dramont's highest point, 136m. above the sea.

Places of interest nearby

The Esterel is a kingdom for walkers and cyclists only. Its roads are closed to traffic and there are no villages within the massif. Outside interest lies along the coast – the fashionable twin towns of Fréjus and St Raphaël and the corniche road itself (N98), with its many spectacular viewpoints.

Fréjus is a town in two parts – Fréjus plage, a glorious and more than popular stretch of golden sand flanked by buildings from the 50s, and the old town of Fréjus where in the narrow streets and square beside the cathedral you will find bustling market stalls on almost any day of the week. To the west and north of the old town are the relics of Fréjus' days of Roman occupation – an arena (still in use for bull-fights), a theatre and an aqueduct. To the east of the *Plage* is the harbour, built in the last twenty years to house almost 2000 floating palaces. The rich and famous are here – you can tell from the restaurants alongside. It has to be worth a look! St Raphaël too has its links with the Romans – it was once a resort frequented by the most affluent of the day. It has a harbour, a long sea-front and an old town, but is particularly known for its water sports – sailing, surfing, water-skiing and especially diving. Boat trips start from the Gare Maritime at the old port, from where you can just take a turn around the bay, head south to St Tropez or north to the fascinating Îles de Lérins (off Cannes)

To guide you around the local area, the Office de Tourisme in Fréjus stocks a truly excellent series of free leaflets in English under the title *Highways and Byways*. Included are a coastal walk, a tour of the Roman sites, a cycle ride through the Esterel and many drives farther afield, seeking out olives, perfumes, gardens, pottery and more. As a bonus, each leaflet also contains a local knowledge quiz and a Provençal recipe.

18. Beside the beautiful Lac de Ste Croix

The beautiful blue Lac de Ste Croix is by far the largest of the lakes on the Verdon River. Starting from Bauduen, the views are changing all the way as you take this ramble around a headland on its eastern shore.

Grade: Moderate (with one fairly strenuous rocky scramble)

Distance: 11.5km (7¼ miles)

Time: 4 hours

Map: IGN Top 25 3442 OT

Start and finish: The lakeside at Bauduen

How to get there: Bauduen is at the southern tip of the Lac de Ste Croix, about 16km north of Aups via the D49. There is a parking area on the lakeside.

Refreshment: A handful of bar/cafés, hotels and restaurants line the esplanade at Bauduen.

Notes: This whole route is on a Grande Randonnée, at first around the headland and then over a wooded hill for the return. Some agility is needed for just one short section – a climb and descent over a rocky outcrop. Paths otherwise are good, but the steeper sections could be slippery after heavy rainfall – walking boots would be the footwear of choice. Carry water with you, put on the sun cream in hot weather (although there is shade in the woods) and take your bathing costume if you want a swim at the end of the day.

Waymarking: The route is waymarked in white on red throughout.

Introduction

With the damming of the Verdon River in 1975 the Lac de Ste Croix was born. Beneath its waters are the old village of Les-Salles-sur-Verdon (now rebuilt on the lakeside), a famous spring, the Fontaine-l'Évêque, and the medieval bridge of Aiguines. Bauduen, once a 'perched village', found itself with an esplanade, a sailing school, a harbour and a beach. Above the lake shore the old village has retained its character with narrow streets and tall houses, archways, fountains and brightly-coloured floral displays. At the top of the hill the church in its rocky niche overlooks the whole scene.

The opalescent turquoise colour of the lake (and of the river itself) is said to be due to the original presence of fluoride molecules in the soil of this area. These were stabilised by micro-organisms during the formation of the rock and now are dissolved out by the running water. Unlike the river, whose waters can be muddied after a storm, the blue of the lake never varies – and is made all the more striking by the pinky-orange tones of its beaches.

The walk here takes you around a headland at the south-east corner of the lake. The path weaves through woodland on the slopes above the shore and there are views first across to the dam and the village of Ste Croix, and later up the length of the lake, backed by the towering ranges of the pre-Alps of Digne. The rocky scramble near the tip of the headland merely adds spice to the walk. The way back climbs the hill across the neck of the headland. Coming down again through a cleft known as the Gorge of Caletty, there are fine views of the lake as you return to Bauduen.

The Walk

1. At Bauduen, walk along the lakeside towards the end of the road. Just before the sailing school, double back to the right uphill, and turn left at the junction. You have now picked up the white on red waymarks of the Grande Randonnée (GR 99), and can follow them along the road, which becomes a track passing several interesting properties. After about 15 minutes you reach some tennis courts beside the lake (It would have been possible to get here along the lake shore past the sailing school, but the views from the top road are better). Now continue on the very pretty track along the lake shore. The wild flowers are splendid and there are occasional clearings with stone picnic tables. Across the water the village of Ste-Croix-de-Verdon seems pressed into the hillside, and you can see the bridge on the D111 with the barrage behind it.

2. At this point the track ends and you continue on a narrow path under the rocks and through the woods. In time this very pretty path climbs a little, increasing the views of the rocky shore. Just before the tip of the headland the path turns inland to meet the rocks. You will need all fours for the short climb. The descent is a little longer and there are one or two sharp drops, but there is nothing remotely dangerous about it – just expect to spend a little time on your bottom! At the end of the descent you are again at the lake shore, at a clearing beside a shingly beach.

3. Bear left here and look out for the waymarks. They will lead you on a path alongside the shore (lake on left). There are now views up the lake to the north-east where the Verdon enters it and, farther back, some impressive mountain ranges. The path soon becomes quite a broad track above the lake shore. Ignore all paths heading inland and keep to this track parallel to the lake edge for around three-quarters of an hour. There are views of an island and, behind it, the promontory where les-Salles-sur-Verdon has been relocated. Eventually the path begins to climb again and, after passing a ruined building on the right, you reach a barrier and a track junction

4. All tracks at this junction bear the white on red waymarks of a Grande Randonnée. Take the track on the right, doubling back to begin climbing the slope. At the fork in just a few minutes, keep to the right, and at a second fork, right again – all is clearly waymarked. A ruined building stands on the right before you pass under the high tension lines and descend to a T-junction of paths.

5. Turn left here on a stony track. After 3 or 4 minutes, keep right at a fork. The path climbs and, deep in the forest, becomes narrower and steeper. Old red waymarks and splashes of green can be seen along with the white on red. After around half an hour of climbing you reach a broad track running along the summit of the ridge (there is a fork just before the summit, but it doesn't matter which way you choose).

6. Turn right on this broad track.. In about 30m, ignore a track on the right and keep ahead. The path now descends through the woods and you keep ahead on the main track (ignoring tracks on left, then right).

7. At a T-junction, bear right and continue downhill. Soon you can see the layered rocky sides of the gorge and there is a stream (often dry) beside you on the left. The lake is in sight ahead as you round the side of the hill with views of Bauduen and its harbour. At the hairpin, the track ahead leads in to the top of the village if you want to explore it. Otherwise continue descending and, at the next bend, turn right (leaving the GR at last). At the next junction, go left, passing a *lavoir* to regain the lakeside.

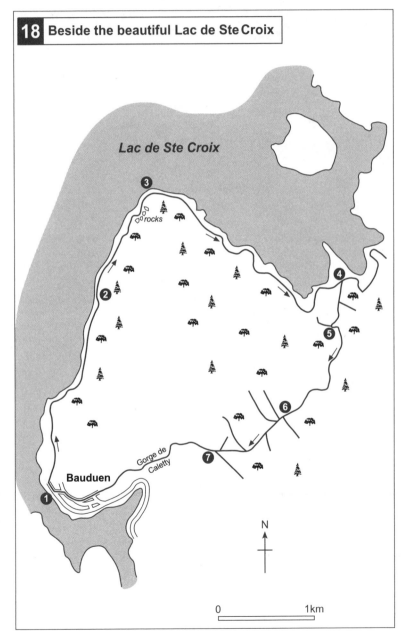

18 Beside the beautiful Lac de Ste Croix

Lac de Ste Croix

Bauduen

Gorge de Caletty

N

0   1km

Lac de Ste Croix

More Walks in the Area

The Topoguide *Gorges, lacs et plateaux du Verdon à pied (Ref. P042)* offers 20 excellent walks along the length of the river, including the classic Sentier Martel (Walk 19). The maps in this topoguide are, as usual, extracts from the IGN series on which the routes have been drawn – making them very easy to follow without reference to the French text. Another energetic choice from this book is a walk starting downriver from the Lac de Ste Croix at the village of Quinson. The circuit is entitled *Ste Maxime et les basses gorges du Verdon* and sets out following the old Canal de Provence along the near-vertical sides of the gorge. This is fairly spectacular stuff, but at the time of writing, although the path had not been closed, there were warnings about the eroded state of the canal banks. But for those with a sense of adventure –

Upstream from Quinson, between there and the Lac de Ste Croix, the village of St Laurent-sur-Verdon is the starting point of two rather gentler walks, each around 6km in length. Here again the Verdon flows through a gorge that is steep-sided although less deep than that at Quinson. Heading north-east from the car park (opposite the château) at St Laurent, you will soon pick up signs for the circuit of *Coteau Chiron* – the path encircles a hill from whose flanks there are good views into the gorge with its blue river. Another circuit starts from the same point but soon turns south and follows the river downstream where the banks are less steep. Both these routes are very well-waymarked with signposts and yellow flashes, so you should have no difficulty following them. They are marked on the appropriate IGN map (3343 OT) and again they appear in the Topoguide.

For those with good comprehension of French, the book *30 Balades en famille le long du Verdon* will further extend your range of walks. But beware the *en famille* – many of these walks are not suitable for young children (the Sentier Martel and the Sentier de l'Imbut are included)

Places of interest nearby

For some good views of the lake it is worth driving clockwise around shores as far as the village of Moustiers-Ste-Marie. Moustiers is tucked deep in a gorge on the River Maire. The church, as ever, has the views, but you will need energy to share them. A seemingly endless flight of steps takes you to its rocky perch, from where it looks over the jumbled roofs and along the length of the gorge, the Ravin de Notre Dame. High above, a single star is suspended on a cable between the opposite rocky faces.

Quinson has its own lake and is also home to the 'state of the art' *Musée de préhistoire des Gorges de Verdon*. 21st century technology is employed to tell the story of man over the last million years. Beyond the museum building, a walk through the garrigue takes you to a cave first occupied some 400,000 years ago. Below the cave, on the riverside, a reconstructed prehistoric village offers the opportunity to try your hand at redundant skills such as throwing a spear or starting a fire without matches. The museum is open every day except Tuesday (every day is summer), but closed from mid-December to 1st February.

The prehistory museum may be closed in winter, but this is just the time to visit the nearby town of Aups with its Thursday truffle market. From November to March its stalls are laden with the unpleasant-looking delicacy – and if you should happen to be here for the truffle fair at the end of January, you can admire the skills of the trained pigs that snout them out.

South-east of Aups, the hillside medieval village of Tourtour has commanding views over the plains of Var to the south. The *table d'orientation* beside the church points out the humpback of the Luberon, the steep-sided Mont Ste Victoire and the ridge of the Ste Baume to the west and to the east, the curve of the Maures. More views are to be had from the huge *boules* pitch – obviously the heart of the village – but you can wander on through ancient streets, past fountains, artists' galleries, an oil mill and more. In July and August, Tourtour is just too popular for comfort – arrange your visit out of season.

19. Martel's path through the Gorges of Verdon

The Verdon Gorges have often been described as Europe's answer to the Grand Canyon. This path devised a century ago by the pioneer Martel has become the most popular hike in the south of France – but you will need a head for heights and plenty of stamina.

Grade: Strenuous

Distance: 14km (8¾ miles)

Time: 6 hours – but allow yourself up to two hours more.

Map: IGN Top 25 3442 OT

Start and finish: Point Sublime – from where you get a bus or taxi to the Chalet de la Maline. (The trail is more demanding when taken in the opposite direction)

How to get there: Point Sublime is on the D952 between la Palud-sur-Verdon and Castellane and there is a large car park. In July and August there are buses from here to the Chalet de la Maline. Throughout the year it is usual to find morning taxis waiting for customers – but if none is there, a number to call is always posted on the taxi stand. It is also possible to park your car at Chalet de la Maline and get transport back at the end of the walk. Another option would be to leave your car at the parking place at the Couloir Samson (Point 5) and climb to Point Sublime before picking up transport, but this car park is more vulnerable to theft. Wherever you park, you are recommended not to leave valuables in your car.

Refreshment: At Point Sublime there is a pleasant auberge and also a kiosk in the car park selling drinks, etc. Down in the gorge you need to be self-sufficient – carry food and at least 2 litres of water per person.

Notes: There is no doubt that this is a tough hike – although you will probably not find it as strenuous as various texts lead you to believe. If you are unsure whether you can make it, check out the three points in the Introduction below. It is in any case forbidden to take children under 10 years of age. Footwear is preferably walking boots, even though you will almost certainly see some people in trainers. When the sun shines it can be very hot in the gorge – wear lightweight clothing and a hat and apply the sun-cream. But the weather can change rapidly in this area, so don't forget to take a warm sweater and a waterproof. Other ingredients of the rucksack should include a good torch (for the tunnels at the end of the walk) and, of course, the camera. On a hot day the blue waters of the Verdon look very inviting – and there are a couple of 'beaches' where you may see folk bathing. Nevertheless, notice boards advise you not to go near the water. Its level is controlled by a dam upstream and can rise very quickly. And finally, this walk is extremely popular. For maximum seclusion (still not a lot), go on a weekday, well out of season – but beware wet weather, when the rocks can be slippery underfoot.

Waymarking: This route is all on a Grande Randonnée (GR 4) and so is waymarked with flashes of white on red – but you can't get lost.

Introduction

Right at the heart of Provence, the blue waters of the Verdon have sliced sharply through a high plateau of limestone. These spectacular gorges vary between 200 and 700 metres in depth and were unknown to the world until the beginning of the twentieth century. At that time the electricity board was devising a scheme to provide hydro-electric power by canalising river water between Carajuan and Galetas. Edouard-Alfred Martel, famous speleologist and hydrologist, was appointed to embark on an expedition of reconnaissance. With him went Isidore Blanc, a schoolteacher from

Beside the river at the Pré d'Issane

nearby Rougon. In August 1905 they spent three days working their way down the whole length of the gorge and as a result of their efforts the project got underway – the tunnels you meet at the end of this walk were a part of it. But the First World War intervened and the work was never completed. After the war Isidore Blanc began to take his own guided tours into the canyon and in 1930 the Touring Club of France took over the trail. From that time its fame has grown. It has recently been estimated that up to 2000 people a day may be on the path in summer, and even in winter solitude is unlikely. (We actually once saw the path completely free of people when we looked down from the Belvédère de Rancoumas (see **More Walks**) on the wettest of very wet days in early spring – but going in the rain is not recommended)

Apart from its challenge, what else makes this walk so popular? The gorges themselves are breathtaking in their depth and stunningly beautiful. As Martel himself said, 'There exists here, I repeat, a marvel without a second in Europe'. The river is a sort of milky blue colour (due to its fluoride content) and appears as a sparkling ribbon threading its way through the greenness of the depths. A couple of times the path descends to its banks, but mostly you are above it, climbing up and down slopes pitted with caves and decked in wild flowers and lush vegetation. Perhaps most beautiful is the spot known as the Mescla where the Verdon turns through a right-angle to head west and its blue waters mingle with the green of the Artuby arriving from the south. At the mid-point of the walk, it makes a perfect picnic place. More imposing than beautiful are the tall pink and grey cliffs of Escalès, where rock-climbers may be seen clinging to the sheer face. And the walk ends with the photogenic Towers of Trescaire and the deep blue river sliding through the narrow rocky channel of the Samson Corridor.

The Martel path is by no means the only route through these gorges. But despite all the warnings of its perils, it is definitely the easiest. If you are wondering whether you can cope with this walk's demands, you might like to consider three particular difficulties. The first of these is the length – you can expect to walk for 5 or 6 hours and there is no practical possibility of a short cut. But if you set out early, you can take your time and have as many rests as you like. The second point is that the route does involve some scrambling over rocks. Although you will need to use your hands, no section is especially arduous. If you are not sure about this, try taking Walk 18 beside the Lac de Ste Croix. On this walk there is just one rocky scramble – and no part of the Martel path exceeds this in difficulty. Finally, there are the ladders and ropes that have been installed to help you over rough sections of rock or scree. These are generally easy to negotiate. The most dramatic (and possibly most daunting) point of the walk comes at the Brèche Imbert where over 200 steps on near-vertical ladders take you down 120m to the river below. The good hand-rails here are invaluable – and most people prefer to turn round rather than look where they are going. If all that sounds too much, you can at least get a taster of the gorges by following the 'Lizard Path' (see **More Walks**). Otherwise, go for it! This walk has to rate as one of life's experiences.

The Walk

1. Your path leaves the road just to the left of the Chalet de la Maline – you will see the white on red flashes of the Grand Randonnée. At first it descends gently just below the road but soon becomes rather steeper as it zigzags down rocky slopes into the denser vegetation at the bottom of the gorge. After about 40 minutes you reach a path junction.

2. To the right, the GR99 goes off to cross the river (the bridge here was under repair in the summer of '02), but you turn left, in the direction of Point Sublime. A pleasant path under the trees follows and high on the cliff opposite you can see the Auberge des Cavaliers, the starting point of the Sentier de l'Imbut (see **More Walks**). Soon you have reached river level and a sign on the right points you to the Pré d'Issane. This is a lovely pebbly beach beside the river, overlooked by the huge towering cliffs of the opposite shore. The path now begins to meander up and down the slopes with one or two rocky climbs. On the other side the cliff holds many caves and, along its rim, a series of square holes where the scenic balcony road passes through a tunnel. After a climb, a couple of metal staircases take you down to the Guègues scree, a short shingly slope crossed with the aid of a fixed rope. A few more minutes walking and you are passing the Baume aux Boeufs, a cave where the bones of early cattle were once found. Soon afterwards you arrive at a junction with a signpost

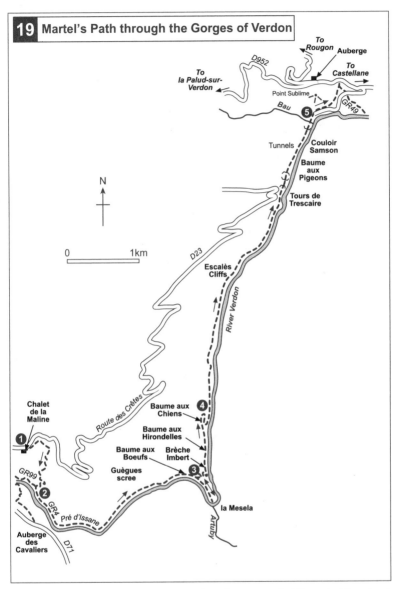

19 Martel's Path through the Gorges of Verdon

3. The main path here continues ahead to Point Sublime (said to be 3 hours away). But it is well worth turning right to descend to the Mescla – it will probably take you less than the 30 minutes suggested on the sign. Mescla comes from a Provençal word for 'mixing' and from the tip of this spur the River Artuby can be seen silently emptying its green waters into the blue Verdon. The rocky slabs overlooking the confluence are bright with shrubs and wild flowers, making a grand place for a picnic.

It must be said that the second part of this journey is rather more demanding than the first. From the Mescla, return to the path junction and turn right. Almost immediately you begin the climb to the Brèche Imbert, where a series of metal ladders descend through an almost vertical shaft in the rock. Over a hundred metres below, the blue river sparkles – but you may not want to look! Nevertheless, both ladders and hand-rails are quite substantial and there is no physical difficulty in the descent. Once at the bottom the path soon begins to climb again passing the arching Baume aux Hirondelles (Swallows' Cave) and there are fine views into the gorge. Farther on, after a hairpin bend, you pass the dripping Baume aux Chiens (Dogs' Cave) and then make a steep rocky knee-pounding descent to river level once more.

4.   Now you can choose to look in on the Plage des Fères before climbing under the pink and grey faces of the mighty cliffs of the Escalès. Suddenly, as you round a corner, you are struck by a blast of cool air from the left (possibly very welcome) – you have reached the first of the tunnels. Enjoy the cool, but don't go into this one. Continuing on the path, another rope helps you across a huge rock before you reach a viewpoint overlooking the curious banded rock formations known as the Tours de Trescaire. More metal steps take you onwards into the depths of the Couloir Samson (Samson Corridor). Soon you arrive at the entrance of the 100m Trescaire Tunnel. Light can be seen at the end, but you will still need a torch. The second tunnel follows immediately, 670m long this time, and full of puddles if there has been any rain. Along its length are three 'windows' – from the first of these more ladders will take you down to the river beside a cave known as the Baume aux Pigeons. Reaching the end of the tunnel, steps now descend again to the river. At this point you are supposed to look back and see Samson, a shadowy giant etched by crevices in the rock face, high on the opposite side. His strength is holding the walls of the corridor apart. You require a strong imagination (or the booklet described in **More Walks**) to make him out. The path soon takes you across a bridge where the Bau stream enters the gorge and then climbs to a parking area.

5.   To the left of the parking area, the waymarked GR4 leaves to climb to the Point Sublime (approx. 40 minutes away). Here you meet the first of the green lizard signs (see **More Walks**). The path soon levels out and passes under a cliff face from where there are fine views back into the gorge. A few minutes beyond the cliff you arrive at a path junction. Ahead the GR 49 goes down to the Pont de Tusset, but you turn left on the GR4 to climb to the road. The auberge and parking at Point Sublime are just a couple of hundred metres to the left.

More Walks in the Area

The kiosk in the parking area at Point Sublime stocks a delightful little book describing the discovery trail (with its green lizard signs) that you may have met briefly at the end of this walk. The trail was originally the work of a local secondary school more than ten years ago and has been well-maintained. The book (*The Verdon Grand Canyon – a discovery trail*) has an English version and is full of interesting facts about the gorges (including a picture of Samson). If you feel the whole Martel path is not for you, with this booklet you can at least follow the paths from Point Sublime with their numbered posts and make the journey into the gorge as far as the Trescaire Towers.

More demanding than the Sentier Martel, but certainly the most beautiful of the gorge paths, is the Sentier de l'Imbut. If you are fit, footsure and free from vertigo, this is probably the one to go for. Highlights are the Styx (dubbed 'hell' by Martel after he arrived at night and first heard the tumult of the waters here) and the Imbut (funnel) where the river disappears underground for 150m The path starts from the Auberge des Cavaliers on the left bank, is well-waymarked (GR99) and will take around 6 hours for a there-and-back trip (the most courageous could choose instead a direct ascent to the road on the Vidal path). The Sentier de l'Imbut is clearly marked on the IGN map (3442 OT) – and is described, with good photos but minimum detail, in a booklet in English entitled *Canyon du Verdon – the most beautiful hikes*. This latter contains 28 walks, and is on sale in the kiosk at Point Sublime and at the Office de Tourisme (in the old château) at la Palud-sur-Verdon.

Another popular route (although not on the same scale as Martel's path) is the 5km Bastidon trail between Mainmorte (on the D23 west of La Palud) and the Maireste viewpoint on the D952. The difference here is that this is a balcony path with some stunning views into the gorges. The route is again described in the *Canyon du Verdon – the most beautiful hikes* book. It also appears in more detail in the Topoguide of this area *Gorges, lacs et plateaux du Verdon à pied* (Ref. P042). In this book it is incorporated into a circuit of 14.5km starting from La Palud and returning on some fairly adventurous forest tracks.

And finally, if you really want to test your head for heights, there is nothing to beat the Belvédère de Rancoumas, a lonely viewpoint 400 vertical metres above the river, and facing the sheer cliffs of Escalès. The setting is blissful – a flower-scattered rocky outcrop on the edge of an alpine meadow, across which are the crumbling stone buildings of the old hamlet of Encastel. Courageous souls who look over the edge can see walkers like so many ants on the Martel path way below. The route to the Belvédère de Rancoumas initially follows the GR49 from Point Sublime across the picturesque Pont de Tusset. The waymarked path then climbs steeply uphill until in around an hour you arrive at a junction with a broad cross-track. Here the GR49 turns left, but you descend on the track to the right as far as a sharp left-hand bend. Go to the right at this point, into the meadow, and find a path along the ridge of rocks on the left, which will take you to the Belvédère. This route is shown on the IGN map and again in the *Most beautiful hikes* book, but has been described here because the last part into the meadow is easily missed and there are no waymarks.

Places of interest nearby

It is possible to take a drive encircling the gorges, stopping at all the many viewpoints around the rims. Starting from Moustiers Ste Marie or Castellane, the total distance is around 150km but with winding roads and crawling traffic in summertime, the journey will almost certainly take all day. On the way you will look down from the Falaise des Cavaliers and go on to the Pont de l'Artuby with its bungee-jumpers. Next comes the superb vantage point above the Mescla. On the north side, Point Sublime is passed, after which you turn on to the Routes des Crêtes with its multiple viewpoints. The one at Escalès is the most vertiginous, looking down on the Sentier Martel some 500m below. The final Belvédère de l'Imbut gives a view of the disappearing river and the Styx.

20. The Grès d'Annot – in the Hall of the Mountain King

Above the old town of Annot, gigantic blocks of gritstone are lodged on the slopes amid the oaks and chestnuts. Narrow passages and chambers in the rock, towering cliffs and the bizarre shapes of the boulders make you feel you have reached another world.

Grade: Moderate

Distance: 6km (3¾ miles)

Time: 3 hours

Map: Top 25 3541 OT

Start and finish: The station at Annot

How to get there: Annot is about 45km east of Barrême, just off the N202 road to Nice. On entering the town from the south, turn right where signed to reach the station, where there is parking. Or you can arrive by train – the line here is that of the magnificent Chemin de Fer de Provence (Train des Pignes) from Nice to Digne, with many stops en route.

Refreshment: Annot is well-endowed with cafés and restaurants.

Notes: This walk climbs fairly steeply through woodland on the valley sides above Annot. Boots are preferable footwear – those wearing trainers will find themselves picking their way through a few boggy patches on the way down. There is just one vertiginous but not dangerous point on the walk where the path (quite wide) skirts a cliff with some bird's-eye views into the valley below. Otherwise it's a woodland wander amid impressive boulders with good shade for a hot day.

Waymarking: This route is waymarked in yellow throughout

Introduction

Running an exciting 150km between Nice and Digne, the Chemin de Fer de Provence passes through some of the region's most dramatic scenery. Every halt along the line has something to offer – Entrevaux with its perched citadel, the blue lake at St André-les-Alpes, Digne itself, at the heart of the geological reserve. Annot (the 't' is pronounced) is a beautiful old Provençal town in the valley of the River Vaire, its streets shaded by ancient plane trees. Around Annot the landscape is dotted with massive gritty boulders – the first can be seen from the panoramic windows of the train, blocks big enough to have houses built into them. Higher up the hill the chaos of boulders is even more impressive, with narrow passages, caves, balanced rocks and arches of stone.

How did these boulders get here? There is a story that when St Peter arrived to evangelise, he could get no response whatsoever from the local population. He left, shaking the sand of the place from his shoes as he went. The grains stuck together as they fell to form these enormous rocks. St Peter's footprint can be seen at a place called Baou de Parou, on the route of another waymarked walk starting from Annot. If this legend does-n't provide all the answers for you, there is a geological explanation. Some 65 million years ago, the sea began to retreat from this region, leaving behind a thick layer of sandy sediment. Millions of years later, this sand

The Train des Pignes

became united with calcareous deposits to form cliffs of gigantic proportions. Under the action of erosion the cliffs broke up into the immense blocks that are the focus of this walk – the Grès d'Annot.

The path you follow at first climbs quite steeply through lovely woodland of chestnut and oaks. Deep green ferns spring from the boulders on either side. As you near the top of the hill it is well worth taking a short diversion to les Oubliettes – a narrow channel between some of the largest rocks, a popular site for *escalade*. A little farther up the path, another boulder-engulfed passage has caves leading off – the site has been given the evocative name of Chambre du Roi. Beyond this rocky chaos the scene changes and you find yourself on a path beneath cliffs whose faces bear strangely human profiles. Far below you two rivers meet and the little village of les Scaffarels gets on with its business. Before returning down the slopes, the path leads you to the most famous of the rocky phenomena, an arch of 'kissing' stones, known as les Portettes.

The Walk

1. Leaving the railway station, walk back downhill on the road and then turn right to walk under the railway, following a sign to the *Grès d'Annot* and the *Chambre du Roi*. At the far side turn right and continue parallel to the railway lines, passing a house built in to one of the huge rocks. After the sign for the Escalade, opposite the last station building, the path bends away left and begins to climb. Yellow waymarks pick out your route as you ascend on a stony track shaded by chestnuts and winding between huge boulders. At a clearing with a big rock on the left the path swings round to the right and then crosses *robines* (ridged slopes of black marl) as it continues to climb. Again the rocks are all around you and, coming up to a cliff face, you meet a sign pointing left to the *Jardin du Roi*. Take a glance that way, and then continue uphill (SP *Chambre du Roi*) to a path junction

2. The path to the left here is signed to *Les Oubliettes (PR 6)* – the circular detour will take about 15 minutes. On the way you walk through a cool corridor between the biggest rocks you have yet seen. A third rock balances precariously overhead. Beyond them big-leaved chestnuts give dappled shade – you begin to feel you are in the land of the trolls! The path curves round and reaches a ferny glade – the Jardin du Roi, where you rejoin the path you were on earlier. Climb now past the junction (Point 2) and continue uphill towards the Chambre du Roi. Soon you reach it – a place where the huge rocks seem to have crashed into each other and the path passes through a narrow crack beneath them. Could this be a scene from Lord of the Rings? Or perhaps you can hear strains of Grieg wafting from the entrance? Look right as you go into it – *ENTRÉE* has been written in red on the rock. If you wriggle through this hole you will find yourself in a rocky room with others beyond. Do not be tempted to continue squeezing through the rock to find an exit – this *chambre* has no safe way out other than the opening through which you came. Now go on through the rocky passage. At its end you are in a sort of amphitheatre with terraced banks.

3. From here the yellow-flashed path becomes a balcony overlooking the valleys of the Vaire and the Coulomp with their accompanying roads and railway. You walk on beneath towering cliffs with this most spectacular view until the path eventually turns inland and enters woods following the bed of a stream uphill. Carved-out footholds lead you up rocks and you continue ahead, picking out the yellow blazes to guide you through the pines and chestnuts. On the right the path passes the crumbling remains of an old shelter between blocks of stone. The path soon swings to the left and becomes less distinct for a brief time. Suddenly it is again clear and you skirt overhanging rock on the left to reach the strange arch of les Portettes and walk beneath it.

4. Beyond the arch, the path bears round to the right, and, flanked by chestnuts, oaks, pines and boulders, it begins to descend gently. After several minutes walking, look out for a sharp turn to the left downhill – the path ahead bears a yellow cross and heads straight for a rock. Now follow the path in its descent, becoming ever steeper as it goes. At each junction you keep to the main track, which is always marked with a yellow flash. Several small streams cross your path – or run along it – and there are waterfalls in the rock beside you. At points the path is boggy where it crosses robines of clay again. The descent seems to go on forever (at least there is shade) but eventually you emerge from the woods just above the town. The grassy slopes now lead you down to buildings – a house on the right and the 12th century chapel of Notre-Dame de Vers-la-Ville on the left. Continue descending on the cobbled track with its Stations of the Cross to reach the railway line.

5. Cross straight over and walk on down the tarmacked road (more Stations of the Cross) into the town. At the main road turn left and then turn left again where signposted to reach the station.

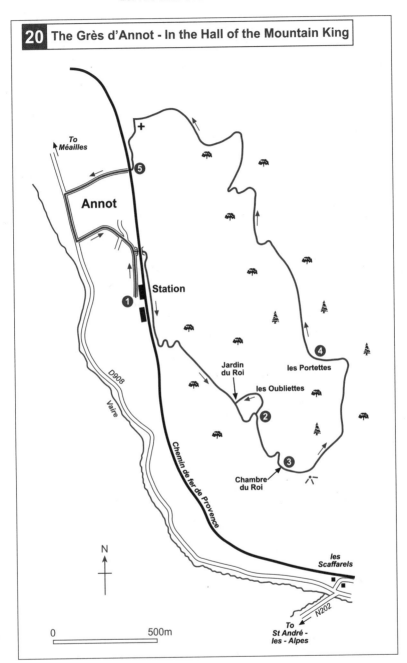

More Walks in the Area

Other walks from Annot include a short (2 hour) there-and-back climb to the Baou de Parou and a long ascent into the mountains on a Grande Randonnée du Pays (waymarked yellow on red) known as the *Grande Traverse des Préalpes*. The Office de Tourisme in Annot (in the main street) is happy to talk to you about both these routes and to offer you a simple photocopied sketch map. Particularly for the long hike, you would also need to get the IGN map of this area (3541 OT), which is on sale in a shop almost opposite the Office de Tourisme.

More walks in the area around Annot can be found in the topoguide *Les Alpes-de-Haute-Provence à pied* (Ref. D004). As usual this topoguide is in French only, but the maps are excellent, and routes included in a topoguide are almost invariably well-waymarked on the ground. One interesting excursion not included in the topoguide is the hike (4 hours there-and-back) to the Grotte de Méailles, off the D908 about 7km north of Annot. Geologists will find this cave particularly fascinating – but for everyone else, it's a marvellous hike into the mountains with a spectacular cave to explore at the end of the trail. Don't forget your torches. Details can be obtained from the Office de Tourisme at Annot.

The village of Méailles is actually a halt on the route of the Train des Pignes – many more excellent walks can be accessed from the stations along this narrow-gauge railway. Its northern terminus at Digne can offer 7 waymarked routes, Barrême has an interesting geological trail (Walk 21 in this book), and from St André-les-Alpes you can walk down to the shores of the Lac du Castillon. Entrevaux, a few kilometres to the east of Annot is a spectacular town itself. You may consider the 20-minute climb up the zigzag path to its citadel quite sufficient exercise for a hot day. But if it's a good substantial mountain hike that you require, a popular fairly adventurous waymarked trail leads from here to the next stop east, Puget Théniers – the return (or outward journey) can be made by rail. The map you want is 3640 OT. The route sets off above the north bank of the river and then climbs to St Louis. Continuing through the Ravine of Augière you head east to pick up the GR 510 at the Col de Velacs and descend to Puget-Théniers. The whole distance is around 12km, for which you should allow at least 5 hours. For more ideas of possible rambles from the stations of the Train des Pignes, a free brochure entitled *Rando Train* (obtainable from OT) should help. If your French is fairly competent, it might also be worth seeking out a book entitled *75 Randonnées Pédestres entre Digne et Nice avec le Train des Pignes*. But this comprehensive little volume dates from 1980 – and, after a lot of searching, it seems quite possible that the one copy we found was the very last!

Places of interest nearby

Entrevaux is a Provençal gem – a 'perched' citadel 150m above a town of narrow streets and tall stone houses. The town originated in the 11th century on a spur almost surrounded by the River Var. Its situation made it a gateway to France, and in medieval times it was attacked, taken and re-taken. At the end of the 17th century, Louis XIV directed Vauban to make this place impregnable. The château on its rocky pinnacle became a fortified citadel, with views up and down the valley. Towers, ramparts, gates, ditches and drawbridges protected the town – and it later resisted the assaults of the Duke of Savoy's army, allies of the Emperor of Austria. Its fortifications have all been preserved – and Entrevaux is well on the tourist trail.

The Train des Pignes is again something quite unique. The narrow-gauge track of the Chemin de Fer de Provence between Digne and Nice was built around 1900. It was a masterful piece of engineering involving the construction of more than fifty tunnels, bridges and via-ducts, and took about 20 years to complete. The first trains were of course steam trains and the name Train des Pignes (Pine-cone Train) probably derives from the occasional use of pine-cones for fuel in wartime. (Its website explains the name with a legend. Apparently one cold Christmas a little girl who lived beside the line was sick, and her family had no fuel to keep the house warm. The train stopped to give them some – and when the train itself ran out, pine cones dropped from the trees kept it going!) Nowadays a smart little diesel with panoramic windows makes the journey in each direction four times a day throughout the year (although on special summer Sundays an original *train à vapeur* dating from 1909 emerges from its shed at Puget-Théniers and ventures as far as Annot and back). The line follows river valleys all the way – from Digne the train climbs beside the Asse and the Verdon, then passes through a tunnel under the watershed and descends beside the Vaire and then the Var all the way down to Nice. Classic views are many – the rocky Clue de Chabrières, the azure Lac de Castillon, the Grès of Annot and the splendours of fortified Entrevaux come before glimpses of the spectacular gorges entering the Var – the gorges of the Cians, the Tinée and the Vésubie. To say the least it's a scenic journey and you might think of taking a map with you to identify the sights (although the train has tiny maps printed on the drinks trays below the windows). The whole journey takes 3 hours and tickets are very reasonably priced – certainly by British standards.

21. In Napoleon's footsteps at Barrême

Napoleon passed through Barrême on his march north to Paris in the spring of 1815. Follow his route into the mountains – and take in a few of the geological phenomena of this region on the way.

Grade: Moderate

Distance: 7km (4½ miles)

Time: 3 hours

Map: IGN Top 25 3441 OT

Start and finish: The Place de l'Église at Barrême

How to get there: The Place de l'Église is in the centre of Barrême on the N202 to Moriez. Park in the square itself, or just a little farther along the road in the car park behind the supermarket.

Refreshment: There are a couple of bar/cafés close to the square, and a restaurant beside the station.

Notes: This walk is all on good tracks with a short return along a minor road – trainers would be quite acceptable in good weather. The steady climb in the first half of the walk results in a height gain of around 200m. The route is partly in forest and partly exposed – it would be as well to take sun-cream and a hat on a hot day, and also to carry plenty of fluid. Water is available in the village of St Jacques, near the end of the walk.

Waymarking: Most of the walk is marked with yellow flashes – see the text.

Introduction

Beside the main road from Digne to Castellane, Barrême seems a rather undistinguished sort of place – that is, until you take a closer look. Its first claim to fame is announced on the wall of a house in the main street – Napoleon spent the night here on his rapid march north in March 1815. The local population even knows what he had for supper – soup, omelette, cod, goat's meat and plenty of wine! His bid to recover his throne as emperor had begun two days earlier (1st March) when he landed near Cannes with an army of around 1200 men. On his arrival, he heard that the Rhône valley was hostile and chose instead this particular route north, believing the mountain roads to have been improved during his former reign. In fact the work had never been done, and Napoleon and his army found themselves on no more than mule tracks through peaks blasted by icy winds and inches deep in snow. Nevertheless, in seven days they reached Grenoble, and on the 20th March, entered Paris itself. The end came at the Battle of Waterloo on 18th June. Defeat at the hands of Wellington resulted in secure imprisonment on the island of St Helena. The route of Napoleon's march has been marked with a white eagle motif, inspired by his words 'L'aigle volera de clocher en clocher, jusqu'aux tours de Notre-Dame' (The eagle will fly from steeple to steeple until it reaches the towers of Notre-Dame.)

Returning to Barrême and more recent history, a display board in the market square shows that this place was a centre of Resistance activity in the last world war. The area is known as the Haute Vallées de l'Asse (three tributaries join to form the River Asse just below the town) and it was

View from the Chapelle St-Jean

awarded the Croix de Guerre at the end of the war, in recognition of courageous conduct. A museum at Castellane tells of the exploits of the Maquisards, with many memorabilia.

Likewise in the square, another board has been erected by the *Reserve Géologique* and shows the route of this walk along with the many geological treasures in this area. Barrême is well-known to geologists, having a particular era named after it – the Barremian era is a stage of the Upper Cretaceous, around 117 – 113 million years ago. Among the characteristic fossils of this era are uncoiled ammonites and many local finds are displayed – curiously – in the waiting room at the station. The station is actually worthy of a visit in its own right. As with others on the route of the classic Train des Pignes, it seems to have come straight from a Second World War film, complete with hand-operated signals.

This short walk from Barrême takes you first to a chapel on a hillock above the town. The old town of Barrême was sited here and there are splendid views into the valleys of the Asse and its tributaries. The path leads on to follow Napoleon's route into the mountains, on the way passing rock strata typical of the Barremian era. A display board gives an explanation in English. High in the mountains, Napoleon went on towards Digne, but you turn downhill through a deep valley to another display of local geology in the form of a rock of very tiny fossils known as nummulites. Passing through the pretty village of St Jacques, you return to Barrême – where it is worth crossing the river to the station before making your way home.

The Walk

1. Leaving the market square, walk past the war memorial and bear left. A sign on the corner directs you to the *Chapelle St Jean* and the *Sentier des Senteurs* (Path of Scents – an evocative title for the route you are about to follow). After passing the *Mairie* on your right you arrive at the Place des Tilleuls (Square of Lime-trees) surrounded by old build-

ings from the 16th and 17th centuries. Cross it to the left and then turn right uphill. Leaving the village, turn left beside the oratory, following a yellow-flashed path to the Chapelle St Jean. The grassy track passes a field of fine lavender (*Lavandula angustifolia*), planted by the town to recall its one time economic dependence on this same lavender that grows wild in the surrounding mountains. Beyond the lavender field, the track bears right and zigzags up the side of the hill, passing several oratories and a junction at which you bear left. The chapel and its calvaries crown the summit. At a splendid viewpoint, an orientation table points out the three valleys of the Asse. To the left, the little village of St Jacques spills down the hillside.

2. To continue with the walk, return along the track on which you came for some 50 metres or so. At the junction, do not turn right, but continue straight ahead (SP Sentier des Senteurs, St Jacques). On coming out of the pinewoods, look for some sandy-coloured rock on the left. This is nummulitic limestone, similar to that you will meet at St Jacques – if it doesn't look that remarkable to you, all will later be revealed. Reaching a junction beside some houses, turn left uphill on a stony track (SP St Jacques). Now just keep to the main broad track through pleasant open prairie and dotted woodland.

3. Eventually you reach a fork – the track ahead leads past a house, the left-hand track turns uphill and bears a notice saying it is forbidden to motor vehicles. This latter is the one you want. It continues to climb with increasing views over the valley to the right. In a few minutes you reach a rocky slope on your left and an information panel beside it tells you that this has the stratotype of the Barremian. Just a little farther on, the main track swings sharply to the left (a path ahead descends rapidly to St Jacques), after which you meet the first white eagle waymarks of the *Voie Imperiale* taken by Napoleon. These lead you on through the pinewoods to a clearing with a wooden signpost.

4. Leave Napoleon here (he went on to Chaudon) and instead turn right in the direction of St Jacques and the Sentier des Senteurs. Yellow waymarks lead you downhill beside the pine woods before the path makes an even steeper descent into a ravine (Ravin de St Martin). Cross over the stream at the bottom and bear right to climb the bank on the opposite side. Continuing on the track, you will soon see on the right a huge ridged bank of marl (a blend of clay materials and silt) behind which the *site nummulitique* is hidden. Meeting another track, keep ahead (i.e. do not turn left) and continue descending between hedges to meet a tarmacked road. Turn right on this road for about 50 metres.

5. Here a signpost directs you right to the nummulitic site – a couple of minutes walking will take you there. Immediately it's not very impressive, but the information panel will tell you where to look out for tiny nummulites, pectin shells, etc. When geologically replete, return to the tarmacked road and turn right, following it uphill through the pretty old village of St Jacques. A fountain and a communal bread oven are found in its central square. As you descend, look out for the newly constructed viewpoint over the *Bassin Barrêmois* on the right (toilets and water have been installed nearby). Continue down the

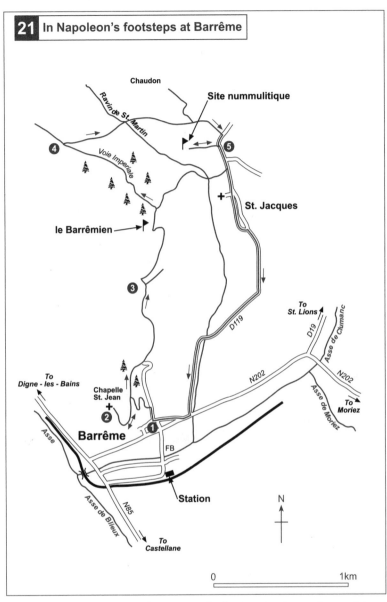

21 | In Napoleon's footsteps at Barrême

(Map labels: Chaudon, Site nummulitique, Ravin de St Martin, Voie Imperiale, le Barrêmien, St. Jacques, D119, To St. Lions, Asse de Chumanc, D19, N202, To Moriez, To Digne-les-Bains, Chapelle St. Jean, Barrême, Asse de Moriez, Asse, FB, Station, N85, Asse de Blieux, To Castellane, N)

0 — 1km

quiet road a further 2km to reach the N202, the main road from Moriez. Turn right here and walk beside the road for 100m or so before taking the road glancing off on the right, quickly returning you to the church and square in the centre of Barrême.

More Walks in the Area

Napoleon's route through the mountains is shown on the relevant map (3441 OT) and is well marked on the ground, but if you want to follow it farther, you will need to get a taxi (ask the *Mairie* in Barrême for help) – or enlist the services of a friend to pick you up. Chaudon is 9km from Barrême and Entrages a further 12km. Digne is around 33km from

Barrême – and if you decide to try this longish trek, remember that Napoleon made the same journey in time for lunch at Digne! In fact, he and his army took just four days to travel from Cannes to Gap, a distance of more than 220km on snowy mountain tracks with only around 12 hours of light a day.

The *Haute Vallées de l'Asse* is a fascinating region and the *Réserve Géologique* has devoted an entire (and weighty) publication to it. If you can read French there's lots of interest here, including comprehensive descriptions of 11 walks visiting the geological sites. Unfortunately the maps are about as sketchy as you can get – merely thin lines of different colours. It's not easy identifying the routes on the IGN map either, but if you can do it, these are very good walks – well waymarked, and well off the usual tourist tracks. Among these walks, Barrême has its own little town trail, calling at the station and the old lavender distillery.

Heading south towards Castellane, the road reaches its highest point at the Col des Lecques. To the west the skyline is dominated by huge rocky outcrops known as the *Cadières de Brandis*. If you park your car in the grassy car park beside the camp site and cross the road, you will immediately pick up signs for the fairly demanding hiking path that encircles these rocks. The whole route will take about 4 hours. This walk is included in the Topoguide *Les Alpes-de-Haute-Provence à pied (Ref. D004),* but the Office de Tourisme in Castellane should be able to find you a route map.

Also starting from the car park on the Col des Lecques is a much shorter and easier walk, a half-hour ramble to the valley of the *Sirènes Fossiles* – the fossils of sea creatures, the forerunners of today's dugongs and manatees. This very scenic path through the woods brings you to a beautiful valley where the bones of these prehistoric animals (jaws, vertebrae, ribs, limb-bones, etc.) are exposed on the rockface, and have been covered in a 'flexi-glass' case for protection. If you have visited this site, you will undoubtedly want to call in at the *Maison des Sirènes et Sirèniens* in Castellane – see the Places of Interest section

Castellane is in a spectacular position beside the blue River Verdon – but not half so spectacular as the old Castellane, of which only the chapel remains, perched seemingly unassailably on its rock above the river. A yellow-waymarked route of 5km (the *Tour du Roc*) will take you up to the Chapelle Notre-Dame du Roc for a bird's-eye view of the town before returning through the ruins of the old settlement. The route is described in the Topoguide *Les Alpes-de-Haute-Provence à pied*, and also in a publication entitled *Vallée du Verdon de Saint-André-les-Alpes à Castellane – Guide des Sentiers de Randonnée*. The latter offers 16 waymarked walks in the region with reasonable maps and French only text. The Office de Tourisme in Castellane should have a copy.

Places of interest nearby

If you are interested in pursuing fossils and geology, the Office de Tourisme in Digne-les-Bains stocks a map of the area (produced by the *Réserve Géologique*) showing on one side all the 18 protected sites. On the other side, all the monuments, walking routes, points of view and other geological curiosities of the region are detailed. Of the latter, the nearest is just a few kilometres north of Barrême – the *recif fossile* at St Lions. As usual, the first sight is unimpressive, merely a bank of sand in the middle of a wood. But an information panel (in both French and English) tells you that this bank was once a coral reef at the bottom of the sea and is full of marine fossils.

The *Maison des Sirènes et Sirèniens* at Castellane manages to mix mythology and palaeontology, persuading you that mermaids and dugongs are one and the same thing – or perhaps that they have a common ancestor. Whatever your thoughts on mermaids and the like, there's plenty of well-presented geological fact here. It must be worth an hour of anyone's time. The *Maison* is in the central square and is open every day from May to September and some days in April and October.

The *Musée de la Résistance* (just north of Castellane, on the road to Barrême) is an unsophisticated establishment crammed with records, recollections, photographs and memorabilia of all kinds. Some knowledge of French would help you to get the best from it, but this is a place to take your time and browse.

Finally, Barrême is the first stop south of Digne for the remarkable little *Train des Pignes* – see Walk 20 at Annot for more details.

22. Deep in the Gorges de Trévans

South of Digne-les-Bains, the River Estoublaïsse has cut a deep gash through the limestone hills. This excellent walk has plenty of drama, but not too much difficulty. And these gorges are much quieter and perhaps even as beautiful as those of the Verdon.

Grade: Moderate

Distance: 8km (5 miles). An optional extension to the Chapelle St André will add another kilometre or so.

Time: 3 hours, plus half an hour for the extension.

Map: IGN Top 25 3441 OT

Start and finish: Parking at the entrance to the gorges, 5km east of Estoublon

How to get there: Estoublon is 7km south of Mézel on the D907. In the village, turn east where signposted to Gorges de Trévans. There is roadside parking near a left-hand bend in around 5km

Refreshment: None on the route. The nearest restaurant is in the village of Estoublon.

Notes: This walk does involve some climbing and descending, but though occasionally the path is steep, there is none of the rocky scrambling that is a feature of most Provençal gorges. Nevertheless, stout footwear is recommended, particularly after wet weather, and a head for heights might be helpful. Although much of the path is through woodland, you would probably still appreciate protection from the sun on a hot day. And don't forget to take plenty of fluid with you.

Waymarking: Red, green and yellow waymarks appear at times on this walk – just follow the text.

Introduction

On this walk you are in the *Pré-Alpes de Digne*, the foothills of the Alps themselves. Way to the south the Verdon has already cut its path through the early limestone massifs. Here the peaks are higher – the Estoublaïsse has its source on the slopes of Chiran, a summit of 1905m.. The gorge it then follows is steep-sided and densely wooded, a splendid hideout for wildlife, including the shy chamois.

In contrast to the Gorges of Verdon, you can enjoy solitude here. At a weekend you may meet the odd walking party and perhaps a few families who venture along the riverside to the first bridges – after that you can expect to be on your own. Even so, the paths are well waymarked – and the combination of scenery and rich vegetation is stunning. At the beginning, the walk follows the tumbling blue river under rocky overhangs to the bridges at the foot of the gorge. If you were to go no farther than this you would still have had a treat. Farther on, the path climbs high along the sides of the valley, overlooked by the high peaks at its head. Glancing backwards you can see that the river has cut a slit of incredible depth, and so narrow the sides almost touch. An extra climb will take you to the ruined Chapelle St André, and the effort is worthwhile – peering over its crumbling walls you have a breathtaking view of the whole length of the gorge. Picnic here with the panorama before you, or continue downhill to a lovely riverside spot near the deserted village of Valbonnette. The scenic path continues and makes a final descent into the gorge of cascading water – don't put your camera away until the very end!

The Walk

1. From the parking area, walk round a barrier – the cross beside it tells you that this was once the site of Camp Josette, one of the many Maquis camps in this area. Beyond the barrier a broad track takes you down alongside the river and then across it on a concrete bridge. On the far side a wooden signboard shows all the tracks in the gorges (confusing, as it is 'upside down') – and tells you that it is possible to bathe in the river 200m upstream from the concrete bridge. Turn to the left in front of this signboard and follow the path beside the river – there are red waymarks. After a few minutes walking the path passes under a rocky overhang and shortly afterwards you reach a fork

2. Take the left hand path here, still following the red waymarks (the yel-low-flashed path is the one on which you return). The path leads downhill and crosses the Estoublaïsse on a wooden footbridge, just upstream of a confluence. On the far side, a very clear path through

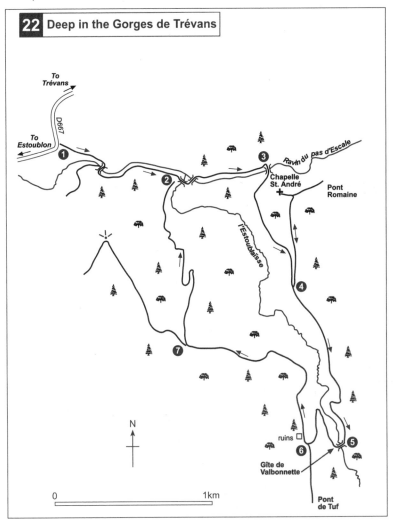

22 Deep in the Gorges de Trévans

the pinewood quickly brings you to a second bridge crossing a tributary of the river. Now the path climbs quite steeply. At the top of the rocky slope a clearing is reached, after which the path, though still gently climbing, is much easier. The descent soon begins, and deep in the pines, you reach the bed of a stream, which may be dry.

3. Cross over the stream and immediately turn right along its bank – there are red waymarks on the stones. Soon you reach the main tributary of the Estoublaïsse (the one you crossed earlier) and can cross it again on double bridges in the Ravin du Pas d'Escale. The path now bears right and climbs steadily. Soon you find yourself on a ledge high above the bed of the Estoublaïsse – you can just get a glimpse of the water if you dare to look. Behind you can see the sharp, deep, curving cleft of the gorge. The path rounds a bend and continues between pinnacles of rock, with views of the wider upper gorge, and of the path you will be taking on its opposite side. After around 20 minutes walking (from the bridges), while the path is still climbing, look out for a junction where a path doubles back on the left (just before a left hand bend in your path)

4. This is where you can choose to take the diversion to the Chapelle St André. Taking the yellow-flashed path on the left you will very soon see the ruins looming above you – surprisingly, it only takes around 15 minutes to get up there and the ascent is a lot easier than it looks. The path brings you to a clearing in the pines at the foot of the rocky outcrop on which the chapel is built. Here a signpost points ahead to the Pont Romaine, but you bear to the left and take a not-too-difficult path that zigzags up the slope to the chapel. Take time to look around – from the back of the chapel you can see down the gorge to the car park where this walk began, looking over the chapel walls your view is into the green bowl of the upper gorge. When you are ready to leave, retrace your steps to Point 4 and turn left, continuing on the track you left earlier. This is still climbing gently, but soon begins a long descent to the river again. There are one or two patches of scree to cross, but the path has been well cut out and nowhere is it dangerous. At length you reach the river and cross it on a footbridge.

5. On the far side is a flat grassy meadow, a perfect place for a picnic. Cross the grassy area, bearing right to where a ruined stone building (the Gîte de Valbonnette) stands at the foot of the slope. Here a path climbs to the right under the pines – you are still following red waymarks. The path rounds a spur and now you have a deep valley beside you on the right. At the head of it you reach a signposted junction of paths.

6. The red-flashed path goes left here, heading for the Pont de Tuf. Leave it to go, and continue on the track along the opposite side of the valley, now following green waymarks. Soon you pass a few ruined stone buildings, the old hamlet of Valbonnette. The path continues to climb with many breathtaking viewpoints – to the north are a line of snow-topped peaks, while across the gorge the Chapelle St André and the path you took earlier can be clearly seen. When you are at about the same height as the chapel, a fork is reached.

7. Take the downhill path to the right here, abandoning the green

waymarks to follow yellow. The path now descends and makes a hairpin around the head of a ravine. The final rocky descent into the gorge is much steeper – but any point of difficulty has thoughtfully been equipped with a metal railing for safety. At length the path widens and, under an overhang of rock, you have a splendid view of the water racing out of the gorge and tumbling to the little bridge below. Beside that bridge you arrive at the path junction you passed at the beginning of the walk (Point 2). Turn left here and retrace your steps to the car park.

Bridge over the Estoublaïsse, Gorges de Trévans

More Walks in the Area

As you could see from the wooden signboard at the start of the walk, there are plenty more waymarked paths in the Gorges de Trévans. The only problem is that most of them are rather more technically difficult than the route chosen – you may have noticed that you were warned not to go up to the Pont de Tuf without ropes. An obvious extension to this walk, and one that offers a quite magnificent viewpoint, can be achieved by taking the green-flashed route (instead of the yellow) from Point 7. The difficulty is the ridge walk that follows the viewpoint – you will need to be sure-footed and have a head for heights. Once the tricky section is passed, you pick up red waymarks at the next junction and quickly return to the starting point. Taking this extension will just about double the length of the walk – the only disadvantage is that you miss those fabulous last views of the gorge itself.

Heading north to Digne, the Office de Tourisme can offer you a large folded sheet entitled *Balades et Randonnées autour de Digne-les-Bains*. On one side is a very bare map showing 16 routes in the vicinity; on the other there is a brief description of each. The saving grace is that each of the routes is well-waymarked on the ground. Nevertheless there are some excellent walks here. A good choice would be route 14, taking you to the summit of le Cousson, with some staggering views from its 1511m height. At the end of the summit ridge the Chapel of St Michel sits alarmingly on an overhanging cliff – but you had better go soon or erosion will get the better of it. This first-class walk is described in much more detail (in

French) in the Topoguide *Les Alpes-de-Haute-Provence à pied (Ref. D004)*. If you are spending any time in the area the outlay on this publication is well worth while – even if the French is incomprehensible, the excellent mapping (along with the waymarking of these routes) will give you access to 36 of the region's best walks.

Digne-les-Bains is the centre of the *Réserve Géologique de Haute-Provence* – don't miss a visit to the 'walk-museum' (see below). Within the vast territory of the reserve are 18 numbered sites of particular interest. A few of these can be reached by car but most are way off the beaten track and are accessible only to walkers. A rather expensive book entitled *A travers la Réserve Géologique de Haute-Provence* will give you details of the routes. If you visit no other, at least go to the site of the Ichthyosaurus fossil, about 8km north of Digne (off the D900A to Barles). From a roadside car park you head up beside a stream to a remote valley where the fossilised skeleton of a huge ichthyosaurus can be seen in the rockface. Perhaps the 'Plexiglass' casing detracts from the scene, but there's no denying that this particular dinosaur found an idyllic last resting place – though, in his day, this valley was under the sea. And if geological trails have taken your fancy, another gem (although not one of the 18) is the walk to the valley of the *Sirènes Fossiles* from the Col des Lecques near Castellane – see Walk 21 for the details

Places of interest nearby

The *Musée-Promenade St Benoît (Centre de Géologie)* in Digne is situated just to the north of the town on the road to Barles. Although called a 'walk museum' there isn't a lot for the legs – just a short climb through very attractively landscaped grounds to reach the museum building, and the opportunity to stop and picnic in pleasant surroundings on the way. The museum itself holds a huge selection of fossilised 'finds', several large aquaria, a contemporary art gallery and a film taking 10 minutes to cover what nature did in 600 million years. In reality, it's pretty sure to inspire you to a little geological thinking, at which point you can head for the shop and all the literature you need to take you round the designated sites. The first of these is the ammonite wall, a kilometre up the road from the museum, but you could go on to footprints of prehistoric birds, a fossilised coral reef and more. Beware – hunting down fossils can be addicting.

If you really can't work up any enthusiasm for fossils, go instead to the house that once belonged to a remarkable lady by the name of Alexandra David-Néel. She was a philosopher and an explorer, spending much of her life in Central Asia, China and Tibet. She died in 1968 at the age of 100 – having just renewed her passport for yet another trip to the orient. All the memorabilia of her long life (including a Tibetan temple) are preserved in her home, 1 kilometre south of the centre of Digne, on the N85 to Barrême. Entry to the house is free and there are at least three guided tours a day throughout the year. It is possible to get a commentary in English.

Finally, Digne is the northern terminus of the *Train des Pignes*, a little train with panoramic windows whose 3-hour journey to Nice is to say the least spectacular. Mountains, gorges, lakes, tunnels, viaducts and old-fashioned stations flash (or rather drift) by the window – it's an amazing ride. Four trains a day leave Digne – and in high season can be very full. For more details, see Walk 20.

23. The unfortunate Penitents of les Mées

Near the village of les Mées, gigantic towers of puddingstone thrust through the vegetation of the hillside – allegedly they are monks turned to stone. You can view them from above and below on this splendidly flower-strewn walk above the valley of the Durance.

Grade: Moderate

Distance: 7km (4½ miles). The short cut will reduce this to only 3km

Time: About 3½ hours for the whole route, including time to explore. Allow 2 hours for the short circuit.

Map: IGN Top 25 3341 OT

Start and finish: Place de la République, Les Mées

How to get there: Les Mées is in the valley of the Durance, about 25km south-west of Digne-les-Bains. There is plenty of parking in the Place de la République, which is in the centre of the village.

Refreshment: There are one or two bars and restaurants in les Mées, but nothing en route.

Notes: The initial climb on this walk is fairly steep, although the path is reasonable. The descent on the short cut is even steeper, but the path is excellent and log steps have been put in to make things easier. Trainers would be suitable footwear in dry summer weather, otherwise something stouter is called for. On a hot day, wear appropriate protection from the sun, and carry fluid with you – there is no refreshment on the route. The short cut is a path descending behind the rocks themselves – it is not recommended in wet weather.

Waymarking: The path is waymarked in yellow throughout

Introduction

On a hillside above the Durance, a group of brown-robed monks, their pointed cowls pulled over their heads, gaze in frozen silence into the valley below. These are the Penitents of les Mées. Theirs wasn't a great crime – they merely turned out to watch seven beautiful Saracen women, prisoners of the local count, being taken down to the river to be deported to Arles. Maybe their hearts did beat a little faster, but old St Donat witnessed the scene from the other side of the Durance and, to prevent further sinful thoughts, had them turned to stone. There are others that will tell you that these are pillars of puddingstone, created some 25 million years ago, and further sculpted by glaciation and erosion – but it seems rather fanciful in comparison.

Les Mées is on the edge of the stony Plateau of Valensole, bordered to the west by the Durance, to the north by the Bléone and to the south by the Verdon. The bedrock of the plateau is puddingstone, a conglomerate of small pebbles and a cement-like sand. The enormous columns of this stone at les Mées are unique – around 100m in height, they can be seen from some distance away on the other side of the river. For even greater effect, they are now floodlit by night.

The walk here climbs the hill above the Penitents and then returns on the track at their feet where they tower above you. On the way you take a lovely ridge-top path with abundant flowers and butterflies. There are splendid views into the valleys on either side and more distant panoramas of the Lure mountains and the Pre-Alps. The ridge you are on runs from west to east, with noticeable contrast between the sparse Mediterranean vegetation on its south slope and the more dense forest of oaks on its north. The short cut on this route is a classic path that descends behind the Penitents themselves and allows you to view them at close-quarters – if you have chosen to take the long walk, you may well want to detour briefly up this path to explore some more.

The Walk

1. From the Place de la République, walk uphill (bar on your left, super-market on right) on the Rue Clovis Picon. A sign soon points out the *Sentier des Pénitents* and you continue uphill, passing a covered *lavoir* (old wash house). After passing a camp site on your left, a sign (now *Sentier des Rochers*) and a yellow waymark direct you to the left, crossing the valley along the top of a wall. At the far side, bear left and soon find yourself zigzagging up the slope. After 3 hairpins the path straightens out and continues climbing across a slope of puddingstone. Aleppo pines are joined by juniper and mastic and the slopes are dotted with wild flowers.

2. At the top of the slope, you reach a path junction under the pine trees. To the left is the short cut path, signposted to *Les Pénitents*. It is very well waymarked and you will have no problem following it through to Point 6 – but remember it is not advisable in wet weather as it could be slippery. The path to the right is signed to *San Peyre* – the main walk continues that way. This is now a splendid ridge-path under the pines – there is wild thyme at your feet, a deep valley to the right and a wide view across the Durance to the left. The path climbs steeply for a few minutes – you can see the Lure to the west across the valley and the foothills of the Alps to the north. Reaching a clearing at the top of the slope, the path now becomes wider and climbs very much more gently. Soon the path moves below the crest of the ridge and over-looks the wooded Ravin de la Combe on the right. Eventually you meet the remains of a wall on the left (the ruins of San Peyre) and then reach a path junction with a signpost.

3. Keep left here, in the direction of *les Mées par Bel Air* (ignore the path signed *la Haute Montagne*). After a couple of minutes the path swings left again and you ignore once more a track dipping to the right. You are now on a high plateau with splendid views of the ring of moun-tains to the north beyond Digne. At the end of the promontory a seat has been placed overlooking the valley of the Durance

4. To the right of the seat a narrow path dips into the woodland on the flank of the promontory – look out for the yellow waymarks. The path winds through the trees and emerges on the flank of the hill – you can see the Canal du Moulin below you and beyond it, the valley where the Durance is joined by the Bléone. Maintain the same direction, descending along the shoulder of the slope – unfortunately forestry work here had overlaid some of the original waymarked path (summer 2002) but it is easy to see where you are heading. Almost at

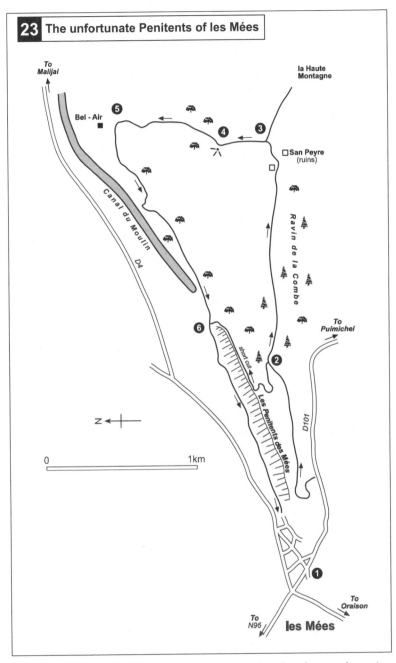

23 The unfortunate Penitents of les Mées

the bottom of the hill you meet a cross-track – ahead are a plantation of fruit trees and the ruined remains of Bel-Air.

5. Do not go into the orchards, but turn left on the track. This now descends through the woods and then continues parallel to and above the canal – at last you have views of the Penitents. Soon the path takes a corner to the right, descending more steeply to meet a wide cross track. Turn left on this, signposted to *les Mées*. The canal is

still below you and you can see that it disappears into the hillside. It is actually on its way to the hydro-electric power station at Oraison and emerges again on the far side of les Mées. The track continues past a barrier excluding cyclists and eventually reaches the foot of the first Penitent.

Looking down from the Penitents across the valley of the Durance

6. The short cut joins from the left here. If you want to view these rocks from above as well as below, climb up the obvious path which eventually runs along behind them. Otherwise continue on the main track feeling very dwarfed by the massive bulk above you. The rocks seem to get more impressive as you go and you can climb up into clearings between them if you feel like diverting. Eventually you arrive at a tarmacked road. Turn left along this and, at a junction in about 100m, turn right towards the centre of the village. At the end of the narrow street, turn right down the Rue du Pavillon. A left turn into the Rue André Lagier will now bring you back to the Place de la République.

More Walks in the Area

The other waymarked (red) walk starting from les Mées is a 15km circuit called the *Chemin de la Colle*. The Office de Tourisme (about 100m downhill from the Place de la République) should be able to find you a sketch map of this – but beware, it's 'upside-down'. It would probably be best to translate this route on to the appropriate IGN map (3341 OT) before setting off. The circuit is set on the western edge of the Plateau de Valensole, an area full of evidence of earlier habitation – stone walls, ruined buildings and the sites of charcoal burners. Open plateau is contrasted with woodland and the return is along the banks of the canal.

For those who are staying here for a while, it would be well worth getting hold of the local topoguide, *Le Val de Durance (Ref. 633)*. Here you have no fewer than 42 walks in the region between Sisteron and Manosque – one of them is the *Haute Montagne* path that you met briefly on this walk.

Just across the river, the very well stocked Office de Tourisme at Forcalquier can find you a folder of walks entitled *Pays de Forcalquier – Montagne de Lure*. The region of Forcalquier is fascinating and three of the walks in this folder start from the town. Two of these visit the Rochers des Mourres, curious dry limestone rocks carved by erosion into a series of bizarre shapes. Other walks visit the Lure mountains – two short circuits on the wooded slopes are described. The highest point of the Lure is Signal de Lure (1826m.), from which there are incredible views of nearby Mont Ventoux, and more distantly, the Cévennes, the Vercors, Mont Pelvoux in the Écrins, Mont Viso on the Italain border, and more. A winding road (D53) will take you to within a few minutes climb of the summit – but if you want a good hike as well, try following the well-marked GR6 from L'Église de Notre Dame de Lure, on the D53 north of Saint Etienne-les-Orgues. The IGN map you require is 3341 OT.

Places of interest nearby

To the east of the Durance, the Plateau of Valensole is best known for its vast fields of lavender. The plateau is not high, and the plant grown here is the hybrid lavandin rather than fine lavender. The lavandin of the Plateau of Valensole is some of the earliest flowering in Provence, often beginning in early June. A free booklet entitled *The Lavender Roads* is obtainable from just about any Office de Tourisme in the area. It offers suggestions for tours, visits to farms and distilleries, dates of festivals and lots of other lavender-based information. Along with the lavender go the bees, and the Plateau of Valensole is also renowned for its honey.

Across the Durance and a little to the south, the Benedictine priory of Ganagobie looks out over the river. The original priory here was built in the 10th century. Most of the buildings now are modern, but the cloisters and part of the old church remain from the Romanesque period. The 12th century floor mosaic is one of the finest in France. The priory is open every afternoon except Monday. While at Ganagobie you might like to take a short walk in the surrounding forest. The 4.5km circuit has been waymarked in yellow – you can get details from the *Mairie* ((beside the car park) in Ganagobie.

South of Ganagobie, the old town of Forcalquier is worth a visit. The Office de Tourisme (in the square opposite the cathedral) can give you details of the Distillerie Domaine de Haute-Provence (a liqueur distillery), the nearby Prieuré de Salagon (herb gardens and perfumes) and, 10km away, the Observatoire de Haute-Provence, an astronomical research centre with guided tours (Wednesday afternoons only). Not far from the latter, the Centre d'Astronomie de St Michel offers lessons in stargazing (and more) on weekday evenings with the exception of Mondays.

24. Alpine pastures at Barcelonnette

In the valley of the Ubaye, tucked beneath the mighty alpine ranges, Barcelonnette is squeezed into the most northerly corner of Provence. On this walk you climb above the tree-line to reach alpine meadows echoing with cowbells and – as you would expect – the views are magnificent.

Grade: Moderate/strenuous. See the 'Notes' below

Distance: 10km (6¼ miles)

Time: 4½ hours

Map: IGN Top 25 3538 ET

Start and finish: Parking at les Dalis, north-west of Barcelonnette

How to get there: From Barcelonnette, head west on the D900. Just before the aerodrome (approx. 2km), turn right and continue ahead on a road that soon crosses and then climbs alongside a mountain torrent (the Riou Bourdoux). At a left hairpin, keep straight ahead, cross the river again and follow the gravelled road, which in a few minutes passes the Maison Forestière de Tréou (the starting point of a *Sentier de Découverte*). From here the track becomes rougher with many hairpins, and in something over 2km reaches the very pleasant parking place at les Dalis.

Refreshment: Near the end of the walk, the Maison Forestière de la Pare is a mountain refuge offering accommodation and serving meals and light refreshment during the summer months (15 June to 15 Sept. approx.).

Notes: This is a reasonably demanding walk at high level – wear walking boots, carry waterproofs, drink and snacks and, on a hot day, include the sun cream. The walk begins on a good track climbing steadily for around 450m to reach the Cabane Neuve. From here a lesser track takes you around the flanks of the hills before descending to la Pare. Although this track is sometimes narrow, it should present no problems – the Office de Tourisme in Barcelonnette recommend the walk and describe it as *sans difficulté*. Nevertheless, you might note that when we followed this route after heavy rain, it appeared that a very short section of otherwise safe path across loose shale had been washed away. On reporting this to the Office National des Forêts in Barcelonnette (the owners of the land), they were very apologetic and promised instant repair – so hopefully you should not have the same problem.

Waymarking: The path between the Cabane Neuve and la Pare is waymarked in yellow. The final descent also bears yellow waymarks and elsewhere you follow the white on red flashes of the GR6 – 56 (see the text).

Introduction

Barcelonnette is curiously the meeting place of three cultures – Provençal, Alpine and Mexican. This latter is due to three brothers from nearby Jausiers, who at the beginning of the 19th century, set out to seek their fortunes in the new world. Success came when they founded the textile industry in Mexico – and 5,000 *Barcelonnettais* set out to do likewise. Those who came home again built their villas in Mexican style – and you will also find Mexican eating houses and a large boutique selling Mexican

View from the Cabane Neuve

leather, carvings and patchwork. The odd sombrero or poncho makes a good change from the usual Provençal souvenirs.

This interesting town is situated in the wide lower valley of the River Ubaye, which descends from the slopes of Mont Viso in Italy. The horizon all around is studded with the magnificent peaks of the southern Alps. In winter the skiers move in on the scene – there are three major ski stations on the nearby slopes. In summer the mountain bikers have their day. Apart from the road alongside the Ubaye, Barcelonnette is connected with the outside world only by seven high cols or passes – any mountain-biker conquering them all is rewarded with a medal. To get the measure of this feat, try leaving Barcelonnette via the road to the south over the redoubtable Col d'Allos – on four wheels rather than two.

Hiking from Barcelonnette is, for the main part, equally heroic – the route here is the easiest suggested by the Office de Tourism, a circular hike skirting the slopes on the north side of the valley. The first part is a steady climb to the forestry office's Cabane Neuve, a white hut in alpine meadows, where you can sit on benches in the sun enjoying views of the rounded hump of the Pain de Sucre and the sloping flanks of the closest giant, the 2685m Chapeau de Gendarme. Farther on a narrower path leads around slopes where arise the tributary streams of the mountain torrent known as the Riou Bourdoux. In former years this particular mountain river was responsible for a catalogue of disasters. The 19th century saw it tamed with the creation of a series of dams and the planting of the ravaged slopes with pines and larch. Even now this vegetation is sometimes carried away by winter avalanches, and the path you follow at times emerges from the trees to cross the denuded slopes. Eventually the path descends to the Maison Forestière de la Pare, a mountain refuge in a splendid location where you can take in the views from the terrace and enjoy a drink before the final descent to the car park.

The Walk

1. Leaving the car park, ignore the wooden signpost to Col de la Pare pointing across the field and instead turn uphill on the gravelled forest road. Now keep to this track disregarding all side turnings – gaps in the trees give you first glimpses of the peaks to the south across the valley as you go. After about 20 minutes a T-junction of tracks is reached

2. Turn left here in the direction of Cabane Neuve – you are now on the Grande Randonnée with its white on red waymarks. After a further 20 minutes walking through the pines and larches you arrive at another track junction.

3. Here you leave the GR and its waymarks and double back to the right – the only sign is a rock bearing the painted words Cabane Neuve. The path continues to climb, and shortly you find yourself in front of an alpine meadow with the high summits ranged behind. It is probably best to keep to the forest track (the alternative is a grassy track through the meadow if the gate is open) – being higher, it offers splendid views back across the valley and you can pick out the white building of the Maison Forestière de la Pare below you in the woods on the opposite flank. Beside the track in the meadow you can see a stone *bergerie* – a barn for sheep. After the two tracks meet, the hard-surfaced track descends to cross a stream and climbs again. At this point a removable section of an electric fence allows you into cattle grazing country – you are in a wide short-cropped meadow with an old part-timbered barn that seems somehow picturesque against the bare mountains behind. Time for a block of chocolate! A final burst of energy is needed to reach the Cabane Neuve, still 100m above you – but the winding track is obvious and extremely pretty, alternating between pine woods and alpine pasture.

4. The simple wooden benches outside the Cabane Neuve demand a pause. Across the Ubaye you can see the Valley of Bachelard winding to the south – to the right of it are the peaks of the Séolanes, to the left is the Pain de Sucre and beside it, the distinctive rakish tilt of the Chapeau de Gendarme. When you are ready to continue, cross the front of the Cabane Neuve and take the path above and to the left of the electric fence – it is waymarked in yellow. After passing through the fence again, the path wanders attractively along the edge of the woods with the high meadows to your left – you may be able to see cattle grazing far above you, or at least, to hear the clanging of their bells. This path is now very well waymarked and you will have no difficulty following it as it winds around the head of the valley, sometimes beneath the trees, occasionally crossing open slopes of shale. After over an hour's walking with little change in altitude, the path begins to zigzag in a steep descent into the valley of the Riou de la Pare. It crosses the river at a ford just before reaching the Maison Forestière, where you may well be glad of another break.

5. In front of the forest refuge the GR goes off left to the Col de la Pare. You now take the main hard-surfaced track in the opposite direction, crossing the Riou de la Pare and other tributaries of the Riou

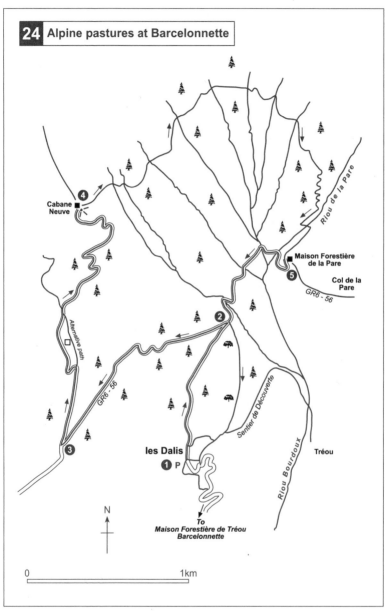

24 Alpine pastures at Barcelonnette

Cabane Neuve

Maison Forestière de la Pare

Col de la Pare

GR6 - 56

Riou de la Pare

Alternative path

GR6 - 56

les Dalis

Sentier de Découverte

Riou Bourdoux

Tréou

N

To
Maison Forestière de Tréou
Barcelonnette

0   1km

Bourdoux as you go. In around 15 minutes you reach Point 2, the junction you passed earlier. This time follow the signpost pointing to les Dalis, left of the main track. This narrower path is waymarked in yellow and bends its way downhill through the trees to cross a stream on a wooden bridge. Soon afterwards you reach a fork – and, of course, there's no waymarking in sight. Keep right (straight ahead) here – the path to the left leads off into the *Sentier de Découverte*. Eventually you can see a forest road ahead. Just before meeting it, turn right on a path climbing a bank. At the top of it you are in a meadow with picnic tables, and can cross it to return to the car park.

More Walks in the Area

There are two other popular routes on this side of the valley. The first of these is the *Sentier de Découverte* that you touched briefly on this walk. It starts lower down the mountain at the Maison Forestière de Tréou and its short 4km will take you around 3 hours on account of the closeness of the contour lines round here (the total ascent is about 300m). More time will be needed for deciphering the ten *panneaux* (information boards) en route, which are in French only. But if you can manage it, the Riou Bourdoux has an interesting tale to tell. The Office National des Forêts has produced a leaflet on the area (*À la découverte du Riou-Bourdoux*) giving a brief outline of the problems faced in disciplining this particularly capricious mountain torrent.

These second popular trail is the hike to the Col de la Pare along the GR6 - 56. If you are contemplating this one – take careful thought. The Office National des Forêts dubs this route *sportive* – and the route you have just taken here is *facile*! This is an out-and-back excursion that should be attempted only by regular mountain walkers. The Col is approximately at the same altitude as the summits of the Pain de Sucre and the Chapeau de Gendarme – and if you make it up there, the views over the valley are superb.

The Office de Tourisme in Barcelonnette can find you a rather uninspiring leaflet describing 8 routes of varying length and difficulty in the area. If your French is good you may be able to work these out on the appropriate IGN map. Particularly note the level of difficulty – and, where it is not stated, assume the worst. One or two of these routes make an appearance in the topoguide of this region, *La Vallée de l'Ubaye à pied* (a book you might almost buy for its photographs alone). Since topoguides always have such excellent maps and waymarking on the ground, these are the easiest routes to follow. One of the most interesting routes described on both leaflet and topoguide (said to be of medium difficulty) starts near the Abbey of Laverq – take the D900 west of Barcelonnette to le Martinet, turn south and continue past the abbey as far as you can drive. From there you climb through the wooded valley to a plateau crossed by the winding water channels left by a one-time glacier – a geological feature known as *les eaux tortes*. The route has been made a *Sentier de Découverte* with panels describing the various points of interest. Once again, this is a day-long hike. Several other routes in the vicinity of Barcelonnette are also described in this topoguide.

Places of interest nearby

The history of this valley from the Iron Age to the Mexican era is told in the Musée de la Vallée, housed in the Villa la Sapinière on the Avenue de la Libération, not far from the Office de Tourisme. On the ground floor of this impressive building is found one of the headquarters of the Mercantour National Park. Both are worth a visit – the Musée de la Vallée is open throughout the year (although not every day – consult the Office de Tourisme), while the park headquarters is open only from mid-June to mid-September.

The valley of the Ubaye is the gateway to Italy and the fortifications some 20km to the north-east bear witness to centuries of border conflict. Pressed into the bare mountainside, the stark buildings of the Forteresse de Tournoux and the nearby batteries of Roche-la-Croix last played their defensive role as part of the Alpine Maginot Line. Guided tours are on offer between mid-June and mid-September – book at the Office de Tourisme in Barcelonnette.

You may have noticed some of the many sundials (*cadrans solaires*) in this area, painted on the walls of houses. There was one on the façade of the Maison Forestière de la Pare, at the end of this walk. Many of these are works of art in themselves – and some have interesting texts to go with the picture. The Barcelonnette tourist office can offer you a leaflet entitled *Route des Cadrans Solaires de la Vallée de l'Ubaye* – a 50km tour seeking out some of the best of these sundials. Since the leaflet is only produced in French, and the directions range from sketchy to non-existent, you can expect to spend at least a whole day on this treasure hunt. Even finding the one in the centre of Barcelonnette is difficult – it certainly isn't where it is said to be. But as an interesting diversion ...

Finally, Barcelonnette is the home of Génépy (*Génépi*), that delightful herby Provençal liqueur often served from a bottle that appears to have a plant growing in it (the *brins*). The Office de Tourisme can direct you to the local factory, where guided tours are offered in summer time. Outside the main season, you can still find Génépy (and a superb range of other local produce) at the *Maison du Produits de Pays* on the main road in Jausiers.

25. A goats' path through the Gorges de St Pierre

These little-known gorges are quite spectacular – and your only requirement for this out-and-back walk is a head for heights as you follow a path cut from the rocky sides, once used for shepherding goats. Those with extra energy can follow the goats' trail onwards to their high alpine pastures.

Grade: Moderate – see the notes below

Distance: 4km each way (plus a little extra for the *sentier botanique*). Climbing to the shepherds' huts in the high pastures will add a further 1km in each direction.

Time: Out-and-back through the gorges, 2½ hours. Add 1½ hours for the extra climb.

Map: IGN Top 25 3541 OT

Start and finish: The parking for the Gorges de St Pierre

How to get there: Take the D908 following the upper valley of the Verdon above St, André-les-Alpes. At Beauvezer (5km south of Colmars), cross the river on the D252 to Villars-Heyssier. Continue through the village on a track that soon becomes quite rough. There is parking at its end, from where you enter the gorge.

Refreshment: None on the walk. If you take your own, there are picnic tables at the *Cabanes de Congerman* at the end of the extended walk, and beside the chapel at the lower end of the gorges.

Notes: This is a walk along a ledge above very deep (and very spectacular) gorges – a sign at the entrance warns off vertigo sufferers and those with young children. It also tells you that the walk should not be attempted in icy weather, and that heavy rain increases the chances of falling rock. If you still feel brave enough to venture forth after all that, you can be reassured that there is nothing technically difficult about it – the ledge is amply wide and the climb is always gradual. In fact, if you are here at the weekend, you will find that this path makes quite a popular local excursion. An optional loop near the beginning of the walk will take you via a *sentier botanique* to a little chapel perched at the entrance to the gorge – and for anyone with time and energy, another extension at the end will lead you to the *cabanes* and pastures 300m above. And for the most experienced (and agile) there are yet more possibilities – see the **More Walks** section.

Waymarking: The path through the gorge has been copiously waymarked in yellow – they must have had paint to spare, since there are definitely no alternatives!

Introduction

With the approach of summer every year, it would be time to take the goats and sheep to the higher pastures. From the little town of Beauvezer the route led through the Gorges de Pierre, along a path that had been hewn from the rock for just that purpose. Those animals must have been sure-footed. Did they wisely adopt single file, or were they jostling for place as they climbed on the narrow ledge way above the tumbling river? It must have been quite a journey. At the end of the 19th century the pastures beyond the end of the gorges were planted with pines and a forest nursery was set up. Now the rocky ledge was widened to allow the passage of donkeys carrying forest produce. And what was once wide enough for a donkey with trees on its back is wide enough for the hikers of today.

In the Gorges de St Pierre, it is not only the path that inspires awe but the helter-skeltering antics of the blue river in its depths on its way to join the Verdon. A series of cascades and pools come into view as you climb and tributary streams join with equal drama. The gorge itself is an almost vertical slit running from east to

The path through the gorge

west – so giving the perfect opportunity to contrast the vegetation of the *ubac* (north-facing slope) and the *adret* (south-facing). The path is cut high on the latter, the sunny side, with its sparse Mediterranean shrubs. The opposing face is in the shadows, humid and clothed in dark pines, some said to be more than 400 years old. At the entrance to the gorge a tiny chapel perches on a rock looking into the deep cleft – it was built here in the 13th century when in such breathtaking places man acknowledged the hand of God.

When you reach the top of the gorges you are close to river-level and you may just want to picnic by the banks before returning. But it is also possible to climb the wooded slopes from here to a site known as the Cabanes de Congerman – ruined huts that were once the shelters of shepherds and a stone house that bears witness to the more recent forest enterprise. Beside the latter a spring splashes into a wooden trough and there are picnic tables from which to enjoy views of the forested slopes and alpine pastures. The most agile can opt for an extension from here (see **More Walks**), but otherwise, the way back lies through the gorge once more.

The Walk

1. Leaving the parking area, continue ahead on the well-signed path. This soon curves around the head of a valley where a waterfall splashes below you into a blue pool. The path continues climbing above the stream, and after a bend to the left, a fork with a signpost is reached.

2. The main track into the gorge continues ahead here, but it is well worthwhile diverting to the right on the *Boucle de l'Ermite* – it descends to the chapel, on which site a hermit once lived. The path is actually a *sentier botanique*, although unfortunately the fine wooden framed information panels bear the plant names in French only. In a splendid setting beside the chapel picnic tables have been provided – when ready to leave, follow the *retour* sign directing you back to Point 2. Now simply follow the balcony path ascending through the gorge. If you can look into the depths you will see waterfalls and deep clefts in the rock created by the river. After about an hour's walking the path curves to the left. The Congerman stream tumbles into the St Pierre on the opposite bank and you can see ahead a wooden bridge over the river.

3. This bridge is effectively the top of the gorge, the place to turn around. If you want to continue to the Cabanes de Congerman, ignore the yellow waymarks (going ahead beside the river) and cross the bridge. At the far side a path begins its zigzag route up the hillside under the pines, with the Congerman Ravine below you on the right. After something in excess of half an hour you emerge suddenly on a grassy pasture, on the far side of which are ruined stone shelters. The path never reaches them but instead turns uphill to enter the trees again. A few minutes later you are beside two large barns, one of wood and one of stone and above them a house with picnic tables outside. The ensemble is known as the Cabanes Forestières de Congerman.

4. Behind the forestry house a signpost points the way to the Lacs de Lignin and to Chabanal. Take either at your peril (see below) – but for most, this is the end of the line and time to turn back again into the gorge and head for home.

More Walks in the Area

When you arrive at the Cabanes de Congerman on this walk there are two options (other than going back). One is to continue on the trail to the Lacs de Lignin, a long hard climb over exposed mountains – and you would have to return the same way. The other is to follow the signpost in the direction of Chabanal – a circular route appearing in the local walks leaflet, masquerading quietly under the classification *difficile*. A few minutes on from the Cabanes de Congerman you are invited to jump through a waterfall on to a narrow path across scree. We didn't bother – but if you feel up to it, there are several more similar feats to perform on this path before you are returned to the bridge at the head of the gorge. Equip yourself with the IGN map (3541 OT) and the leaflet *Haute Vallée du Verdon – 50 Promenades et Randonnées à pied*.

The above-mentioned leaflet can be found in the excellent Office de

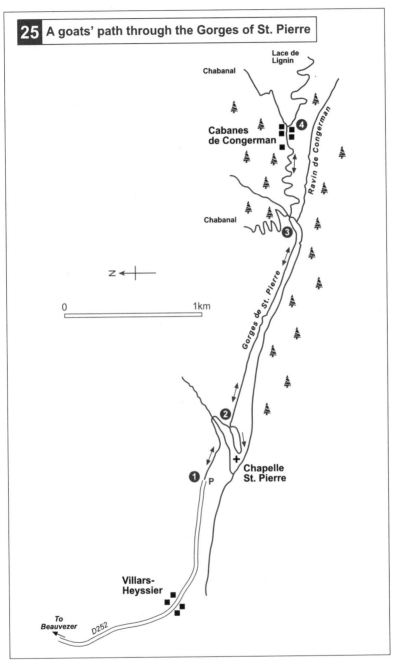

25 A goats' path through the Gorges of St. Pierre

Lace de Lignin

Chabanal

Ravin de Congerman

Cabanes de Congerman

4

Chabanal

3

Gorges de St. Pierre

N

0   1km

2

+ Chapelle St. Pierre

1 P

Villars-Heyssier

To Beauvezer   D252

Tourisme situated beside the main road at Colmars – it actually defines 51 walks in the region of the Verdon valley between that town and Thorame-Haute. There is minimal text relating to each walk – but they have been given a level of difficulty which you should particularly note (see above). The waymarking of these walks on the ground is generally good, so with the aid of the IGN map, you should easily be able to follow any of them.

One good choice from the above leaflet – described as *facile*, but not exactly a soft option – is the climb to the viewpoint at the Croix du Puy above Villars-Colmars. You first gain as much height as possible by driving up to the church at the top end of the village, an area known as la Tête. From here a further ascent on foot (around 370m) will take you up to the cross, plainly visible on a sharp peak towering almost vertically above. The circular route will take about 3 hours and is well-waymarked in yellow. It can be picked out on the appropriate IGN map (3540 OT) and also appears in the topoguide of the region, *Les Alpes-de-Haute-Provence à pied* (Ref. D004)

Going on beyond Colmars, there is one walk that everyone must take – the hike to the glorious Lac d'Allos. From the town of Allos, 13 tortuous kilometres will take you take you to the Parking du Laus, high in the mountains and within the confines of the Mercantour National Park. From here it is around half an hour's walk to the lake on a track dotted with informative display boards (in French only). First views of the lake are stunning – a circle of brilliant blue water backed by the curiously 'striped' rocky humps known as the Tours du Lac. Beside the lake is a refuge (open only in the height of summer) and behind it the little stone chapel of Notre-Dame. For more walking, a track encircles the lake – and it is possible to take a wilder route back by following the signed path uphill past the chapel in the direction of Mont Pélat. At the cross-tracks in about half an hour, turn left to return to the car park – or continue ahead (beware – *difficile*) to take in the fantastic panorama from the summit of Mont Pélat, a further 800m above you at this point. All paths are shown on the IGN map (3540 OT). Note that access to the Lac d'Allos is only allowed for about four months of the year, approximately from mid-June to mid-October.

Places of interest nearby

Colmars is well worth a visit – the town is still hiding behind walls that have stood for half a millennium. At the end of the 17th century the ubiquitous Vauban was asked to provide further protection when invasion was threatened by the Piedmontese. A fort was built at each end of the town, each connected by a protected passage entering the ramparts. Both forts are well-preserved and you can take a guided tour in summer time to admire the architecture of the northern edifice, the Fort of Savoy. For simpler pleasures, the gates of Colmars are always open – and you can wander at will through the narrow medieval streets of high houses and walk short sections of the ramparts. And when you have seen it all, cross the road to the Office de Tourisme and follow the signs to the Cascade de la Lance. It's a very pleasant 20 minutes walk to the spot where a gushing torrent (its volume depending on recent rainfall) descends to a deep blue pool. A rather wobbly iron bridge has been provided to improve the view. Colmars is quite a tourist attraction and can become crowded in July and August – although there are plenty of car parks. Visiting is more pleasant out of season.

26. A coastal stroll to Monte Carlo

This is the very best way to arrive at Monte Carlo. Forget the crowded roads and limited parking and treat yourself instead to the beautiful coastal path around the green headland of Cap Martin. Once at Monte Carlo, the tranquillity continues in the peaceful seafront Japanese Garden – but you can get up to speed again with a visit to the Casino before catching the train home.

Grade: Easy

Distance: 7km (4½ miles). Shorter walk (Carnolès to Cabbé) 4.5 km

Time: 3 hours (you won't want to hurry)

Map: IGN Top 25 3742 OT

Start and finish: The train station (*Gare SNCF*) at Carnolès. The walk ends at the station in Monte Carlo, with a ten-minute train ride back to Carnolès.

How to get there: From Menton, head west on the coast road into Carnolès. Turn right where signposted to the *Gare*. There is parking at the station and in side-roads close by. (If this should fail, continue on the coast road to Cap Martin where there is a parking area (Point 2))

Refreshment: A plethora of sea-front cafés at Carnolès and similar (possibly more expensive) at Monte Carlo.

Notes: This easy walk is suitable for everyone and you certainly don't need your walking boots. Tracks are good and obvious. Arriving in Monte Carlo there is a little road walking before you reach the seafront promenade. Allow time to look around the Japanese Gardens, the Casino and any of the other attractions you fancy (see below) before returning by train. If you want a shorter walk (or can't face the bustle of Monte Carlo), you can catch the same train back from the station at Cabbé (Point 4). Trains run from Monte-Carlo stopping at Cabbé (Roquebrune-Cap Martin) and Carnolès approximately every half an hour in the late afternoon – but less frequently at weekends. And finally, this glorious walk is exposed to the elements – don't forget the sun cream.

Waymarking: You can't possibly get lost, but there are signposts along the route giving expected times to Cabbé and Monte Carlo.

Introduction

The opening of the Casino in 1865 transformed Monaco. Previously it had been the poorest state in Europe – within a year became the most glamorous spot on the Continent. Today it is bustling with the yachting fraternity and with holidaymakers, a popular conference centre and a magnet for everyone with money to lose. Maybe it would be more suitable to draw up in front of the Casino in a long black limousine with darkened windows, but taking this path around this coast is much more of a treat, a gentle ramble above the brilliant blue Mediterranean flanked by a lush vegetation of pines, mastic and cacti.

The path here takes you around the rocky shores of Cap Martin, a green thumb of land jutting into the Mediterranean and guarding the Bay of Roquebrune. There are glorious views of Monaco as you go. On the cliffs are the villas of the rich and famous – and in absolute contrast, you pass the 15 sq. m. log cabin (*cabanon*) that was the self-designed summer retreat of le Corbusier, most celebrated of French architects. There is no publicity for *le cabanon*, but it is quite recognisable, and anyone intrigued to see inside can apply for a guided tour from the Office de Tourisme in Roquebrune.

Beyond the Cap is the very lovely Plage de la Buse, and behind it, the station at Cabbé (Roquebrune-Cap Martin) for those who want a quick return. Otherwise your path goes on, dipping up and down between the coast and the railway line, until it reaches Monte Carlo, which is actually the eastern part of Monaco. Its wide esplanade is home to a giant glass-house known as the Grimaldi Centre, and, beside it, the small but exquisite Japanese Gardens. Formally blessed by a Shinto priest, they were created with the intention of providing a haven for contemplation amid the hurly-burly of urban life. Not far away is the Casino, but unless you have been walking in jacket and tie you won't be going into the gaming rooms – even so, it's worth making a foray into the vast ornate entrance hall with its comings and goings. Anyone wanting to see some action at the tables can go instead to the nearby Café de Paris, which is much less formal. If you have time, go on into Monaco and visit the Princely Palace and perhaps the famous Oceanographic Museum. At the end of the day, a short train ride from Monaco's state-of-the-art station will return you to your starting point.

The Walk

1. From the station walk down to the sea front (approx. 200m) and turn right in the direction of Cap Martin. An old palace built in 1891 looks down on you from the hillside ahead. You are now on the Avenue Winston Churchill, which swings left towards the Cap. Immediately after the old archway, bear left on to the sea-front wall (SP Cap Martin). Briefly you come up to the road again before dipping once more to the left and then reaching a parking area (you could use this as an alternative to parking at the station).

2. After a last restaurant, the path again dips left and passes under an overhanging veranda. You are now surrounded by scented pines and mastic and, as you round the Cap, Monaco comes into view across the Bay of Roquebrune. The hard-surfaced path dips up and down by a series of steps and you pass a curious residence in two halves joined by what appear to be cloisters. The path is now flanked on the right by the cacti-filled gardens of villas high above. Arriving at a clearing with seats, bear left on what is soon a balcony path above the blue bay. Farther on, as you approach the cove known as the Anse de Cabbé, there are summer-houses below you on the left. The one belonging to le Corbusier is built of dark pine logs and is sheltered by a large carob tree. It doesn't look that impressive, but apparently the interior design of this tiny cabin is remarkable. You can walk down the steps for a closer look. Immediately beyond the *cabanon* you reach the cross-tracks of Massolin.

3. Keeping ahead here you soon reach a signed path descending to the Plage du Buse. It is possible to go that way, cross the beach and climb the flight of steps beside the restaurant at its far end. But if you want to find the station (Roquebrune – Cap Martin) to return from here, you will need to ignore the beach path and keep straight ahead. The path

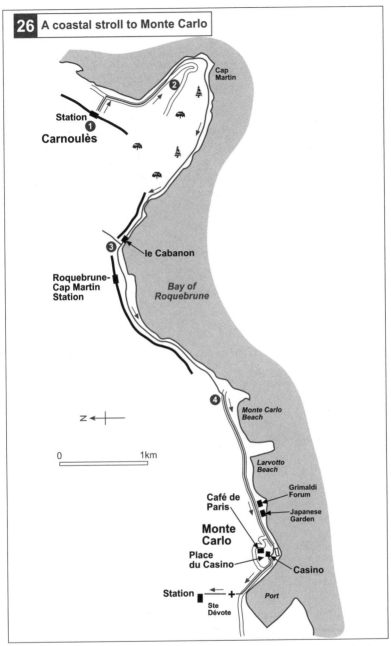

26 A coastal stroll to Monte Carlo

Station
❶
Carnoulès

❷

Cap
Martin

❸
le Cabanon

**Roquebrune-
Cap Martin
Station**

*Bay of
Roquebrune*

❹

*Monte Carlo
Beach*

N

0   1km

*Larvotto
Beach*

Grimaldi
Forum

**Café de
Paris**

Japanese
Garden

**Monte
Carlo**

**Place
du Casino**

Casino

Station

Ste
Dévote

Port

passes the station and those carrying on to Monte Carlo will afterwards come out beside the vast Hotel Diodato. Look up from here to see the grey building of the Château de Roquebrune on the hill behind the town. To continue from here keep the railway on your right and follow the signposts to Monte Carlo at any doubtful junction. You are led on narrow streets and a path between the railway and some houses – and always there are views of the sea. At length, the path descends some steps to a road.

The casino at Monte Carlo

4. Turning right in the direction of Monte Carlo you soon find yourself in front of the Monte Carlo Beach complex – if you fancy a swim you will only need the odd 50 euros. From here continue along the main road, passing a row of hotels, until thankfully you can escape on to the broad esplanade above Larvotto beach. At its far end the glass panes of the Grimaldi Forum glitter in the sun. Keep to the left of the building to reach the Japanese Gardens – a side entrance lets you in. When you are ready, carry on down the road and cross where signed to the Casino (before the road goes into the tunnel). Ahead of you the ornate building dates from the latter half of the 19th century and houses both the lavish Casino and the even more sumptuous Salle Garnier (both were designed by Charles Garnier, architect of the Paris Opéra). Walk around the building to reach the Place du Casino, where you will find the entrance to the Casino, and, close by, the Café de Paris.

To reach the station from here, leave via the road to the right of the Casino. This leads downhill to the port where ranks of white-hulled yachts line the quays, under the eye of the Princely Palace high above. At the bottom of the hill the church of Ste Dévote is set back on the right hand side. Leave the main road and walk past it – a few flights of steps will now take you up to the station.

More Walks in the Area

The other popular – and fascinating – coastal stroll from Monaco heads west to the Plage Mala. Rocks and headlands, luxurious vegetation and extravagant villas are the ingredients of this 2-hour out-and-back walk, which was apparently a favourite of Winston Churchill. The Office de Tourisme in Monte Carlo (from Place du Casino, walk uphill and turn right) publishes a short guide to the path, including the historical and geological details to be found on the display boards along the route.

Walking other than along the coast from Monte Carlo is going to involve some pretty stiff climbing. The excellent free booklet *Rando – Pays*

Côtier, obtainable from any Office de Tourisme in the area, suggests a route starting from the station at Monte Carlo and rising to the little town of la Turbie an almost vertical 460m above. La Turbie is famed for its Roman monument, la Trophée d'Auguste (see below) – look up and see it on the skyline before deciding to take the walk.

Those looking for something even more ambitious can enjoy a real treat in this part of the world. Menton sees the start of the GR 51, a long-distance path given the epithet Balcons de la Côte d'Azur – the first waymarks are found on the road just east of Menton–Garavan station. This magnificent high-level path seeks out the best viewpoints along the length of the Mediterranean coast to Marseille. The first section is as splendid as any – 6 hours from Menton will take you to the lovely old perched village of St Agnès, said to be the highest on the coast, where you can get overnight accommodation. The route continues through pines and olive groves to picturesque Gorbio and on to la Turbie (5 hours in total) from where you can walk down to Monte-Carlo (see above) to catch the train back to Menton. The route is clearly shown on the appropriate map (3742 OT) and, being a Grande Randonnée, is well-waymarked all the way.

Places of interest nearby

If the walk up to la Turbie doesn't appeal, the same place is easily reached by car. At the highest point of the village, accessed by many narrow alley-ways of old houses, stands the massive Trophée d'Auguste. This was built about 6 BC to commemorate the conquest of the tribes of the Maritime Alps by the Roman emperor Augustus – an important victory since it freed the roads into Gaul and Spain. This massive monument was once topped by a statue of Augustus himself while below him stood effigies of the generals who had taken part in the campaign. All were raised on a gigantic plinth bearing a suitably lengthy inscription. Time took its natural toll, and along with the removal of the stone for building and the destructive urges of Louis XIV, reduced the fine monument to little more than a pile of rubble. Although only some restoration has taken place, you can still be staggered by the sheer bulk of this one. Possibly more staggering is the view from the gardens (or, without paying the entrance fee, from the table d'orientation just along the road). More than five hundred metres below you, the cobalt sea frames Cap Martin to the east and Cap Ferrat to the west, while behind sweep the mountains from the Alps to the Esterel and beneath you the buildings of Monaco cling to their rock. By night the view is even more impressive.

Although you would probably appreciate fine weather for this walk, there is nowhere better for a rainy day than Monaco. Within a short distance of each other are the Musée Océanographique (90 huge tanks of fish, a complete coral reef from the Red Sea, skeletons of whales, etc.), the Palais du Prince (sumptuous state rooms, Napoleonic memorabilia – and 'Changing the Guard' ceremony at 11.55am every day), the Collection des Voitures Anciennes (100 vintage vehicles collected by Prince Rainier himself) and the Monte Carlo Story (film and display about the Grimaldi dynasty in Monaco). Add to that lot the National Museum of Monaco, a Museum of Stamps and Coins, a Wax Museum, a Naval Museum and more. Most of these are open all year round – confirm dates and times at the Office de Tourisme.

27. Ups and downs at the Italian border

Here is a wander in the woods and olive groves of the hilly country to the east of Sospel. Highlights are the stunning views from the Col de Paula and a visit to Piène-Haute, a village alarmingly perched four hundred metres above the valley of the Roya.

Grade: Moderate – but includes one fairly steep climb

Distance: 13.5km (8½ miles) including the detour to Piène-Haute (approx. 1km)

Time: 5 hours

Map: IGN Top 25 3741 ET

Start and finish: The Pont de Caï, on the River Bévèra east of Sospel

How to get there: From Sospel, take the D2204 heading east and in 2 km turn right on the D93 to Olivetta. After a further 2km there is a wooden signpost where the GR510 reaches the road – the place is called le Pont de Caï on the map, but there are no signs (if you cross the river, you have gone too far). Before and after this signpost there are parking bays under the cliffs on the side of the road – choose any one of them.

Refreshment: The Restaurant de la Château in Piène-Haute sells ice-creams and drinks, and offers the usual restaurant fare at weekends only.

Notes: This is a walk with quite a bit of climbing and descending, but the gradients are not particularly steep apart from one short climb to the Col de Paula. Underfoot the tracks are clear and generally well-surfaced (with just a little road walking), but stout footwear must be the order of the day. Carry adequate food and lots of fluid (which can be topped up at the tap in the square at Piène-Haute). And if the sun is shining, don't forget the sun-cream for this long walk.

Waymarking: Initially you are following yellow waymarks but the latter part of the journey is almost entirely on Grande Randonnée, waymarked in white on red.

Introduction

Here you are in the extreme south-east corner of France, and the borderland in which you are walking has changed ownership several times. Until the mid-nineteenth century, this territory was part of Savoy, itself a province of the kingdom of Sardinia. The alliance of Napoleon III with Victor Emmanuel of Sardinia (later to be Victor Emmanuel II of Italy) was decisive in his conflict with the Austrians – and in 1860, Savoy and the *comté* of Nice were restored to France in return. But the upper valley of the Roya had long been a favourite royal hunting ground, and was not included in the deal. It was only in 1947, in the post-war peace treaty between France and Italy, that the border was pushed back to the watershed on the mountain peaks and the Roya valley came to belong entirely to the French. The 'perched' village of Piène-Haute, the gem of this walk, was formerly the Italian Piena, and those names engraved on the war memorial in the church square are of men who gave their lives not for France but for Italy.

The objective of this walk may be Piène-Haute, but the outward and return routes are packed with interest. The whole walk actually encircles

'Perched village' of Piène-Haute

a peak of 862m known as Mont Grazian (you can divert to the summit if you wish). The path first climbs the western flank of the mountain following the very pretty valley of the River Bassèra before a short steep ascent takes you to the Col de Paula. Here the views extend over the valley of the Roya and you can see the red roofs of Piène-Haute on its spur in the distance. When you reach the village, a walk through alleyways bright with geraniums brings you to the square before the church with its war memorial and shady seats from which to take in the splendid views. The old ruined château sits on the tip of the spur beside with just a narrow ridge of rock separating it from the village. Cross it if you dare – on each side the land falls vertically and the wind sweeps across the rocky saddle. The access can only be left open as a challenge, since entry to the crumbling ruins is forbidden. From Piène-Haute the route descends through olive terraces to the Italian border above the aptly named village of Olivetta. Beyond is another col leading into the valley of the Bévèra. Here a Grande Randonnée (GR 510) weaves its way along the rocky sides, leading you past many viewpoints to return to the Pont de Caï – and on the way, the many information panels of a *sentier botanique* offer a lesson in Mediterranean botany.

The Walk

1. From any of the parking spots beside the D93 head for the signpost where the GR510 meets the road. On the opposite side another signpost directs you up some steps in the direction of the Vallon de Bassèra and the Col de Paula – there are yellow waymarks. This very pleasant path now leads under the trees with plentiful wild flowers at your feet. At first the path runs parallel to but above the road, later it approaches the river bank beside the ruined barns of Caï Supérieur. After passing a little waterfall, continue beside the river for a couple more minutes to a place where the rocks make it easy to cross over. The path now continues on the opposite side, climbing high above

the river with lovely glimpses of pools, rocks and waterfalls through the trees. Two streams are crossed before reaching a particularly beautiful spot where water cascades down a rocky chasm into a deep blue pool. Shortly afterwards you reach a grassy area around the ivy-clad ruins of the one-time hamlet of Garba. At a fork five minutes farther on, take the right hand path, ascending, and at a second fork immediately afterwards, bear right again – all is well waymarked. Ten minutes farther along, a more confusing junction is reached

2. Here there is again a choice of two paths – and both bear yellow waymarks. The right-hand path heading uphill is the one you want and it now zigzags up the slope to reach a pleasant clearing. Beyond it you plunge into the woods again on a path that gradually descends, passes more ruins, and then arrives at a junction with the GR52A in a pretty spot beside the river.

3. Do not cross the river but continue ahead here following signs to Piène-Haute and the Col de Paula (Post 96) – there are now white on red waymarks. The path continues through the woods to a junction where the waymarked path doubles back to the right – and the hard climb has begun. Initially the ascent is made by means of a series of hairpin bends, but eventually the path straightens and heads directly for the summit. You can smell victory as you arrive – the fresh breeze from the south blowing over the col. There are views of the high peaks to the south as you swing left on a beautiful path flanked by broom, cistus, thyme and juniper. The path then climbs a little, bearing left then right to reach a clearing area. From here the GR waymarks lead you left to a path descending to meet the gravelled track at the Col de Paula.

4. The broad track to the right leads to the summit of Mont Grazian, 1.5km away, and 120m above you. But for this walk, cross over the road and take the wide descending track opposite, signed to Piène-Haute (you can see the village in the distance). About 10 minutes down this track you have the option to cut off one of its bends by taking the path over the hillock ahead. Another short-cut path cuts out the next bend and you arrive at the track again beside a concrete building and a helicopter pad. Cross straight over, again continuing on an earthen track. Arriving at the main track a third time, cross over it again, taking the obvious track opposite. This leads over the brow of a hillock to a cross-tracks – and there are no waymarks. Do not continue uphill here, but turn left and descend gently on a lesser track, vaguely in the direction of Piène-Haute, which you can see on its spur over to the left. The track bends around and eventually reaches a tar-macked road at Post 115, half a kilometre west of Piène-Haute.

5. A few minutes walking will take you out to the village – and it really is worth the diversion. When you are ready, return to Point 5 and continue along the road for a further 500m or so to another signed junction (Post 440). Here leave the road and descend a gravelled track to the left in the direction of Olivetta – you can soon see its yellow buildings with red roofs nestling in the valley below. Arriving at the pink-faced Chapel of St Jérôme, the gravelled track ends, and you continue on an earthen track dropping down through terraces of olive

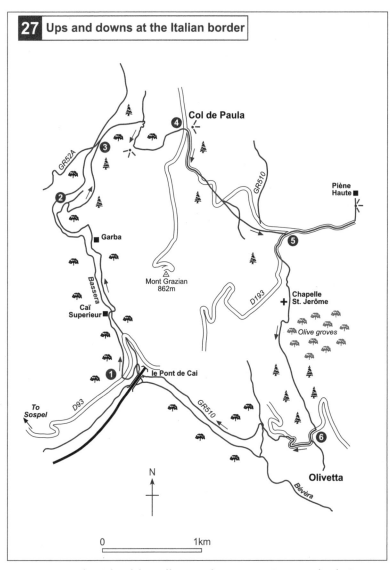

27 | Ups and downs at the Italian border

Col de Paula

GR52A

Piène
Haute ■

Garba

Bassera

Mont Grazian
862m

Caï
Superieur ■

GR510

D193

Chapelle
St. Jerôme

Olive groves

le Pont de Cai

To
Sospel

D93

GR510

Olivetta

Bévèra

N

0   1km

groves on the side of the valley. Farther on are pine woods, their scent combining with that of the aromatic mastic, thyme and rosemary. This delightful track meets the road in what appears to be no man's land – to the left is the Italian border post above the village of Olivetta, to the right is a sign welcoming you to France.

6. Walking into France you soon reach a little col (Post 442) where a path on the left leads down to Olivetta – divert if you wish. Otherwise continue on the road heading downhill, round a couple of bends and past old lime kilns to reach Post 443. Take the path on the left here, the GR 510 in the direction of Pont de Caï and Sospel. The path hugs the side of the valley and you soon meet the information panels of the *sentier botanique* – the scientific names are given with the French. On the opposite side are terraces of olives and the ruins of the farms that once owned them. The path crosses a stream (Ruisseau de Scuisse) and bends back again, soon becoming cobbled and rising to a splendid viewpoint over the valley of the Bévèra. Here you are on the old road to Sospel, an obvious path now dotted with the sign-boards of the *sentier botanique*, and offering views into the valley and along to the distant railway bridge of the Pont de Caï. Reaching that bridge, the path passes under it and then heads downhill beside a rushing stream. The stream short-cuts to the left, but you continue instead into the valley where a little waterfall drops into a pool. Cross the bridge and climb the slope on the far side to reach the point on the D93 from which you started.

More Walks in the Area

This is a splendid area for walking and there is no more helpful book than *Rando – Moyen Pays*, one of three free volumes of 'Guides RandOxygène' produced by the Conseil General des Alpes-Maritimes (the others are *Haut Pays* and *Pays Côtier*). Every Office de Tourisme in the region stocks these books, but if you want to get one before you leave home, write directly to the Conseil General, Services des Randonnées, BP 3007, 06201 NICE CEDEX 3. Rando – Moyen Pays offers a choice of 60 circuits between the Italian border in the east and Puget-Théniers in the west and from the Loup valley in the south to the lower valleys of the Roya, Vésubie and Tinée in the north. The text is fairly dense French, but the route maps are very clear – although you should also get the appropriate IGN map for any walk you are thinking of undertaking. Height gained and lost is clearly stated with each walk, as is an expected time (on the ambitious side). Above all, take a good look at the level of *difficulté* – *Rando facile* and *Rando moyenne* walks are well within the compass of any regular rambler, but *Rando sportive* definitely needs more stamina and possibly a bit of rock climbing (and *Rando alpine*, found in walks in the Haut Pays book, speaks for itself).

One of the most popular hikes in the vicinity of Sospel is included in the *Moyen Pays* book under the title *Boucle de Mont Agaisen*. Mont Agaisen is an almost conical mountain rising some 350m above Sospel on its north side. At its summit there are fortifications that were once part of the Maginot line – and some fine views over Sospel and the Bevèra valley to the south and the Col de Brouis to the north. You can drive up Mont Agaisen on one of those narrow, serpentine, precipitous roads so common around here. But the walk follows the GR52 to the north side of the mountain, a rather gentler route classified (perhaps optimistically) as a *Rando facile*.

One other publication well deserves a mention – a booklet this time translated into English under the title *The Paths of the Perched Villages*. *The Paths* turns out to be a well-worked-out 5-day itinerary for hikers, taking you down the valley of the Roya from Tende to Breil, then on to Sospel and Castellar. All the information you would need for this truly excellent and not-too-arduous ramble is here – places to eat and sleep are included with telephone numbers and there are details of museums and monuments and interesting snippets on the villages passed through. Any Office de Tourisme should be able to find you a copy – or write instead to Association pour le Développement Touristique des Vallées Roya-Bévèra, Boulevard Rouvier, 06540 BREIL-SUR-ROYA.

Places of interest nearby

Sospel's 11th century bridge over the River Bévèra has made the town famous – it's a photograph seen in many tourist brochures. Unfortunately the original was destroyed in the last world war, and the present bridge is a faithful reconstruction, complete with the little toll tower (now housing a tiny but well-stocked Office de Tourisme). Other buildings worth visiting in Sospel are the Cathedral and the Palais Ricci (both in the splendid Place St Michel) and the traditionally-coloured Chapel of the White Penitents tucked away in the Place Ste Croix, north of the river.

One kilometre south of Sospel on the D2204, the Fort St Roch is a building worth visiting for quite a different reason. Part of the Alpine Maginot Line, its ugly bare concrete façade conceals a whole underground warren of rooms and passageways, effectively a complete town where the military could live for up to three months at a time. The Fort St Roch is open every afternoon during the summer months and at weekends only in April, May and June.

28. Prehistory in the Valley of Fontanalbe

In the east of the Mercantour National Park are two remote valleys where Bronze Age man has left thousands of mysterious engravings on the rocks. The Valley of Fontanalbe is the more easily accessible of the two sites and in addition to the carvings, this walk passes beautiful high alpine lakes and offers the chance to spot chamois and even ibex.

Grade: Moderate/strenuous

Distance: 13.5km (8½ miles)

Time: 5½ hours walking, plus time for looking at the engravings

Map: IGN Top 25 3841 OT or Didier Richard no. 9, *Mercantour massif et parc national* (1: 50,000)

Start and finish: The village of Casterino

How to get there: Casterino is near the Italian border to the north of Menton. From Breil-sur-Roya, head north on the N204 and in St Dalmas-de-Tende, turn west on the D91 (SP Casterino). Half an hour on this winding climbing road will bring you to the village, where there is plenty of parking.

Refreshment: Casterino boasts a couple of restaurants and a bar. En route you will pass the Refuge de Fontanalbe, open in summer, where it should be possible to get resuscitation – but don't take it for granted.

Notes: This walk is only possible between the months of June and October – outside that time the site is likely to be snow-covered. The total ascent here is 670m, a steady climb lasting around 2½ hours. Most of the route is on wide forest tracks, but nevertheless, walking boots must always be the recommended footwear in the mountains. The walk reaches an altitude of 2220m where the temperature will be well below that at St Dalmas-de-Tende or even Casterino, so come well-equipped. And sudden storms are common in these mountains, so whatever the weather when you set out, carry a waterproof. The Valley of Fontanalbe is a protected site – you are forbidden by law to stray from the marked pathways, and to walk on, or even touch, the engravings. And lastly, bring binoculars – the views are stupendous and you may also want to get a closer look at the wildlife.

Waymarking: The route is waymarked in yellow, but there is no difficulty in route-finding here.

Introduction

High in the Mercantour, two remarkable valleys lie at the foot of sharp-peaked Mont Bégo – the more extensive of these is the bare rocky Vallée des Merveilles, the lesser but easier to reach is the green larch-clad Vallon de Fontanalbe. Some four thousand years ago, these wild valleys were a sacred site, a place where Bronze Age man came to worship his god – a bull-god, personified by the 'horn' of Mont Bégo. Mont Bégo is a 'ferritic' mountain and the sudden violent storms with lightning centred on this spot must have added to the mystique. Arriving here from their homes in the lower valleys, the Bronze Age pilgrims chiselled tiny pieces from the orange glacier-polished rock, producing simple outlines of things that

Guides' hut and the Lacs Jumeaux

were relevant to their pastoral and agricultural lives. More than 40,000 engravings have been separately identified and among them there are four distinct themes – 'corniforms' or horned figures relating to the bull-god, geometric figures representing an 'earth-god' that controlled their farming enterprises, the tools and weapons they used every day, and, very much less frequently, curious humanoid forms that have since been given nicknames (the sorcerer, the dancer, the Christ). Both these valleys are now protected sites, with only limited access to the engravings allowed to the casual rambler. If you want to see the most and the best, you would be wise to join one of the summer guided tours that take you off the marked paths into the protected area (see the Places of Interest section below). But if you prefer to do it yourself, there is still plenty to see and the route suggested here leads past some of the most exciting sites in the Valley of Fontanalbe. For anyone who can manage it, there is a certain magic in being here out of season when there are no other visitors.

Aside from the rock engravings, this is also a magnificent ramble in its own right. The Mercantour National Park has a rich variety of flora and fauna – the Valley of Fontanalbe itself is filled with pines and larches that are particularly glorious in autumn colours. Chamois roam the slopes and, on a personal note, we were lucky enough to get quite close to a couple of ibex. At the top of the long climb, the plateau where the engravings are found is truly beautiful – there are stunning views of Mont Bégo and other peaks, and the path takes you past the Lacs Jumeaux, where a wooden-tiled guides' hut nestles beside two small alpine lakes. The third alpine lake at the summit, the Lac Vert, is the most delightful of all – a stretch of green water in a rocky valley ringed with larches.

To get the most from this walk and to get an idea of what you are about to see, it would be wise visit the superb new Musée des Merveilles in Tende before setting off – and the nearby Office de Tourisme could also give you helpful information on the wildlife and vegetation of the Mercantour.

The Walk

1. From the parking area opposite the auberge of Les Melèzes, walk downhill on the road in the direction of St Dalmas. At the bottom of the village where the road bears left, take a gravelled track climbing on the right, signposted (Post 391) to the Refuge de Fontanalbe. An information panel offers an introduction to the area. The wide track now climbs steadily under the larches and as you get higher some of the loops, necessary for 4x4 vehicles, can be cut by walkers preferring to take a shorter but slightly steeper route. At a clearing you have a sudden view across the valley to the high peaks near the Italian border before diving into the pines again. In another half an hour or so another track joins you from the left and you are now walking along the boundary of the National Park as indicated by the green-painted spots. As you climb a hut comes into view on a hillock on the right and the path soon bears round to pass it and reach a track junction at Post 390.

2. Do not cross the river ahead, but bear left in the direction of the Refuge de Fontanalbe to pass under the wooden barrier marking the boundary of the National Park. The path doubles back to the south, and you are now heading for the strange silhouettes of the Cime de Chanvrairaie. At a corner you reach the roughly-built stone hut that is the Refuge de Fontanalbe. Below the refuge Post 389 directs you onwards to up the main track, which now becomes more gravely. You are above 2000m at this point and the vegetation seems less luxurious. The climb continues for almost another half an hour before you see a bridge ahead with a mountain stream cascading over a chaos of boulders below.

3. At the junction marked by Post 387, turn right to cross the bridge and enter the protected sector. A few metres farther along, Post 388 tells you that the Lac Vert is up a track to the left. Ignore it (you will be coming back that way) and continue on the main track signed to Gias des Pasteurs. A few moments farther on you reach the Vacherie Supérieure – a stone cattle shelter fronted by a skeleton of timber. In front of it an information board shows the sites of the best engravings.

4. Leave the main path here and take the track heading up the valley on the left – you are going looking for the first of the engravings. After about 5 minutes walking, at the top of a slope, look out for an information panel below you on the left. It marks the site of the engravings known as les Attelages – you may have seen a recreation of it in the museum at Tende. The engravings are not particularly clear – but just look around you, there are plenty more on the rocks nearby. If you now return to the path you can continue ahead to find some more modern engravings. The work entitled Le Cathédrale is dated 1776. When you want to return to the Bronze Age, walk back down the path to the Vacherie Supérieure and turn left on to the main track again. Continuing to climb you pass a small lake and soon have sweeping views down the Valley of Fontanalbe on the right. A long stone building is pressed into the rock on the left and the path swings left towards the hut of the Mercantour Guides.

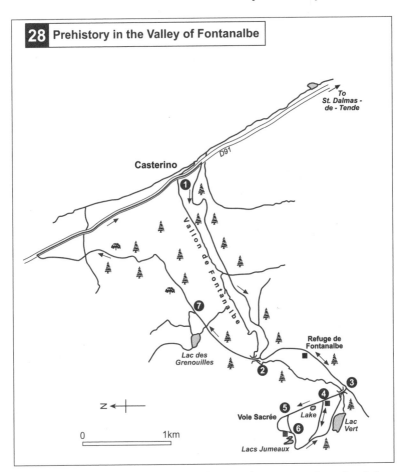

28 Prehistory in the Valley of Fontanalbe

5. As the path turns, look for a path leaving the main track on the right – it is sign-posted to the Voie Sacrée. Following the path around you soon reach the foot of a huge slab of orange schist (*chiappe*) bearing hundreds of engravings. Turn up the hill to climb alongside it, passing three information panels as you go. These are the best carvings you will see in this valley – take your time. At the top of the slope you reach a beautiful ceramic *table d'orientation* which points out the holy Mont Bégo (a huge mountain of 2872m) and all the surrounding peaks. The path then descends to the guides' hut beside the Lacs Jumeaux.

6. Turn right and continue on the path beside the lakes. It soon descends through a marshy valley where it becomes rather indistinct at times, but posts have been set in the ground to guide you. A path signed to the *Parcours de Découverte* goes off on the left – ignore it, this is the path you were on earlier heading for the Vacherie Supérieure. Keeping ahead you soon arrive at a lovely viewpoint above the Lac Vert and then descend to its shores. The path leads you on, sometimes clambering over rocks, to reach the main track again, where you turn right to return to Point 3. Now retrace your steps down past the Refuge de Fontanalbe to leave the Park at Point 2. This time turn left

at Post 390 and cross the river (this variation in the homeward route will lengthen the walk by about an hour). The wide path climbs very gently and you can look across the valley to the path you took earlier.

7. The track crosses stream and, reaching Post 392, a path goes left to the Lac des Grenouilles. Follow it if you want an extra short diversion, but otherwise keep ahead on the main track. About half an hour after leaving the Park the path turns north – you are now overlooking the Valley of Casterino and can see the village itself below you. After a further half an hour or so on this splendid balcony path you descend to meet a narrow tarmacked road at Post 395. Turn right here and follow the road downhill all the way back to Casterino.

More Walks in the Area

The Fontanalbe area contains only about one third of the engravings. Around 60% and some of the most famous are to be found in the Vallée des Merveilles on the other side of Mont Bégo. It is possible to walk to the Refuge des Merveilles in about 2½ hours, following a long jeep track starting above the Lac des Mesches (on the road to Casterino). From here the route continues on a path high above the Lac Long to reach the protected area of engravings (known as l'Arpette). Without a guide you must keep to the main track, on which there are again information panels describing the engravings. Those with energy and some agility can now complete a magnificent circular walk heading north past the three lakes to the Refuge de Valmasque, and then east down the Valmasque Valley to meet the road above Casterino. The whole circuit including the Vallée des Merveilles itself will take something like 8 or 9 hours – rather too much for one day. If you are contemplating it, you should stay overnight at the Refuge des Merveilles and get a look at the engravings in the morning before completing the tour. This route appears in the excellent free booklet *Rando – Haut Pays* (French only) produced by the Conseil General des Alpes-Maritimes and available at any Office de Tourisme in the region. But it would also be as well to acquire the relevant IGN or Didier Richard map before setting out.

Getting away from the rock engravings, many interesting walks in this area are made possible by the route of the Nice-Cuneo railway. This incredible line manages to climb its way into the mountains by a series of underground spirals and innumerable tunnels. From a walker's point of view, the line makes it possible to follow the GR 52A all the way down the valley from Tende to Breil-sur-Roya. A good choice here might be the section from la Brigue to Saorge, a fairly energetic day's hike. For something less ambitious, you could choose to walk from Tende to St Dalmas by the Chemin des Bois or from St Dalmas to la Brigue through the Armaneïra Woods. Both these easy rambles are described in the free leaflet *Randonnée Pédestre – Commune de Tende*. The text of this leaflet is in French, but the paths used are clearly shown on the IGN map (3841 OT) – if you have difficulty, perhaps someone at the Office de Tourisme in Tende could help you identify them.

Places of interest nearby

A visit to the stylish Musée des Merveilles in Tende is a must. Outside, gendarmes prowl in the road at the French border post (although Italy is still 10km away), inside you are in another world. Recreations of all the major carvings are displayed, along with archaeological finds, geological maps of the area and splendid tableaux of life in prehistoric times. The Musée des Merveilles is open virtually every day throughout the year except Tuesdays (but note that annual holidays may be taken for two weeks at the end of March and at the end of November).

Just down the road from the Musée des Merveilles, the Office de Tourisme in Tende can give you details of the regular guided visits to the engravings in both the Fontanalbe and Merveilles areas. Generally speaking, these are available only from the beginning of June to the end of September. In the Vallée des Merveilles, the tours start from the Refuge de Merveilles (2½ hours from the Lac des Mesches) and at Fontanalbe the morning tours start from the Fontanalbe Refuge, with later ones starting from the hut at the Lacs Jumeaux (2½ hours from Casterino). In each case the visits are scheduled to take between 2½ and 3½ hours. Private visits can also be arranged with the Mercantour Guides, and for those wanting to avoid the long climb on foot to the sites, approved guides have access using 4x4 vehicles. The Office de Tourisme has all the details.

The upper valley of the Roya belonged to Italy until the peace treaty of 1947. There is lots to explore – the forts near the Italian border, Tende itself with its houses of green schist, the 15th century wall paintings in the lonely Chapel of Notre-Dame-des-Fontaines 4 km east of la Brigue, the gorges of Saorge on the N204 and the old houses of the village itself clinging precariously to the hillside. Sports enthusiasts are well catered for with canoeing, caving and canyoning and those who must test their head for heights have Via Ferrata circuits at la Brigue and at Tende.

29. High in the Mercantour
– The Lac de Trécolpas

Wild, remote and beautiful, the mountains of the Mercantour National Park sweep to their summit level at the Italian border. Here you are close to that watershed as you climb beside the rushing Boréon stream to a high mountain refuge and continue to the glacial Lac de Trécolpas, cradled by rocky peaks.

Grade: Moderate / strenuous

Distance: 9km (5½ miles)

Time: 4½ hours

Map: IGN Top 25 3741 OT or Didier Richard no. 9 *Mercantour massif et parc national.*

Start and finish: Parking Supérieur at le Boréon

How to get there: From St Martin-Vésubie, head north-east on the D89. Continue past the waterfall and through the hamlet of le Boréon. At the junction above the village, bear right on a narrow road leading to the Vacherie du Boréon, a group of stone barns. Take the rough track climbing to the right of these, which in a couple of minutes brings you to a large parking area, the Parking Supérieur.

Refreshment: It should be possible to get both food and drink (and accommodation) at the new Refuge de Cougourde, due to open in October 2002. It seems likely that this large hostel will be continuously open during the summer months, and on reservation between November and May – but do not rely on it. Check first (the Office de Tourisme at St Martin-Vésubie should be able to help), or carry your own refreshment with you. There are several bars and restaurants in St Martin-Vésubie itself and an auberge at le Boréon.

Notes: This walk is only possible between the months of June and October, when there should be no snow. It involves a steady climb of around 400m to the refuge, followed by a virtually horizontal section to the lake and the descent home. The climb has only one or two steep sections, which are short and not difficult to negotiate. Paths are clearly marked and obvious except for the final ascent to the refuge, but you can't really get lost. Note that you are walking at high altitude (the Lac de Trécolpas is at 2150m) – take extra warm clothing, include waterproofs even if the sun is shining and get a weather forecast before you go (posted in the window of the Office de Tourisme at St Martin-Vésubie). Do not venture out in heavy rain or mist. And think of including binoculars in your pack – you are almost certain to see chamois and the views are outstanding.

Waymarking: Much of the route is on the Grande Randonnée, waymarked in white on red. Otherwise, there are signposts at every track junction.

Introduction

From a walker's point of view, this has to be the most exciting corner of Provence. Here the tail of the Alpine arc drops 3000 metres to the sea, its flanks cut through by parallel rivers tumbling south to the Mediterranean. The valleys of the Cians, the Tinée, the Vésubie and the Roya form some of the most spectacular gorges in Provence. The Mercantour National Park

The snow-covered 'thumb' of the Cougourde looks down on the larches in the valley below

encompasses the upper valleys of these rivers as it stretches for 80km along the line of the Italian border. On the far side the Italians have their own equivalent – the Argentera or Parco Naturale delle Alpi Maritime. International co-operation in the management of a grand European park is envisaged for the future.

The Mercantour is the last of the series of six national parks created in France in the 60s and 70s (a seventh park, the island of Guadeloup was added in 1989).and like most of the others, it is divided into an outer and an inner zone. In the outer zone of the Mercantour are 28 communes, attractive villages often perched on hilltops, offering hospitality for both summer hikers and winter skiers. The inner zone is the province of nature alone. There are no habitations here – man can only enter on foot, and strict regulations forbid dogs, mountain bikes, fires, camping, picking flowers, leaving litter and more. Wildlife abounds in this protected area. The incredibly agile chamois are everywhere and you may also spot the less common ibex, which, although heavier, are even more nimble and often seem quite tame. Others to be seen are mouflons (Corsican sheep), marmots, hares and red squirrels – and a handful of wolves that wander over from Italy every summer causing consternation among the mountain shepherds. Birds include bearded vultures and golden eagles. The flora of the Mercantour are as splendid as the fauna – over 2000 species are here of which 40 are unique to the area. The Mercantour has adopted one of these, the multi-flowered *saxifraga florulenta* as its emblem.

This walk to the Lac de Trécolpas is one of the region's classics. The journey begins with the beautiful valley of the Borréon Torrent, rock-strewn, dotted with larches and carpeted with wild flowers early in the year. Climbing above it you reach a mountain refuge at the foot of a thick thumb of rock known as the Cougourde – its distinctive form appears on just about every brochure of the Mercantour (the name is a corruption of *courge* – a vegetable marrow). The old refuge here was a character-full bright yellow metal shack. The palace of larchwood that is its replacement now stands close by. From the refuges the path curves round the slopes to its climax at the Lac de Trécolpas. Bright blue under a clear sky, darker and more sinister under the clouds, this high alpine lake is not lacking in atmosphere. Surrounding it are the sharp ridges of the glacial peaks and the path goes on to skirt the lake and climb steeply up the Pas des Ladres on its far side. But you must leave it to go, and instead turn downhill into the valley of the Boréon to return to your starting point.

The Walk

1. Leave the Parking Supérieur by the wide track heading east up the valley – a signpost (420) points the way. A little farther on, in the larch forest you meet two posts labelled '421' in quick succession – keep straight ahead at each. Beyond the second post the path is narrower. At a fork it matters not whether you choose right or left – both arrive at an open stony area ringed by larches and dominated ahead by the rocky hump of the Cougourde. At the far side of the plateau the path leads on to the Chalet Vidron, a small stone hut set between its own tranquil pool and the cascading waters of the Boréon Torrent.

2. Beside a wooden bridge over the end of the pool, post 422 directs you onward and upward under the larches and pines. The path is sometimes a little less than obvious, but you can't really go wrong. Eventually you find yourself heading for a bridge over the torrent on your left.

3. Cross the bridge (the Pont de Peïrastreche) and, directed by post 423, take the path to the right. You are now on the route of the GR52 (white on red waymarks), which leads you through the very beautiful valley of the Boréon, crossing several tributary streams as you go. At post 424 a path to the Lacs Bessons climbs to the left but you continue ahead to Post 425, just before another bridge across the Boréon.

4. You will return across that bridge later, but now you turn left, leaving the GR and heading for the Refuge de la Cougourde. Immediately the path is not apparent – do not cross the boggy ground, but head up the steeper slope to the right of it (there is a white and red cross on the rock). In a few metres you are on a distinct track. Five minutes on and once more you are pathless. Bear right and keep climbing – a plank bridge will take you across a stream in a marshy area. Again bearing right and continuing to climb, a wooden handrail soon comes into view on a ledge ahead. Reaching it you are confronted by this bright yellow hut perched at the foot of the Caïre des Gaisses, while the towering 2921m rock of the Cougourde looks down from behind. The new refuge, surprising in its relative complexity, is set a couple of hundred metres to the left.

5. Behind the old refuge, post 426 directs you across the stream in the direction of the Lac de Trécolpas. The path now sweeps quite safely across the scree of the hillside with splendid views all around (and often flocks of chamois, skipping nimbly over the loose boulders). After about half an hour you reach a fork post 427.

6. From here its just a short haul up over the rocky rim to the Lac de Trécolpas in its magnificent setting. The craggy mountains on the right of the lake are the Cime de Juisse (2580m) and the Cime de

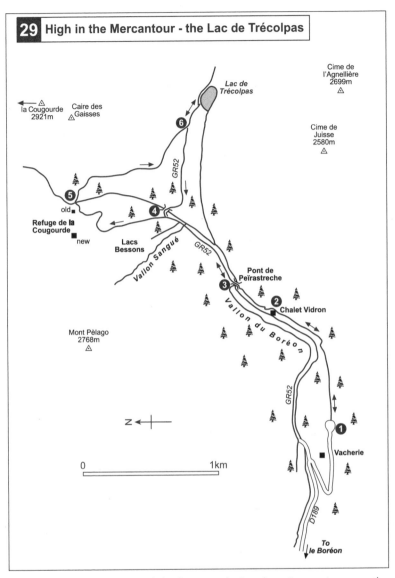

29 High in the Mercantour - the Lac de Trécolpas

l'Agnellière (2699m) while the Grande Randonnée continues to the left around the flanks of the Tête de Trécolpas, climbing its way through another 300m to the Col de Fenestre at the Italian border. When you are ready to leave this awe-inspiring scene, retrace your steps to post 427 (Point 6) and now turn downhill to the left. You are on the GR52 again and have the waymarks to guide you, but the stony path is quite obvious as it descends into the valley with the solid bulk of Mont Pélago directly ahead. Eventually you are alongside the Boréon Torrent once more. Reaching the bridge, cross it to reach post 425 again (Point 4). Now simply turn left and return the way you came, remembering to cross the river at the Pont de Peïrastreche, leaving the GR52 at that point. Just over an hour should see you back at the car park.

More Walks in the Area

The other day-length walk starting from le Boréon itself is the climb to the Col de Cerise on the Italian border. This is classified as a *rando sportive*, mostly on account of the height gain (of the order of 1000m), but technically should not prove too difficult. You are rewarded with some impressive views of the high peaks on the Italian side of the border and can take in a diversion to the Lac de Mercantour on the way down. The route is clearly shown on both the suggested maps for this walk (3741 OT and Didier Richard's *Mercantour*).

More walks start from la Madone de Fenestre, reached by the narrow D94 heading north-east up the valley from St Martin-Vésubie. This is a spot worth visiting in its own right, a magnificent cirque, dominated in the north by one of the highest peaks in these parts, the Cime du Gélas (3143m). The buildings in this wild place are those of a one-time religious community now used as a mountain refuge – behind them a wide stony path sets off for the Col de Fenestre and the Italian border. On the road below the buildings, a couple of hundred metres beyond the stream, post 361 marks the start of another of this region's classic hikes, the circuit of the Lacs de Prals, or the Five Lakes Walk. Here you climb the valley of the Prals, another mountain torrent and continue crossing the contours to reach the five small lakes, over 400m above the starting point. The climb is not too arduous, and the path is clear and marked with cairns. The 4-hour route appears in the free booklet *Rando – Haut Pays* (available from any tourist office) – in which it they also suggest that the shallow lakes are suitable for hardy swimmers.

Places of interest nearby

St Martin-Vésubie is an attractive little town stretching down the hillside above the confluence of two mountain torrents forming the River Vésubie. If you aren't staying in the town, at least spare a few minutes to amble down the one-time main street, the Rue du Docteur Cagnoli, still with its medieval central guttering. Ancient houses, ornate chapels, curious shops and tiny bistros generate mixed aromas of fresh bread, perfume, incense, herbs and haute-cuisine. At its lower end stands the parish church, in which for more than nine months of the year, lives the 12th century polychrome wooden figure of the Madone de Fenestre (her niche is just to the right of the altar). Every year, at the end of June, she is ceremoniously carried to her summer home in the sanctuary of the mountains (see **More Walks**), returning amid yet more festivities in the middle of September. Below the church is the Maison des Gubernatis, former home of a count of that name, while behind, the Rue du Plan leads off to the Place de la Frairie, a square of Ligurian-coloured buildings from where there is a view over the rushing Madone de Fenestre Torrent.

A drive of less than 5km from St Martin-Vésubie will take you to the little village of Venanson. Sitting high on a tiny spur of level land, it has a commanding view of the valley of the Vésubie, St Martin-Vésubie and, beyond the town, the valleys of the Boréon and the Madone de Fenestre separated by the high ridge of the Cime de Piagu. Those with abundant energy can overdose on views by climbing a further 600m to the peak of le Conquet (again see the *Rando – Haut Pays* book), while less dynamic individuals can settle for a tour of the 15th century frescoes in the Chapelle St Sébastien (if not open, ask at the Bella Vista restaurant), and follow up with a leisurely lunch.

30. Gourdon and the Chemin du Paradis

Gourdon, one of the most famous of the *villages perchés*, sits on a clifftop
some 600 metres above the Valley of the Loup. Up that near-vertical face
winds an ancient mule-track – the Chemin du Paradis.

Grade: Moderate – on account of the gradient. See notes below

Distance: 6.5km (4 miles)

Time: 3½ hours plus time to look around Gourdon

Map: IGN Top 25 3643 ET

Start and finish: Parking area beside the cemetery at Bar-sur-Loup

How to get there: From the central square at Bar-sur-Loup, head
downhill in the direction of Pont-du-Loup. Take the first road glancing
off on the left – there is parking just near the turn, before the
cemetery.

Refreshment: All you could possibly need in Bar-sur-Loup and in
Gourdon.

Notes: The climb up the Chemin du Paradis is in no way technically
difficult, and there is generally no need for footwear other than
trainers. Even so, it is a fairly steep and demanding ascent – carry fluid
to refresh you en route (even though there are bars in Gourdon). The
descent on this track can be hard on the knees, and there are even
steeper sections as you head farther downhill towards the old railway
track. The total height gained (and lost) is around 520m Take
appropriate precautions against sunburn on a hot day, and don't
forget the binoculars – the views from the top make it all more than
worthwhile.

Waymarking: The route is waymarked in yellow throughout, with a
short section on the GR51 marked in white on red.

Introduction

The allusion to 'paradise' in this trail must relate to the views. There's not
much of the sublime about the effort needed to make the ascent, and on a
hot summer's day – well, don't even think it! But the slopes are lightly
wooded with interesting vegetation and the dappled shade makes the
climb more comfortable than it would otherwise be. And out of season,
surprising as it may seem, the Chemin du Paradis can be quite crowded on
a Sunday morning. Whole families, including children, grandmother and
dog, are out on the trail – it obviously provides the perfect aperitif to the
five-course lunch with all trimmings that *maman* is preparing for them
back in the kitchen.

The route here is not only a matter of crossing the contours. Starting
from Bar-sur-Loup, a village permanently fragranced by its perfume factory, the path at the outset climbs only gently. For some distance you are
walking on a level balcony path on top of the Canal du Loup, a conduit
supplying water to the village. And the final stretch home is along the
track-bed of an old railway line. But the objective of this walk is Gourdon
on its rocky perch – and zigzagging up the cliff-face to reach it is the
Chemin du Paradis.

Gourdon is a maze of narrow medieval streets whose buildings are
now, sadly but inevitably, totally taken over by the demands of tourism.

On the Chemin du Paradis

There are apparently more than 300 inhabitants of Gourdon, but goodness knows where they buy their bread. Instead their shops teem with Provençal cottons, santons, painted pottery, lavender, olive oil, perfumes, herbs and the rest – but you have to admit it makes interesting browsing, and there are plenty of places to enjoy a drink after the climb. At the heart of the village is the château, built on the site of an original Saracen stronghold. It houses a couple of museums, worth a visit if you have time, but the splendid terraced gardens are more inviting. Designed by le Nôtre, they also enjoy Gourdon's special panorama. And it is the panorama that everyone is here for. Gourdon's village square is effectively a viewing terrace, equipped with telescopes trained on the distant azure sea. All the coast from Cap Ferrat, past Antibes to Cap Roux in the Esterel stretches before you while in the north-east, a craggy line of Alps frames the horizon.

The Walk

1. From the parking area continue up the little road (Chemin du Bessurane) in the direction of the Chapelle St Claude, as shown by the signpost on the corner of the road. Arriving in front of the chapel, bear left up a near-vertical slope that is very fortunately no longer than about 20 metres. At the top you are on an obvious track marked with yellow flashes. In a couple of minutes you reach a fork where a track on the left goes steeply up the slope – and, of course, there is not a waymark in sight. Your path here is the easier option – keep straight ahead beside the fence, climbing gently. A few minutes later the waymarks reappear, and you arrive at a track junction with a signpost.

2. Turn right here in the direction of Gourdon. You are now walking along the route of the Canal du Loup, although at this point it is not visible. Continuing along this balcony path you can soon see Gourdon

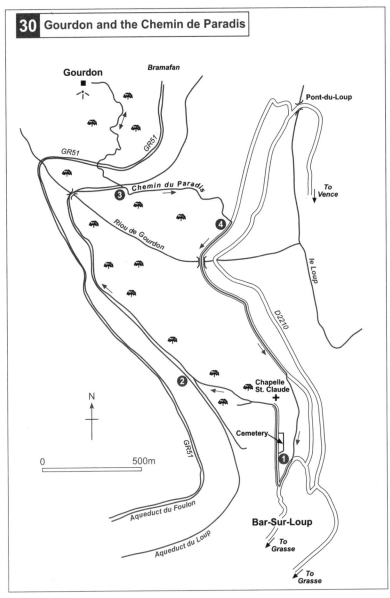

30 Gourdon and the Chemin de Paradis

on its clifftop ahead – and it seems an awful long way up. Turn away and instead look down the valley of the Loup to the not-too-distant sea. At length you reach a metal bridge crossing the bed of the Riou de Gourdon and the path swings round to meet the Chemin du Paradis at a cross-tracks.

3. Turn up to the left here. The broad stony path now zigzags its way up the steep slope and soon reaches the thick pipe of the Aqueduct du Foulon. This particular watercourse was originally installed to supply the flower fields of Grasse. Water splashes from a spout here and you can take a drink or at least, splash your face. The path now continues behind and above the pipe, from here climbing relentlessly up the

slope in a seemingly never-ending series of hairpins. The views increase with every step. Eventually the path comes up under the walls of Gourdon and swings around to enter the village from the rear. Make your way to the square in front of the church from where you can pick out Nice with its airport, Antibes, Cannes and beyond it, the coast of the Esterel. When you have taken your fill of the other delights of Gourdon (château, gardens, shops, and restaurants), retrace your steps down the Chemin de Paradis past the Aqueduct du Foulon and as far as the junction at point 3. Now keep straight ahead on the broad track waymarked in yellow – this is the continuation of the Chemin du Paradis. Coming down to a house, the path veers right and descends very steeply indeed until it reaches a tarmacked road.

4. Turn right on this road, which actually runs along the track-bed of the old railway. Cross the viaduct and continue towards Bar-sur-Loup. Reaching a gravelled clearing on the right, bear right up the Chemin des Fontaites – it is waymarked, and a sign points to the *Cimetière*. When you are faced with a concrete drive ahead and another to the right, look left – a narrow track continues beside a wall and again there is a waymark. The track leads you to a road and you continue to climb to reach your parking area on the right.

More Walks in the Area

Anyone planning a stay in this area should get hold of the excellent booklet *Rando – Pays Côtier* from the series *Guides Randoxygène* produced by the Conseil Général des Alpes-Maritimes. It is offered free in every Office de Tourisme in the district, or it can be sent for in advance – the address is given in the **More Walks** section of Walk 27. This book contains a selection of 60 walks in the hills and on the coast between Cannes and the Italian border. The maps in this book are very good, and the routes can easily be picked out on the appropriate IGN maps. Moreover each route has been well waymarked on the ground, so there should be no trouble in following them. But to get the most from the walks, and even to find out what you are going to see, it would be helpful to read the text, which is in French only. Get a dictionary and have a go – it's worth it for these excellent walks. And whatever you do, check out the level of difficulty (*niveau*) before setting off – it's seldom overestimated.

If you are used to mountain walking and want more of a challenge, you will enjoy the route in this book entitled Balcons du Loup. It follows the Aqueduct du Foulon high on the side of the Loup valley between Pont-du-Loup and Bramafan. A torch is needed for the tunnels (around 20 of them), and a head for heights is the requirement for the bits in between, where there are splendid views into the valley. The route returns to Pont-du-Loup via Courmes and the Plateau des Courmettes on the left bank of the river, making a rather long hike of 23.5km. But if you just want a look at the balcony path along the Aqueduct du Foulon, you can simply pick it up on this walk (near Point 3) and follow it as far as you like (or dare)

One of the few circuits designated *facile* in this area starts near Gourdon, just off the D12 to Caussols, and crosses the limestone plateau to the summit of Haut Montet (1335m). Crowned by radar installations, it offers breathtaking views of both coast and mountains. The total distance of this walk is a mere 4.7km – but allow 2½ hours.

Places of interest nearby

The Château of Gourdon was restored in the 17th century. The ground floor houses the Musée Historique (mostly a collection of arms) while the floor above is home to the Musée de d'Art Naïve. At the time of restoration the terraced gardens were designed by le Nôtre – now they are famed for their collection of alpine plants. The château and grounds are open daily.

Grasse is only a few kilometres away (you can almost smell it) and three of the perfumeries offer free guided tours. Arguably the most famous (by virtue of its omnipresent brochures) is Fragonard near the centre of town (Blvd. de Fragonard). Molinard offers you the chance to create your own perfume (for a fair-sized fee) and is to be found on the Blvd. Victor-Hugo, to the south of the town. Galimard is 3km out of town on the Route de Cannes. In each case there is plenty of free-spraying in anticipation of sales – and there will be no disguising where you've been.

There is so much to see in the vicinity of the Loup valley and space here is limited. But it is only 16km to Vence, where one building particularly deserves mention – the atmospheric Chapelle du Rosaire designed by Henri Matisse. Matisse was in his late seventies and had recently moved to Vence when he met again the woman who had nursed him through illness in wartime. She had become a Dominican nun – Sister Jacques-Marie – and it was she who begged him to design and decorate this chapel for her order. The work took four years of his life and was completed in 1951, three years before he died. The tiny white building with a blue and white tiled roof stands beside the road to St Jeannet north of Vence, just 200 metres from where the artist himself lived. The bare white walls inside are decorated with Matisse's black line drawings – the Virgin Mary in the nave, St Dominic behind the altar and the deliberately jumbled stations of the cross on the wall opposite. Stained glass windows take up the remaining wall, a design of brilliant yellow leaves on a background of green and deep blue. The white walls reflect their colours. In the rooms outside are displayed the priests' vestments designed by Matisse, more of his sketches and an assortment of photographs. The Chapelle du Rosaire is open on Tuesday and Thursday and on other days in the school holidays. Check with the Office de Tourisme at Vence for times.

31. The green waters of the Siagne

West of Grasse, the River Siagne has cut a deep furrow through the underlying limestone. A cool tree-shaded path follows the river through the depths offering you relief from the hot Provençal sun – and even the possibility of a swim.

Grade: Moderate

Distance: 7km (4½ miles)

Time: 2½ hours

Map: IGN Top 25 3543 ET

Start and finish: Place Général de Gaulle, beside the church at St Cézaire-sur-Siagne.

How to get there: St Cézaire is on the D13 approx. 16km west of Grasse. It can also be reached from the Draguinan road, the D562, turning where signed. There is a large car park near the centre of the town.

Refreshment: Bars and restaurants in St Cézaire-sur-Siagne

Notes: St Cézaire-sur-Siagne is about 300m above the river. This walk comprises an initial descent into the gorge, a long riverside path and a sustained but not too steep climb to return to the starting point. Tracks are good and no special footwear is needed in dry summer weather – but it might be a different matter after heavy rain. Carry water with you – you may particularly appreciate it on the way back. And in hot weather, apply the sun-cream (even though there is shade) – and maybe take your swimming costume. There is not much in the way of a riverside beach, but it is possible to swim from the rocks.

Waymarking: The route is waymarked in yellow throughout – but take care to follow the text as other local routes have the same waymarking.

Introduction

'And green and deep, the stream mysterious glides beneath'. The words Rupert Brooke wrote about a very-English Grantchester apply just as well to the River Siagne at the Pont des Tuves. Beside this bridge the river forms a series of deep pools and the mystery is in their colour, an eerie bright emerald green that is almost luminescent. Everything around is green as well – a dense deciduous vegetation thriving in the cool of these gorges. All in all, it's the ideal place to visit on a hot day.

The walk starts from St Cézaire-sur-Siagne, a lovely medieval village on the rim of the gorge, 300 metres above the river. The site has been occupied since prehistoric times, but it was the Romans that made the greatest impact on this place. They introduced olives and vines to the ter-raced slopes of the gorge, and wheat on the plateau above. All went to feed the Roman legions at Fréjus – St Cézaire is said to have derived its name from its role as 'Caesar's granary'. Even today the highest slopes of the gorge are stepped with olive groves – you will see them as you set out on this walk.

The path you take into the gorge is an old mule-track that once went over to Callian and Mons on the far side of the river. Wide and still partly paved, it leads through the olive groves to a region of lovely Mediterra-

The Siagne at the Pont des Tuves

nean vegetation – juniper and mastic, holm oaks, wild asparagus and Spanish broom, with an undergrowth of lavender and thyme. Along the slopes runs the picturesque Canal de la Siagne, carrying water to Cannes – as its forerunner did in Roman times. Below the canal the path approaches the river and the vegetation changes again to a damp green jungle hung with climbing plants. The river itself is beautiful, calm in places, elsewhere rushing and bouncing over the rocks, but always that incredible colour. Beside the high-arching Pont des Tuves, waterfalls tumble down the banks and the path takes you behind one of them. Farther on are the ruins of old stone water-mills and the attractive Pont du Moulin where the river is racing at a great pace. The climb comes at the end of the walk – and it can be warm work after the cool of the gorge. There are plenty of places to refresh you in St Cézaire – but if you really want another breath of chilling air, go along to the Grottes de St Cézaire, 3km away, where you can view the stalactite formations at a constant temperature of 14ºC

The Walk

1. Stand in the Place Général de Gaulle with the church on your right. Ahead of you to the right is the Rue de l'Égalité – walk along it for about 50m and then turn down some steps on the right, marked with a flash of yellow. Turn left at the bottom and you will see a signpost (no. 10) directing you to la Siagne and the Pont des Tuves (among other places). Now you descend on a wide stony path between terraces of olive trees with splendid views into the deep valley below and occasional glimpses of the green river. Behind you are the pre-Alpine ranges above Grasse, and in the opposite direction the view extends to the Maures and the Esterel.

2. Reaching the track junction at post no. 9, turn right, again in the direc-

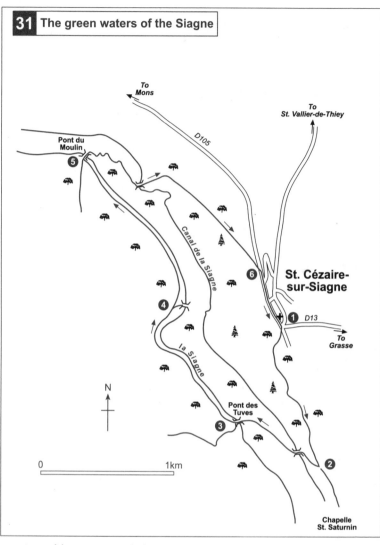

31 **The green waters of the Siagne**

tion of la Siagne and the Pont des Tuves. A further 15 minutes of descent will bring you to the Canal de la Siagne and the little bridge across it. On the far side the downhill path continues towards the river. Soon you can hear it rushing loudly and as you reach the Pont des Tuves a waterfall spills across the path. Going behind the fall is probably the driest option.

3. The river is at its loveliest here – at the far side of the bridge yet another waterfall is tumbling into a sparkling green pool. Cross the bridge and take the track on the right. To confuse you there are several (allowing access to the riverside for bathing etc.), but all join quite quickly to form the main riverside path. The occasional yellow waymark confirms your route, but you can't really get it wrong. The onward path has been well managed, winding up and down between the trees, with log steps put in on the steepest slopes. In about 20 minutes, just after passing a ruin on the left, the path forks.

4. Keep left here (the right hand path goes to a bridge over the river). Your path crosses a small clearing and continues under the trees. At another fork, again keep to the main path, following the waymarks. The large ruin you now meet was once a paper mill – and after passing it, the path climbs a little above the river, passes a holiday home (la Chêne) on the left, and arrives at the Pont du Moulin.

5. Ignore the yellow-flashed path to the left (it is route no. 3 in the local leaflet) and instead cross the bridge and take the path doubling back on the far side. There are yellow waymarks here too. In a moment you are climbing again. Beyond the Canal de la Siagne the path straightens and the ascent brings fine views into the valley you have just left – the little bridge over the green water and the old mill. At the top you reach a tarmacked road.

6. Continue ahead on the road, but where it takes a hairpin to the left leave it and keep straight on. Very soon the waymarks direct you to double back to the left beside post no. 20 (although you can keep ahead here to find the *table d'orientation*). At the top of the slope bear right and then bear left again to return to the church in the middle of town.

More Walks in the Area

The Office de Tourisme at St Cézaire (on the Rue de la République – you passed it at the end of the walk) stocks a leaflet of local walks entitled *Sentiers et Circuits de Randonnée Pédestre*. The leaflet gives only rough sketch maps and accompanying French text, but the excellent waymarking (by the Conseil Général des Alpes-Maritimes) makes everything possible. Just take note of the level of difficulty along with each walk. You would need to transfer the routes to the appropriate IGN map, but they largely follow Grandes Randonnées and other signposted tracks (marked in red on the maps) so this should pose no problems

Cabris, 6km east of St Cézaire, is a splendid example of a *village perché* and its Office de Tourisme likewise produces its own walks leaflet. Unfortunately, no level of difficulty has been given for the individual walks here. But it is quite easy to follow the GR 51 between Cabris and St Vallier-de-Thiey (6km) or between Cabris and St Cézaire (8km) Choosing the former route you would have the fine view from the Croix de Cabris, while the latter route passes near the Grottes de St Cézaire for added interest. Cabris and St Cézaire are connected by a bus route (get times from the Office de Tourisme) – otherwise you would need to return along the same track or get a friend to pick you up at the other end

Between St Cézaire and Cabris is the village of le Tignet. From here another walk along the banks of the Siagne is described in the booklet *Rando – Pays Côtier* which you will find in any Office de Tourisme in Alpes-Maritimes (as the Siagne here is the boundary between the departments of Var and Alpes-Maritimes, look for it only in places east of the river). The walk is an easy one taking about 2½ hours and, in addition to the riverside stretch, offers plenty of shade as it wanders through woods of cork-oak and pine and returns through groves of mimosa. The walk is well waymarked, but it might be as well to get the relevant IGN map, 3543 ET.

Places of interest nearby

The Grottes de St Cézaire were first discovered by farmers clearing the land just over a hundred years ago. They are now a popular attraction, and are well-signed off the D13 just to the east of the town. Steps lead down to galleries of curiously deep pink stalactites (their colour due to the presence of iron ore), with some exotically named formations – the Drapery Room, the Fairies' Alcove, etc.. In the Organ Gallery you will be given a short recital on the resonant 'pipes' and asked to put a name to the tunes (not easy!). 40 metres below the ground the path ends at a big hole leading who knows where. The caves are closed from November to mid-February, but otherwise open daily. Guided tours are usually in French, but an English translation is offered.

Other caves are to be found to the north, off the D5 to St Vallier-de-Thiey. The Grotte Baume Obscure was more recently discovered (1958) and offers nine galleries with stalactites and subterranean water courses, embellished by lights and music. Beyond St Vallier-de-Thiey is the Plateau de Caussols, whose strange limestone landscape seems to belong to another world. And thinking of other worlds, would-be astronomers can see them through telescopes and be shown all the latest star-inspired technology at the *Observatoire du CERGA* at the centre of the plateau. Tours take place in the summer months only.

Taking the winding road through the Siagne gorge and up the other side will bring you to Mons, another splendid *village perché* with its *table d'orientation*. The Office de Tourisme here can offer you information on several prehistoric dolmens nearby. South of Mons, beside the D56, a dilapidated sign announces the Roche Taillée – a huge rock hewn out by the Romans to create an aqueduct taking water to the coastal towns. You can walk underneath the massive boulder and continue along the top of the aqueduct on the well-signed GR49, with some splendid views into the valley of the Siagnole.